BAKKE & THE POLITICS OF EQUALITY

BAKKE &
THE POLITICS OF
EQUALITY

*Friends and Foes in
the Classroom of Litigation*

TIMOTHY J. O'NEILL

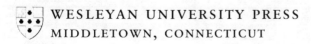

WESLEYAN UNIVERSITY PRESS
MIDDLETOWN, CONNECTICUT

All inquiries and permissions requests should be addressed to the Publisher, Wesleyan University Press, 110 Mt. Vernon Street, Middletown, Connecticut 06457.

Distributed by Harper & Row Publishers, Keystone Industrial Park, Scranton, Pennsylvania 18512.

LIBRARY OF CONGRESS CATALOGING IN PUBLICATION DATA

O'Neill, Timothy J.
  Bakke and the politics of equality.

  Bibliography: p.
  Includes index.
  1. Judicial process—United States. 2. Law and politics.
3. Sociological jurisprudence. 4. Affirmative action
programs—Law and legislation—United States.
5. Bakke, Allan Paul. I. Title.
KF8700.O53 1984   347.73'5   83-26122
ISBN 0-8195-5116-3 (alk. paper)   347.3075

Manufactured in the United States of America

First Edition

For Lynn, William, and James

CONTENTS

FIGURES AND TABLES

Figures

Tables

AMICI ORGANIZATIONS IN *BAKKE*

"Democratic"

American Indian Bar Association
American Indian Law Students Association
American Jewish Committee
American Jewish Congress
Anti-Defamation League
Asian American Bar Association of the Greater Bay Area
Association of American Law Schools
Association of American Medical Colleges
Black Law Students Association at the University of California, Berkeley School of Law
Black Law Students Union of Yale University Law School
Cleveland State University Chapter of the Black American Law Students Association
Columbia University
Committee for Academic Nondiscrimination and Integrity
Congressional Black Caucus
Council of Supervisors and Administrators of the City of New York, Local 1, AFSA, AFL-CIO
Equal Employment Advisory Council
Hellenic Bar Association of Illinois
Japanese American Citizens League
Jewish Labor Council
La Raza National Lawyers Association
Lawyers' Committee for Civil Rights Under Law
Minority Contractors Association of Northern California
National Advocates Society
National Association for the Advancement of Colored People
National Association for Equal Educational Opportunity

National Association for Equal Opportunity in Higher Education
National Association of Affirmative Action Officers
National Association of Minority Contractors
National Bar Association
National Conference of Black Lawyers
National Council of La Raza
National Jewish Commission on Law and Public Affairs
National Lawyers Guild
National Urban League
Native American Law Students of the University of California
    at Davis
Native American Student Union of the University of California
    at Davis
North Carolina Association of Black Lawyers
Order Sons of Italy in America
Polish American Affairs Council
Polish-American Congress
Society of American Law Teachers
UCLA Black Law Students Association
Ukrainian Congress Committee of America (Chicago Division)
UNICO International
Union Women's Alliance to Gain Equality
United States [Carter Administration]
Young Americans for Freedom

"Oligarchic"

American Association of University Professors
American Bar Association
American Civil Liberties Union
American Civil Liberties Union of Northern California
American Civil Liberties Union of Southern California
American Coalition of Citizens with Disabilities
American Federation of State, County, and Municipal Employees,
    AFL-CIO
American Federation of Teachers, AFL-CIO
American Medical Student Association
American Public Health Association
Americans for Democratic Action
American Subcontractors Association
Association of Mexican American Educators
Antioch School of Law

Aspira of America
Bar Association of San Francisco
Board of Governors of Rutgers, The State University of New Jersey
Chamber of Commerce of the United States
Conference of Pennsylvania State Police Lodges
County of Santa Clara, California
Fraternal Order of Police
G.I. Forum
Harvard University
Howard University
IMAGE
International Association of Chiefs of Police
International Conference of Police Associations
International Union of Electrical, Radio, and Machine Workers,
    AFL-CIO, CLC (IUE)
International Union, United Automobile, Aerospace, Agricultural
    Implement Workers of America (UAW)
League of United Latin American Citizens
Los Angeles County Bar Association
Los Angeles Mecha Council
Mexican-American Political Association
National Council of Churches of Christ in the United States
    of America
National Council of Negro Women
National Education Association
National Legal Aid and Defender Association
National Medical and Dental Association
National Medical Association
National Organization for Women
Polish American Educators Association
Rutgers Law School Alumni Association
Stanford University
State of Washington
Student Bar Association of Rutgers School of Law-Newark
UCLA Black Law Student Alumni Association
UNITAS
United Farm Workers of America, AFL-CIO
United Mine Workers of America
United States National Student Association
University of Pennsylvania
University of Washington
Young Women's Christian Association

"Managerial"

American Indian Law Center
Children's Defense Fund
Council on Legal Education Opportunity
Fair Employment Practice Commission of California
Italian-American Foundation (now National Italian American Foundation)
Law School Admission Council
Legal Services Corporation
Mexican-American Legal Defense and Educational Fund
Mid-American Legal Foundation
NAACP Legal Defense and Educational Fund, Inc. (now Legal Defense and Educational Fund, Inc.)
National Employment Law Project, Inc.
National Fund for Minority Engineering Students
National Health Law Program
Pacific Legal Foundation
Puerto Rican Legal Defense and Education Fund

Note: The Queens Jewish Community Council and the Jewish Rights Council are not included.

PREFACE

In several respects, this book about political education in *Bakke* is the product of my own political education. My interest in understanding whether and how amici organizations educated their members about affirmative action is not altogether scholarly. It has deep personal roots as well. As a student of politics and law, I was fascinated by the case's political dynamic, the individuals and organizations that participated in it, and the public controversy over preference programs. As a citizen, I sought guidance on how to resolve a perplexing issue. And as a white male now approaching Allan Bakke's age at the time he first applied to medical school, I wanted to know how my life and fortunes would be affected.

My study is based on materials gathered between 1977 and 1979. In June 1977 a questionnaire was mailed to those individuals whose names appeared on the briefs filed in the case; 69.5 percent replied. The respondents were asked to identify who composed the brief, who was involved in approving and endorsing it, and who were the prime movers and major dissidents in the brief-writing process. In September 1977 and January 1978, I interviewed the respondents and those individuals who had been characterized as active participants in the brief-authoring and authorizing process. Individuals were asked during the course of these follow-up interviews for the names of others influential in the brief-formation process until a relatively stable roster of some 450 names was achieved. In every case, at least the brief writer, an organizational leader, and one member of a local branch or affiliate were interviewed. The only organizations I was unable to contact were the Queens Jewish Community Council and the Jewish Rights Council.

During my stay at the Brookings Institution in 1978 and 1979, I made more intensive contacts with members from the amici organizations. The 361 respondents were selected from the 450 names elicited during the first series of interviews. Most of these were "self-selected"; they were willing to contribute at least an hour to an interview. Based on the initial questionnaires, however, the sampling of respondents reflected the principal participants in each organization's decision making. On several occasions, a respondent was able to provide information about several organizations, another example of the interlocking web of organizational ties which form elite organizational politics in America.

The interviews were semistructured. Respondents were encouraged to expand on their statements by relating stories about their involvement in *Bakke*. Access to private notes, office files, public newsletters, news releases, and other statements of organizational policy were used to check the authenticity of informants' explanations. The data accumulated in all three investigations (June 1977; September 1977–January 1978; 1978–79) were used to develop the materials in chapters 2, 3, and 4. Chapter 5 is based almost wholly on the 1978–79 follow-up interviews. As in the preceding interviews, respondents were subjected to an open-ended and flexible set of questions, but, departing from past procedure, these respondents were promised anonymity for their responses. The questions asked are presented in the tables. Insofar as Chapter 5 is concerned with the participants' perceptions of leaders in *Bakke*, and not, as the preceding chapters were, with the reality of organizational decision making, the data were not corrected by an independent assessment of what other sources reported about an organization.

In an endeavor such as this, there is an element of subjectivity. I have explained in the text and notes the indicators I have used to assign organizations to each of these categories. As a check on personal bias, a panel of twenty-five individuals were given a sheet explaining the criteria for assigning organizations to categories and the complete data on a random sample (thirty-five of one hundred fifteen) of *Bakke* amici organizations. I thank members of my course in Law and Society at Tulane University for serving in this capacity. The students were "blind"—they were not told why they were engaged in this task until after the test was concluded. Their assignments matched mine in all but three cases—the Asian American Bar Association of the Greater Bay Area, the Young Women's Christian Association, and the Polish American Educators Association. In one of these cases— the Asian American Bar Association—I was persuaded to change my assignment of the "scope" score. In the other two, the students divided evenly in their assignments. I conducted further telephone interviews with representatives of these organizations before assigning them final scores. All interview data, coding materials, and panel assignments are held in my files.[1]

Bakke took five years to wend its way from its beginnings in a California trial court to its conclusion in the United States Supreme Court. My study of *Bakke* consumed six years. This indicates either my commitment to the worthiness of the enterprise or my dogged determination to finish the task. I prefer to believe it is the former. Whether my impetus was high-minded dedication or simple-minded doggedness, I have several persons to thank for their advice and encouragement. I thank Warren Breed of the Pericles Foundation and the staff of the Governmental Studies Program of the Brookings Institution for their financial and intellectual assistance. Hanna Pitkin and Robert Kagan strove to ensure that what I wrote was clear, concise, and reasonably interesting. Jeannette Hopkins of the Wesleyan University Press wielded her blue pen to good effect, and this book has been improved considerably by her stylistic and organizational suggestions. I owe a special thanks to William K. Muir, Jr. Without his gentle prodding, this book may have taken even longer to complete. I also recognize an intellectual debt to my many

1. Notes are on pages 267–309.

teachers and students; I hope I have not distorted unduly their teachings and counsel. Finally, I thank Lynn, William, and James. These last six years have produced not only this book but two sons whom I cherish. Lynn's direct assistance in this matter, and her indirect support in so many others, impose an irredeemable debt of love and respect which I happily assume.

Wellesley, Massachusetts   TIMOTHY J. O'NEILL

BAKKE & THE
POLITICS OF EQUALITY

LITIGATION AS A CLASSROOM

The courts are identified as centers of moral debate and political education in America. Eugene Rostow has called them "teachers in a vital national seminar"; "the discussion of problems and the declaration of broad principles by the courts is a vital element in the community experience through which American policy is made."[1] Ralph Lerner sees the court as a "republican schoolmaster," intended by the Founders to be "an educator, molder, and guardian of the manners, morals, and beliefs that sustain republican government."[2] A prominent political scientist rhapsodizes that the "rulings and opinions . . . of the [Supreme] Court constitute our most important source of standards about what is good and bad for the public."[3]

Bakke *and the Politics of Equality* seeks to determine whether, in the affirmative action case *Regents of the University of California* v. *Bakke*, litigation did serve as the schoolmaster in a vital national seminar. The *Bakke* case attracted one of the largest set of amici curiae in the history of the Supreme Court. One hundred seventeen organizations alone or collaboratively submitted fifty-one "friends-of-the-court" briefs,[4] ensuring a broader expression of arguments, evidence, social interests, and concerns than the adversary process of two-party conflict normally allows. Organizations as diverse in their purposes and memberships as the American Civil Liberties Union, the Chamber of Commerce of the United States, the Council of Supervisors and Administrators of the City of New York, and the American Coalition of Citizens with Disabilities pressed for judicial endorsement of policies they preferred on the issue of equality. *Bakke* was not simply the story of one man and his efforts to win admission to medical school, but a tale of individuals and organizations striving to achieve or maintain cherished principles and interests through litigation.

Bakke involved more than the conflict among interests or between existing rules. Rules had to be created and interests had to be reassessed. The grand principles of individual merit and the humanitarian concern for the victims of racial injustice were themselves challenged. The case seemed to force a choice between unacceptable alternatives: That endorsement of "race-conscious though 'benign'" programs would further legitimate race as a test for the apportionment of benefits and burdens in American society, or that rejection of affirmative action programs on a "color-blind" principle would condemn blacks to a continuing status as an underclass. In *Bakke* the nation had to develop new principles or radically recast old ones.

Like the nation, many of the amici organizations participating in *Bakke* were internally divided. Because of the extraordinary character of the issues posed, most had no reservoir of routine responses upon which to call. Policies calling for affirmative action and championing equal opportunity had to be rethought in addressing the legitimacy of programs of "positive discrimination," which sought to aid and not hinder minority achievement. The National Association for the Advancement of Colored People debated whether the needs of the black community would be best served by endorsing race-conscious preference programs or whether such programs would threaten to reestablish the discredited notion of individual distinctions based on race. The American Civil Liberties Union struggled over the issue of whose individual rights were paramount: Allan Bakke's right to racially neutral treatment by the state or the qualified minority member's right to a remedy for past and continuing societal discrimination. The American Jewish Congress was torn by the conflict between its mistrust of quotas, born of restrictive "ceilings" imposed on Jews in the early twentieth century, and the need to find effective ways of establishing racial justice. Such conflicting interests and values were not easily reconcilable.

The absence of existing principles or policies to settle the dispute forced organizations to mobilize their intellectual reserves. Litigation became a form of education for the members of amici organizations. It matters how citizens learn about and form judgments on the issues they find important. It matters who assists and who obstructs them in the process of becoming politically literate. Liberal democracy depends on the informed consent of the governed. Informed consent entails the presence of choices and the citizen's capacity to choose. Sometimes it may mean no more than the act of voting or the informed decision to abstain from voting. The activity of vicarious participation in public-policy making may suffice.

Citizen participation in a liberal democracy, therefore, is a kind of second guessing or kibbitzing. Michael Walzer argues that "[w]ith only a modest imaginative effort, the citizen can put himself in the place of his elected representative. Because he can do that, and commonly does it, he engages in . . . anticipative and retrospective decision-making. He asks, 'What would I do in his place?' and then, later on, he asks, 'Would I have done what he did?'" Such citizen participation demands a special kind of political education. It must be capable of laying the groundwork for the "democratic business of taking stands and shaping policies." It must seek "not only to prepare future citizens for decision-making, but actively to initiate them into the on-going process of (vicarious) decision-making."[5] It must turn bystanders into a jury of peers, deliberating on and deciding the fate of the democratic leader before the bar of an educated public opinion.

Politics is learning. Politics in a liberal democracy involves education—the exchange of facts, ideas, and perspectives among citizens, and between citizens and their rulers. We engage in politics not only to champion specific policies but also to learn about problems and alternative solutions. The solution to one problem often creates new problems. The more we know, the more we discover that we don't know enough. And, as with education, politics often "tests" us, obliging us to act, or to state a judgment, or to take a stand before all the facts are in or before all the consequences are identified. What is more, politics calls upon us to decide issues that are not only abstractly important or interesting, but also vital to our lives and fortunes. With the right to decide we submit to the duty to be responsible.

This book examines the quality of the political education afforded the members of the organizations that offered amici curiae or "friends-of-the-court" briefs in the case *Regents of the University of California* v. *Bakke*. It emphasizes not what the arguments taught the courts or what the courts taught the nation, but the learning process *within* litigating organizations. It considers if and how the use of the amicus process educated the *users* about racial preferences and whether organizations' members learned about the choices to be made and the consequences of those choices. If *Bakke* did teach and the members of amici organizations did learn, then litigation can help the nation learn to identify and assess problems of public policy and to choose from among alternatives. If *Bakke* did not teach about the issue of equality, claims that the courts are "teachers in a vital national seminar" must be viewed skeptically.

Education or Effectiveness? The Unenviable Choice

The Regents of the University of California v. *Bakke* was one of the most celebrated court cases of the seventies. Hailed by the media as a case equal in importance to *Brown* v. *Board of Education*,[6] *Bakke* provoked a national debate over the legal, social, and ethical justifications for preferential treatment of racially disadvantaged groups. It posed in concrete form a vital issue: What type of equality ought the nation to pursue, and in what manner?

Most discussions of *Bakke* have been dominated by the social and moral dilemmas posed by the case, namely, if the equal protection clause of the Constitution allows or demands that some groups be granted preference over whites in the competition for scarce public benefits so that the subtle and pervasive influence of past and continuing racial discrimination can be overcome. If so, it further asks, what are the proper limits for such preferential treatment, and how is an acceptable balance to be drawn between the competing values of individual merit and of traditional definitions of equality as straightforward nondiscrimination?

To emphasize the legal debate as a surrogate for a popular debate over affirmative action may be misleading. Although the amici briefs sought to be more than intellectual challenges to or justifications of affirmative action,[7] few were faithful reflections of the discussions within their sponsoring organizations. Few briefs depicted the uncertainties that had to be resolved in their creation. An amicus brief, as a legal document enlisted in support of a legal argument within the legal process, is a policy statement intended for the courtroom, not for a legislative hearing or a private conversation with the President. It represents the resolution of, and does not reflect the debate within, an organization. Nor are organizations mere vehicles for the pure expression of their members' sentiments. In *Bakke* pressures of time and resources prevented some organizations from consulting their members. These members did not "learn." In the case of other organizations, the need to appease powerful groups or influential outside clienteles restricted membership participation in policy making.

Clement Vose's 1959 study of litigation politics demonstrated how organizations lobby the courts in the same way that they lobby legislatures or administrative agencies.[8] The assets of time, money, attention span, and expertise are influential in the courtroom as in other political arenas. Litigation has become the strategy of choice for many organizations who work to preserve or change the status quo when they fail to gain access to, or expect to lose in, other political forums. However, as organizational advocacy through litigation has expanded, an organization's capacity to teach and to be effective has become limited. Litigation of any kind, but especially through the amicus process, seldom motivates an organization's leadership to solicit membership views. Ideas, not votes, count in courtrooms. The leadership mobilizes an organization's intellectual resources, not its membership numbers. Advocacy organizations that pursue litigation strategies seem to be presented with an unenviable choice: to teach—fostering the expression, refinement, or development of their members' views, or to be effective—achieving the many other, occasionally contradictory, purposes of the organization. The relationship of litigation to political education in *Bakke* is found both in the process and in the product of organizational decision making. How did organizations develop the positions they took? Did it make a difference that some organizations encouraged while others discouraged broad membership involvement? If litigation can educate, the milieu of advocacy may impoverish or enhance learning.

The discussions of broad social issues in the legal process are confined by the linguistic boundaries of constitutional argument and by the special roles played by lawyers. The nature of legal language and the restraining influence of lawyers as organizational leaders ensured that some possibilities and not others would be explored in the effort to develop policies concerning preferential treatment. Any search for important differences and uniformities among amici organizations must recognize not only the distinction between the authorizing—the organizational acceptance—and the authoring—the actual writing—stages of the development of legal briefs. It must also consider the "might have beens"—"what might have happened, but did not." [9] *Bakke* offered an opportunity for learning—the discovery of unrecognized features of the controversy gave rise to new ideas, formulations, and arrangements acceptable to amici members.

The Organization as a Schoolhouse

The concept of "political education" is not fashionable in political science. Education has a kind of "sinister meaning," connoting propaganda, manipulation, or "brainwashing." [10] It is frequently reduced to the inculcation of unexamined attitudes and beliefs or to propagandistic exhortations. The competing notion of political *socialization* is more attractive to many. *Socialization* deals with the ways social conduct is learned, the dictates of authoritative institutions, the patterns of attitudes and behaviors that create a political "self" and form political orientations and a political culture. Socialization includes education but suggests a process apart from the individual acting upon the individual, a process by which human beings are made into political beings.[11] But political education is too valuable an idea to be discarded so cavalierly. It refuses to view individuals as sponges. Individuals are not acted upon only; they act, for they are generators of ideas; they shape, as well as respond to, their environments.[12] Political learning is more than the process of training individuals in political mores. It also includes nurturing the desire and intent to be politically active.

If political education is not another term for socialization, neither is it solely the activity of acquiring knowledge, of becoming politically "literate." A knowledge "of" is not always synonymous with the knowledge "how." Nor is political education simply the development of well-considered and supported opinions. As one axiom of American politics instructs us: Opinion unharnessed to action is unheeded. Political education is more than indoctrination. It draws upon, but is not identified with, the scholar's pursuit of knowledge for its own sake, since it uses knowledge as a means to other ends. Being a self-consciously guided political activity, it is directed toward creating informed participation in decision making, if only through the "vicarious," indirect manner of passing upon the prior actions, or predicting the future policies, of elected or appointed leaders. Political education aims at instruction in the techniques of successful political action and in the development of an *ideology*— a set of values and ideas which help guide individual actions by providing the means for evaluating alternatives. It is prudent, eliciting an awareness of the openness of human life and human society. It should foster not closed-minded dogmatism, but a willingness to abandon ideology when necessary—recognizing the need for visions of the "best" while counseling against too disdainful a treatment of the "second best" or the practical. It is also mutual. Part of the ability to learn is the capacity to teach, to communicate reliable information and ideas that help others to act.[13] Political education as here defined is similar to Aristotle's description of citizenship as being in turn the ruler and the ruled.

Alexis de Tocqueville noted a hundred and fifty years ago that voluntary associations are the schoolhouses of public virtue in an extended commercial republic.[14] Studies exploring the development of public attitudes on political issues have identified a cadre of citizens who are not only knowledgeable about politics but are motivated to act politically. These *activists* tend to be heavily engaged in campaigns, to lobby aggressively on issues attracting their interest, and to be skilled in political techniques. They take more consistent positions on issues than the average citizen does, perhaps because they have access to more and better information about issues or a greater willingness to inform themselves.[15] Activists are overwhelmingly well educated and middle-aged, with high incomes.[16] Americans least likely to participate in politics, seldom voting and showing little interest in discussing issues, are those who are poorly educated, young, from low income groups, "and disproportionately black or women."[17] Activists and *inactives* are opposing ends of a continuum: most Americans are neither, but somewhere in between. Activists are also "joiners." Individuals who join organizations tend to have the same high incomes, high status, and high levels of education as activists.[18] Conversely, joiners tend to be activists, especially (and obviously) those who become members of associations organized to influence the government.[19]

Studies in education support the supposition that organizations serve as centers for political education. For example, Jean Piaget concludes that, in the moral development of children, peer interaction is a prerequisite to a mature moral sense.[20] Joel Auerbach argues that adults who are least active in organizations are least likely to participate in politics. The sense of belonging and sharing characteristic of organizational affiliation overcomes the feeling of helplessness that discourages political action.[21] Individuals most concerned with politics also tend to act out that concern within organizational contexts. The importance of organizations to all forms of education is underscored by the educational process of mutual exchange and support. James MacGregor Burns points out that "people are taught by shared experiences and interaction motivations."[22] Organizations are the human associations most conducive to education.

HYPOTHESIS 1:
The more "business-like" an organization is, the less "school-like" it will be. The narrower or more focused an organization's purposes, the less likely it can provide an environment conducive to mutual exchanges and enlightenment, but the more likely it will actually represent its members' interests.

The greater specificity of interests and goals associated with narrower organizations may in some ways better equip these groups to teach their members. Members will be more intensely involved in the activities of organizations which represent their material interests. Narrower organizations also receive greater benefits from being well informed, especially when they must compete with others for scarce resources. Knowing the opponents' strengths and weaknesses and providing alternatives to competitors' proposals would promise to sharpen the information-gathering and policy-making processes of an organization. Organizations that concentrate on narrower goals do educate their members in a superior fashion when already established interests must be defended or advanced. But in the *Bakke* case it was not always clear how interests were affected. The ability of an organization committed to specific interests to educate its members is diminished in such uncertain circumstances.

In order to teach its members, an organization's concerns must be broad enough to draw upon the arguments, interests, and facts necessary to form new beliefs, yet narrow enough to provide its members with manageable evidence and arguments. The organization must protect the member from information overload. Studies on organizational decision making like that of Cyert and March suggest that most organizations err on the "narrow" rather than the "broad" side of the problem.[23] An organization with a broader set of goals is more likely to have a broader view of what is happening in its world and therefore access to greater resources for education. The broader the values pursued by an organization, the more likely that its members or clients will be exposed to ideas and knowledge conducive to learning. Organizations that are outward looking and promotional in their perspectives will be more receptive to new ideas or to new sources of knowledge than more inward-looking organizations.

HYPOTHESIS II:
"Good faith" conflict encourages education. Certain types of conflict contribute to personal growth and understanding. Some individuals use conflict to clarify their beliefs and attitudes, and some types of conflict induce healthy adjustment of opinions and evoke stronger, more consistent, and therefore more rational, understandings of issues.

Conflict serves several vital social interests as well. An adversary process of challenges and counterchallenges can give rise to hitherto unrecognized solutions to broad social problems—one tenet of the liberal belief in the marketplace of ideas. It can also moderate extreme views, forcing proponents to grapple with the limits of the ideal in a world of finite resources and conflicting demands. Perhaps most important, conflict can educate by challenging behavior. Inconsistencies between personal values and behavior, such as the conflict between beliefs about equal opportunity and practices that victimize blacks, can produce changes in behavior as it tries to correspond to the dictates of values.[24] But not just any type of conflict leads to learning. Conflict and a healthy, democratic politics are not always compatible, certain writers notwithstanding.[25] A fear of conflict can cause individuals to avoid informed debate and decision making on difficult issues. Sullivan, Nakamura, and Winters offer evidence that in the New England town meeting—ironically, the paradigmatic situation cited by advocates of participatory democracy—participants fear conflict, because conflict tends to become personal, transforming debates into attacks on individuals with whom one must live. An occasional issue might attract the interest of the members and thus promote higher participation, yet at the same time lead to greater polarization. Polarization, in turn, results in lower levels of participation as the political process returns to normal. Having had such unpleasant experiences with conflict, individuals prefer to settle problems informally, outside of the town meeting. Only those adversely affected by an issue find participation sufficiently important to risk involvement in policy making: "Consequently, alternatives to proposed policies are rarely put forward effectively, and the town meeting serves to ratify decisions made elsewhere by a dominant socioeconomic elite." Sullivan, Nakamura, and Winters conclude, "the process of deliberation does not inform the voters." The town meeting is a ratifying convention, not a deliberative legislature.[26]

Many decisions, of course, are not the subject of controversy. In the legislative process, controversy is rare, not routine. Jewell and Patterson have shown that the great bulk of the Congress's business is conducted by unanimous or near-unanimous votes.[27] Aaron Wildavsky's study of the budgetary process found that most of the national budget is passed with little challenge. Seldom are any aspects of the budget, except some marginal increases, the subject of political conflict.[28] Conflict may capture our attention, but it is not the norm for democratic decision making.

The type of conflict that encourages learning within an organization will depend on the character of the decision-making process and the characteristics of the membership. As Grant McConnell has said about small-group policy making in general, the more homogeneous an organization's members and the greater the importance they attach to consensus, the less able will the organization be to develop well-informed decisions.[29] Personalized conflict, which results in attacks on the participants rather than challenges of ideas, facts, and values, causes withdrawal from the decision-making process and lessened opportunities for learning. Supportive environments in which conflicts are viewed as disagreements among individuals of good faith, on the other hand, encourage exchanges and learning. It is nonpersonalized conflict which produces learning. The higher the level of education, ego integration, and civic awareness of an organization's membership, the greater the opportunity for learning. There should, therefore, be a direct relationship between these membership characteristics and tolerance to con-troversy.[30] Organizations of highly educated, psychologically well-integrated, and civically aware participants should foster education.

Hypotheses I and II suggest the need for a third hypothesis, one dealing with the special role played by leadership. Most participants in an organization cannot afford and would not be willing to commit their energies to organizational purposes. As in all other complex human enterprises, duties must be dis-tributed within the organization. But a division of labor entails problems of governance as well as of administration. Organiza-tions need staffs and leaders equipped to make decisions on rou-tine matters for the members; they also need to ensure that staffs and leaders are equipped to bring members the facts, ideas, and issues that warrant their attention.

In what I consider to be the most important contemporary study of the nature of leadership, James MacGregor Burns iden-tifies leadership with teaching. Burns defines leadership "as the tapping of existing and potential motive and power bases of fol-lowers . . . for the purpose of achieving intended change." He notes that we think of education "in essentially the same terms" and that "ultimately education and leadership shade into each other." It is not altogether clear whether the analogy between a leader and a teacher is a persuasive one.[31] One danger in per-ceiving the leader as a teacher is the implication that there is something to teach, and that implies the existence not only of a discipline of knowledge and ideas but of individuals who pos-sess a mastery over the discipline.[32] But what of issues and areas in which there is no such discipline or body of knowledge to be mastered? Is the authority of the teacher like that of the leader? Should it be?

Some organizational theorists like Philip Selznick, while rec-ognizing this problem, insist on distinguishing *managerial* from *organizational* types of leadership. Most leaders serve in mana-gerial capacities: they concentrate on the routine matters of or-ganizational life. However, some leaders are obliged "to define the ends of group existence, to design an enterprise distinctively adapted to these ends, and to see that the design becomes a living reality." Such creative leadership emphasizes the development of policies for, and consent within, the organization.[33] But when ought leaders be unrepresentative, when should they take a stand on the basis of personal convictions and not their constituents' views? The problem is, of course, a recurrent one in democratic theory, but it has a special relevance to the idea of political education, which implies mutuality, sensitivity to consequences, and responsibility to principles and other values. If there is a tension between leadership and representation, education resolves them. The leader who chooses to make an important judgment rather than to echo his constituents' sentiments must teach his followers about the wisdom of that judgment. Max Weber recognized the necessity of teaching "citizens to evaluate speech and action intelligently, and at the same time creat-[ing] a system that would make political leadership possible."[34]

HYPOTHESIS III:

Democracy need not be sacrificed in order for an organization to teach and to be effective. An organization's leader is often called upon to play multiple roles. Some may choose to call those roles "managerial" and "organizational," as Selznick does, while others may prefer "transactional" and "transforming"[35] or "mobilizing" and "articulating."[36] Whatever the name, these roles require a leader to reaffirm the organization's primary values and maintain member commitment to them while providing opportunities for the members to reshape those values. If leadership is, in some way, to be equated with teaching, we need to know not only whether the members' desires are communicated to the leaders but also whether the leader is capable of involving his or her followers in the pursuit of group values. This is the problem of organizational cohesion—the maintenance of willing participation in group activities. It involves not only questions of how well leaders satisfy members' preferences but also whether there is the freedom and opportunity for dissent from, as well as consent to, the leader's activities. As the staff size and the number of elected or appointed officers increase, there will be less opportunity for membership participation and, consequently, poorer opportunities for learning by both the leaders and the members. Moreover, patterns of participation will differ among members as well as between members and leaders. The more active members will have more opportunities than less active members to learn and teach. Leaders who encourage broad but relatively minor (unintensive) involvement by their members in organizational policy making will discourage education.

Hypothesis III suggests a possible contradiction with Hypothesis I, which says that a diversified organizational membership with many goals will encourage membership exchange and therefore foster learning, but that the more similar members' goals are for affiliating with an organization, the more likely it will be that the organization will represent these goals accurately. The choice is an awkward one, requiring trade-offs between two equally attractive organizational objectives.

One would expect that the *scope* of the debate within an organization—the breadth and diversity of ideas and information supplied to the participants—would substantiate Hypothesis I's emphasis on organizational purposes. Complementarily, the *intensity* of conflict within an organization, as measured by the sharpness of the *Bakke* debate, and by the tolerance or intolerance of differing viewpoints, would indicate the explanatory power of Hypothesis II. Polarization and personalization of the issue would support the centrality of conflict to political education. An examination of the *nature* of participation by the membership in organizational policy making—what did the members do, were they actively or passively involved—would test the strength of Hypothesis III. If there is a strong relationship between organizational goals and the scope of debate, then Hypothesis I is substantiated. If the relationship between the degree of conflict personalization and the intensity of conflict is positive, then Hypothesis II is supported. A significant relationship between the type of organizational leadership style and the level and character of members' participation would confirm Hypothesis III. Any two or all three factors may affect political education.

Political education is an abstract concept. It cannot wholly be observed and therefore cannot wholly be measured. Scope, intensity, and participation are in some degree observable, how-

ever. What remains unobservable is the degree to which leaders
and members act responsibly on the basis of principles and values. I depend on the perceptions of persons in the amici organizations, and therefore on verification through introspection, to
analyze what is unobservable. By relying on the vicarious introspection test, we make use of the special advantage social science has over its rivals in nature and biology. Leo Strauss points
out that a human being can say why he acts as he does while a
mouse is incapable of explaining why he runs his maze as he
does. The human response may be a misleading one, but it is a
plausible place to begin. If the response is corroborated by more
observable evidence, its credibility can be established.

Political Education and the Amicus Process

Litigation would appear to be an ideal context in which to test
these hypotheses on political education. The legal process
promises to provide the kinds of quality information, competing teachings, and encouragement to participation which are
prerequisites to the political education of organizational members. The successful litigant—as an individual or an organization—must be prepared to make the opponent's case at least as
well as the opponent can. By understanding the strengths and
weaknesses of the opposition, the individual and organization
can discover the strengths and shortcomings of their own positions. The advocacy process is dialectical, prompting the arguments and counterarguments, evidence and counterevidence
necessary for learning. The popular image of the legal process as
the principal moral forum for the nation reinforces this perception of litigation as a mode of education. Laurence Tribe has
faith in the power of the courtroom confrontation: "By debat-
ing our deepest differences in the shared language of constitutional rights and responsibilities, we create the possibility of
persuasion and even moral education in our national life."[37] Kamisar, Inbau, and Arnold express the same sentiment in somewhat different terms. Some court cases, they write, are "like the
miracle or morality plays of ancient times." They "dramatically
present the conflicting values of a community in a way that

could not be done by logical formulation."[38] If they can teach the nation, surely they must teach the participants in the litigation.

Litigation is also a good test for political education because it has become increasingly attractive to organizations. Governments effectively serve those who concentrate and emphasize their interests through organized efforts. As the courts assume the responsibility to distribute important public benefits and burdens, organizations seek access to them for the same purposes for which they seek access to legislative and bureaucratic decision makers—to obtain or preserve values. Judicial review permits struggles that begin in the legislature to spill over into courtrooms. The power of the courts to overthrow or modify legislative and administrative actions invites the continuation of political conflict through litigation. Organizations may initiate "class action" suits on behalf of themselves and/or others who share an actual or threatened injury. They can take over the control of a suit initiated by others or they may decide to sponsor a *test case* in order to develop a favorable precedent on a constitutional or statutory issue affecting the organization's interests. They may pursue nondirect strategies for gaining influence in the judicial process, such as attempting to affect the judicial nomination process or sponsoring law review articles. But the use of the amicus brief seems to be the participatory mechanism of choice, as shown by its expanded usage. Herbert Jacob reports that 87 cases with 315 briefs faced the Supreme Court in its 1973 term, compared with only 63 cases with 105 briefs during the 1963 term.[39] Members of the Office of the Clerk of the Supreme Court have noted increasing numbers of amici briefs filed since the 1975 term.[40]

The amicus process responds to cherished values. Standard works on litigation politics accentuate the role of the amicus brief as a mechanism fostering pluralistic decision making, a concept developed in *Federalist Papers* Ten and Fifty-one and integral to most accounts of the American political system. Clement Vose asserts that organized participation through the amicus process links "broad interests in society to individual parties of interest in Supreme Court cases."[41] For Samuel Krislov the brief is "a vehicle for broad representation of interests, particularly in disputes where political ramifications are wider than a narrow view of common law litigation might indicate."[42] The First Amendment's guarantees of "freedom of speech" and the "right of citizens to petition the government for a redress of grievances" provide the constitutional basis for group action[43] and legitimate use of the amicus brief to further group interests.

Amici litigation has disadvantages. The process is episodic and proceeds at an unusually brisk pace for most organizations. The necessary prominence of those with legal training and the restraining influences of legal vocabularies and practices determine outcomes, placing the fate of the organization in the hands of a very small cadre of political experts. An organization may enter the amicus process not only to represent group values, but also to provide a public relations document that will inform the attentive public of the organization's views. It may publicize the existence of a new organization or appease traditional allies. Briefs actually intended to affect the outcome of a case may be exceptions rather than the norm. The amici organizations in *Bakke* labored under all of these burdens and more.

CHAPTER I

BAKKE, THE UNIVERSITY, AND THE PROBLEMS OF RACIAL EQUALITY

The question of affirmative action divided Americans in unaccustomed ways. It raised issues which resisted solution through traditional, jurisprudential approaches. In the broadest sense, *Bakke* challenged conventional understandings of law, politics, and equality. Because it did so, it offered opportunities for citizen education—for the members of the participating amici organizations to discover new values or to redefine existing principles.

The *Bakke* litigation did contribute to the education of many organizations' members, but not in all cases or in the same degree. In the five years between the University of California, Davis Medical School's rejection of Allan Bakke's application in 1973 and the United States Supreme Court's decision in 1978 to allow him to enter, the debate over affirmative action was only one episode in the continuing controversy over the meanings of equality and the moral limits of politics.

The case of *Regents of the University of California* v. *Bakke* resulted from the efforts of a white, thirty-two-year-old man, Allan Paul Bakke, to win admission to the University of California Medical School at Davis. Just under six feet tall, stocky, blue-eyed, blond but balding, Bakke was characterized in the press as the archetypical Caucasian male. In many respects, his background was archetypical, too. His father was a mailman and his mother a teacher. He majored in engineering at the University of Minnesota in the early sixties, graduated with a 3.51 grade point average (an impressive average in a less "grade-inflated" era), and, after a year of graduate work in mechanical engineering at Minnesota, joined the Marine Corps to fulfill his Naval ROTC obligation. Bakke served four years with the corps. During seven months service as a commanding officer of an antiaircraft battery in Vietnam, he first began to think about attending medical school.[1] He was honorably discharged with the rank of captain and "enlisted in the nation's race to the moon."[2]

With a newly earned master's degree from Stanford, he settled in the San Francisco suburb of Sunnyvale and joined the Ames Research Center, a National Aeronautics and Space Administration (NASA) laboratory near Palo Alto. His work designing equipment used in NASA research programs brought him into daily contact with physicians studying the effects of radiation and outer space on animals and the human body, and Bakke decided that he wanted to be a physician. In his letter to the Davis admissions committee, he explained, "In 1971 my continuously increasing interest in and motivation toward medicine became a firm decision and commitment. I have since completed the premedical course work, under conditions which I believe demonstrate the strength of my motivation and commitment to obtaining a medical education and becoming a physician. While employed full-time as an engineer, I undertook a near full-time course load of medical pre-requisites—biology and chemistry. To make up class and commuting hours, I worked early mornings and also evenings at my job. This was an extremely taxing schedule in terms of time and effort, and involved a significant financial commitment as well."[3] Bakke's enthusiasm was intense. He also worked as a volunteer in a local hospital emergency room.

On November 26, 1972, the Davis admissions office received

his application, one of the 2,664 received at the school that year. Bakke was one of the more than 40,000 Americans applying for 14,000 places in medical schools in 1972. Davis was only one of eleven schools to which he had applied. Bakke's credentials placed him above the ninetieth percentile of all applicants nationally in the Medical College Admissions Test (MCAT) in three of the four categories: ninety-seventh percentile in scientific knowledge, ninety-sixth in verbal ability, and ninety-fourth in quantitative analysis. He ranked in the seventy-second percentile in general knowledge. His statement of purpose was articulate and his letters of recommendation were strong. In March of 1973 Bakke was invited for an interview. The faculty member who conducted the interview described him as "a well-qualified candidate for admission whose main hardship is the unavoidable fact that he is now 33. . . . On the grounds of motivation, academic records, potential promise, endorsement by persons capable of reasonable judgments, personal appearance and decorum, maturity, and probable contribution to balance in the class, I believe Mr. Bakke must be considered as a very desirable applicant and I shall so recommend him."[4] However, despite 468 points out of a possible 500 on the admissions committee's rating scale, Bakke was not admitted. Bakke completed his application late because his mother was ill. Earlier in the year, a rating of 470 had won "automatic admission" with some promising applicants being admitted with lower scores.[5] But by March the number of remaining slots were few, and Bakke received notice of his rejection on May 14, 1973. He was rejected also by the other ten schools to which he had applied.

Bakke persisted, determined to enter the school to which he had so narrowly missed being admitted. Because of its proximity to his home and its state-subsidized tuition, Davis was his first choice. Bakke wrote letters in May and July to the chairman of admissions requesting reconsideration. His second letter challenged the existence of a special admissions program for disadvantaged minority applicants at Davis. "Applicants chosen to be our doctors should be those presenting the best qualifications, both academic and personal," he wrote. "Most are selected according to this standard, but I am convinced that a significant fraction is judged by a separate criteria [sic]. I am refering to quotas, open or covert, for racial minorities. I realize that the rationale for these quotas is that they attempt to atone for past discrimination; but insisting on a new racial bias in favor of minorities is not a just situation." Bakke warned the chairman that he was considering suing the university. His letter ended with a candid confession: "My main reason for undertaking such action would be to secure admission for myself; I consider the goal worth fighting for in every legal and ethical way."[6] As his attorney later reiterated, Bakke was "a private man who felt that he'd been dealt with unfairly. He has stuck with it [the legal case] because it's his dream to become a doctor. He's a determined gentleman."[7]

Bakke's first letter had been ignored. His July letter drew the sympathetic attention of the assistant dean, Peter C. Storandt. As one of the few people who sat on both the regular and special admissions committees, Storandt "knew what was going on."

I had the job of explaining to rejected applicants how we picked from among them. I tried to be fairly open. But I felt frustrated. Task force admissions weren't based on economic and educational disadvantage, although that's a part of it. . . . An applicant who was black . . . regardless of his economic status . . . would be considered first by the special task force. For all practical purposes, and regardless of economic status, no whites were ever considered by the task force. . . . A youngster from a poor white family who hadn't achieved well . . . ends up competing with high-achieving whites despite his disadvantages. . . . It seemed to me that Davis faculty were of the conviction that "disadvantaged" means "membership in a minority race."

Storandt "told Bakke his candidacy had come close and urged him to reapply. If he were not accepted, he could then research the legal question. He had been a good candidate. I thought he'd be accepted and that would end the matter."[8]

Storandt gave Bakke the names of two lawyers who were interested in the issue of affirmative action. The candor of his advice to Bakke led several groups later to charge collusion between Bakke and the university. Ralph Smith, a law professor at the University of Pennsylvania and chairman of the National

Conference of Black Lawyers' Task Force on Legal Education and Bar Admissions insisted that "Allan Bakke was virtually invited to sue the U.C. Davis Medical School by a University official." Smith concluded that it was the university, not Bakke, "who is opposed to minority admissions programs."[9] The general counsel for the University of California, Donald L. Reidhaar, called such charges "ridiculous."[10] He later said, "I don't think Storandt meant to injure the university. It's simply an example of a non-lawyer advising on legal matters."[11] Storandt agreed: "I simply gave Allan the response you'd give an irate customer, to try and cool his anger. I realized the university might be vulnerable to legal attack because of its quota, and I had the feeling by then that somebody somewhere would sue the school, but I surely didn't know this would be the case."[12] Whatever the truth behind the charges of collusion, Storandt was demoted and later resigned to accept a position as associate dean of admissions at Oberlin College.[13]

In a letter to Storandt dated August 7, 1973, Bakke outlined his plan. He would reapply to Davis under an early admissions program. He would simultaneously prepare to sue Davis, Stanford University Medical School, or the University of California Medical School at San Francisco, should he fail in his second application.[14] Having reapplied, Bakke was again invited for an interview. The student interviewer described Bakke as "friendly, well-tempered, conscientious and delightful to speak with," and concluded, "I would give him a sound recommendation for [a] medical career."[15] The faculty interviewer was less enthusiastic. The chairman of the admissions committee, Dr. George H. Lowrey, decided to interview Bakke himself. He found Bakke "disturbing," noting, "[H]e had very definite opinions which were based more on his personal viewpoint than upon the total problem. He was very unsympathetic to the concept of recruiting minority students so that they hopefully would go back to practice in the neglected areas of the country. . . . My own impression of Mr. Bakke is that he is a rather rigidly oriented young man who has a tendency to arrive at conclusions based more upon his personal impressions than upon thoughtful processes using available sources of information."[16] None of the parties in the lawsuit nor the organizations filing amicus curiae briefs, save one, explored the First Amendment and due process issues raised by Lowrey's interviewing of Bakke, and that one did so only in passing.[17]

Using a newly expanded rating system, the five members of the committee gave Bakke scores of 96, 94, 92, 87, and 86 out of a possible 100 points. Storandt gave Bakke the 92; the student member gave him the 94; the lowest rating, 86, came from Lowrey. Bakke received an aggregate score of 549 out of a possible 600 and was denied admission for a second time.[18] His attorneys would later argue that, despite the fact that Bakke's grade point average and performance on the MCAT were higher than those of the average regular admittee, Lowrey had intentionally "penalize[d]" Bakke for challenging the special admissions program by "downgrading" his interview score. This was enough, his attorneys asserted, to make the difference between acceptance or rejection by the school.[19]

After his appeal for reconsideration was rejected later in the year, Bakke retained a lawyer from San Francisco, Reynold Colvin, who, although not a civil rights law specialist, agreed to take on the case because of a personal interest in affirmative action. A past president of the San Francisco chapter of the American Jewish Committee and a former member of the city's board of education, Colvin had helped prevent the institution of a program proposed by the school superintendent, which would allegedly have resulted in the demotion of white administrators and the placement of minorities in high-level administrative posts.[20] Colvin was assisted in the *Bakke* case by Robert Links, so fresh out of UCLA Law School that he did not have the three years experience in private practice required to appear before the Supreme Court.

On the advice of his attorneys, Bakke filed a complaint with the U.S. Department of Health, Education, and Welfare (HEW), charging Davis with violating Title VI of the 1964 Civil Rights Act. The regional office of HEW informed Bakke that he had no administrative recourse. He then sued the school in the Yolo County Superior Court, arguing that the institution's policy of reserving sixteen percent of the entering class for blacks, American Indians, Chicanos, and Asian-Americans "who are judged apart from and permitted to meet lower standards of admission than Bakke" deprived him of his right to the equal protection of the law.[21] Bakke contended that Title VI prohibited any racially or ethnically apportioned preferences in programs supported by federal funds. His suit was officially filed in the summer of 1974.

In Search of a Fair Deal

The University of California Medical School at Davis opened in 1968, with one of its stated purposes improvement of the quality of physician care available to rural upstate California.

The 1968 entering class of fifty students included three Asian-Americans but no blacks or Chicanos, although three blacks and one Chicano had applied. In 1969, fourteen of thirty-four minority applicants were accepted, including two blacks and one Chicano. No American Indians had applied. According to the court record, the faculty at Davis was concerned that the number of successful minority applicants was "insignificant" and was convinced that the existing admissions criteria unfairly hindered minority access to a medical education. They therefore voted to establish a special admissions "task force" program. The intent was to compensate the victims of unjust societal discrimination.[22] Although the notes from the faculty meeting authorizing the task force are not available, the Davis faculty was no doubt responding to the same civil rights activity that led to the formation of similar programs at one hundred other medical schools throughout the nation.

The school's catalogue and application forms for the 1970 academic year characterized the task force program as designed broadly for the "economically or educationally disadvantaged." In a new form prepared for Davis by the American College Application Service in 1974, applicants for the special program were asked to classify themselves as "Black/Afro-American, American Indian, White/Caucasian, Mexican/American or Chicano, Oriental/Asian American, Puerto Rican (Mainland), Puerto Rican (Commonwealth), Cuban, or other." The trial record indicated that while 272 whites considered by Davis as disadvantaged had applied to the program during the years 1971 to

1974, none had been accepted under the special admissions rationale. It is not clear whether disadvantaged white applicants had been interviewed by the task force. Dr. Lowrey said no;[23] a member of the committee asserted that they had been.[24]

The number of minority students admitted between the years 1968 and 1974 increased twelve-fold under the program (table 1). Only three blacks and seven Chicanos had been admitted under the regular program during these years, but twenty-six blacks and thirty-four Chicanos were admitted through the task force program. Asian-Americans did well under both programs; fifty-four were admitted through the regular process, eleven through special admissions.

In 1973 and 1974, the lowest-ranking regular candidate's grade point average (GPA) in science courses was three- to five-tenths of a point higher than the lowest-ranking special admittee's: the average science grade point score of all regular admittees was 3.51 in 1973 and 3.36 in 1974; the averages for all special admittees were 2.62 and 2.42 (table 2). The special admittees fare more poorly when Medical College Admission Test scores are compared. However, quantitative measures were only one part of the evaluation of applicants.

The regular and task force admissions programs were separate and distinct processes up until the final decisions. Applicants with less than a 2.50 overall GPA were rejected under the regular program. Invitations for interviews were offered to the survivors on the basis of grades, test scores, letters of recommendation, and personal statements of purpose. One-sixth of the regular applicants were invited. Following the interview, members of the regular admissions committee rated all remaining applicants on the basis of their statistical records (grades and test scores) and nonstatistical records (recommendations, personal statements, and interviews). Candidates with the highest ratings were generally admitted. Occasionally, exceptions to this rank-ordering process were made for veterans and applicants with unusual records.[25] The Los Angeles Times also reported that the medical school dean intervened on behalf of the sons and daughters of the university's "special friends" to improve their admissions chances.[26]

Minority applicants who answered "yes" to the application

TABLE I Minority Admissions to Davis Medical School, 1968–1974

	Task Force Program				Regular Program					
Year	Black	Chicano	Asian-American	Total	Black	Chicano	Asian-American	Total	Total Minorities	Total Admittees
1968	—	—	—	—	0	0	2	2	2	50
1969	—	—	—	—	2	1	11	14	14	50
1970[a]	5	3	0	8	0	0	4	4	24	52
1971	4	9	2	15	1	0	8	9	24	100
1972	5	6	5	16	0	0	11	11	27	100
1973	6	8	2	16	0	2	13	15	27	100
1974	6	7	2	15[b]	0	4	5	9	24	100
Total	26	34[c]	11	70	3	7	54	48	118	552

SOURCE: *Record, Bakke* (Yolo County, Calif., Superior Ct.), pp. 215–18. "Brief of Petitioner," *Bakke* (U.S. Supr. Ct.) pp. 3–4, supplied the figures for 1974.
  [a]"Task Force" Program began.
  [b]Sixteen minority members accepted under program, one withdrew and was replaced by nonminority applicant from regular program.
  [c]Includes one applicant listed as both Chicano and American Indian.

question "Do you wish to be considered as a minority group applicant?" were referred to the task force program. A special committee of white and minority faculty members and minority medical students evaluated these applicants. An applicant with a good chance for admission through the regular program was referred to the regular admissions committee. No minority applicant with less than a 2.50 GPA was summarily rejected by the task force. Following the interviews, the special committee assigned its own "benchmark" ratings to the applicants and then recommended candidates to the regular admissions committee until the sixteen admissions slots reserved for minorities were filled. All applicants who were admitted were considered "qualified" for medical training—"qualified" indicating a prediction that the individual was capable of high-quality work.[27]

Bakke's legal challenge of the Davis admissions program was defended by the general counsel for the University of California, Donald L. Reidhaar, who had earlier expressed his doubts about the constitutionality of racial preferences. "In my opinion," he wrote in a memorandum to then University of California President Charles Hitch, " . . . both the Equal Protection Clause of the Fourteenth Amendment to the United States Constitution and Title VI of the Civil Rights Act of 1964 and regu-

TABLE 2 Comparative Quantitative Scores of Regular and Special
(Task Force) Admittees, 1973 and 1974

	Regular Admittees (1973)	Task Force Admittees (1973)	Regular Admittees (1974)	Task Force Admittees (1974)
Science Grade				
Point Average	3.51	2.62	3.36	2.42
Range	2.57 to 4.00	2.11 to 2.93	2.50 to 4.00	2.20 to 3.89
Overall Grade				
Point Average	3.49	2.88	3.29	2.62
Range	2.81 to 3.99	2.11 to 3.76	2.79 to 4.00	2.21 to 3.45
MCAT Scores[a]				
Verbal	81	46	69	34
Quantitative	76	24	67	30
Science	83	35	82	37
General	69	33	72	18

SOURCE: *Record, Bakke* (Yolo County, Calif., Superior Ct.), pp. 210, 213.
[a] MCAT scores stated as a percentile rank.

lations issued thereunder prohibit a state university from granting preference in student admissions on the basis of race."[28] As
the university's chief attorney, it was his task to defend the Davis
program nonetheless.

The Struggle in the Courtroom

Only two superior court judges were assigned to Yolo County at
the time Bakke brought his suit, one of whom was occupied
with several cases and the other of whom disqualified himself
because of an unspecified relationship with the university. The
case was given to a retired judge from Santa Rosa County who
had been called up for the day, Judge F. Leslie Manker. "He
walked in on this [the *Bakke* case], expecting the usual run-of-
the-mill cases," observed Reynold Colvin. "From the look on
his face I think he felt he had been done in."[29]

Since there was little disagreement about the facts of the case,
the principal evidence was a statement and deposition by Dr.
Lowrey on the history of the Task Force and records document-
ing Bakke's attempts to get into the school.

The heart of Bakke's argument was simple: equal protection
means nondiscrimination. According to his attorneys and sup-

porters, the Fourteenth Amendment's language is unequivocal when it insists that "No State shall . . . deny to any person within its jurisdiction the equal protection of the laws." What could this mean except the rejection of racial or ethnic ancestry as a relevant basis for awarding a state benefit? Individual, not group-based, attributes are the only permissible factors to be counted.

Bakke was appealing to one strand of constitutional interpretation. A precursor to *Brown* v. *Board of Education* had laid down the doctrine that the "rights created by the first section of the Fourteenth Amendment are, by its terms, guaranteed to the individual. The rights established are personal rights." [30] An even earlier case, *Strauder* v. *West Virginia*, had defended the principle that equal protection means "all persons, whether colored or white, shall stand equal before the laws of the States." A law depriving a "white man" of a right or benefit would be "a denial" of equal protection. [31] Justice William O. Douglas summed up this line of argument in *DeFunis* v. *Odegaard*, a precursor to the *Bakke* case.

[T]here is no superior person by constitutional standards. A . . . [person] who is white is entitled to no advantage by reason of that fact; nor is he subject to any disability, no matter what his race or color. [32]

The university's response took the form of an appeal to a mixture of policy and legal considerations. The policy arguments emphasized the wisdom and utility of using race as a basis for apportioning public benefits. The regents' attorneys stressed that preferences produced significant social benefits that outweighed any harm inflicted on Bakke. The Davis program preserved "social peace"; by offering a special admissions process, the state established its sensitivity to the needs, and therefore its claim on the allegiances, of minority Californians. The program also stimulated social mobility by providing successful role-models who could inspire minority youths. The increased number of minority physicians would improve medical services in the traditionally underserved minority community. The university's spokesmen pleaded that programs such as Davis's were the only administratively feasible means to the goal of a racially integrated California.

Together with these points, the university invoked constitutional arguments to support the Davis admissions process. The university's brief agreed with Bakke that the equal protection clause is fundamentally a meritocratic guarantee. Public benefits, offices, favors, services, or burdens ought to be distributed among a state's citizens according to the individualized criteria of need, capacity, or contribution. However, the university's argument broke from Bakke's by insisting that preferences for minorities are meritorious under the Fourteenth Amendment. The traditional indications of merit of a potential physician overlooked other capabilities. The black from Watts had to overcome educational, economic, and social disadvantages not confronted by his white competitor. A special admissions process manned by individuals sensitive to the plight of disadvantaged members of minority groups provided a second chance to document real worth. The separate track for disadvantaged minorities was not so much a preference as an opportunity for a more accurate assessment of the minority applicant's credentials.

Special attention to the minority applicant was merited on two other grounds. Medical training should provide more than a familiarization with the physiology and chemistry of the human body. The physician must know something about his patient and the world in which the patient lives if he is expected to treat an illness. Bringing with him a set of distinctive experiences, the minority member enriches the education of all the students. Just as achieving geographical and academic diversity in the student body is considered in admissions decisions, so too cultural diversity is a merit qualification for admission. More broadly, the minority physician offers a valuable contribution to public and private decision making. Physicians and other professionals play a crucial role in American society; the more diversified the medical profession is in viewpoints, experiences, and interests, the richer are the resources of the marketplace of ideas—a cardinal tenet of the American belief in social pluralism. Similar arguments had convinced another court in a prior case to uphold the constitutionality of race preferences in higher education.[33]

If the Davis program was defensible under a meritocratic interpretation of the Fourteenth Amendment, it also was responsive to the remedial spirit of the Reconstruction amendments. Guido Calabresi has argued that slaves and their descendants were granted a special constitutional status as a group and are the proper beneficiaries of an extraordinary exception to the individual merit principle contained in the equal protection clause.[34] The Fourteenth Amendment's thrust is a corrective one; it allows government redress for past racial wrongs. State agencies may attempt voluntarily to compensate blacks and other stigmatized groups for the years of deprivation and discrimination they have suffered. "[T]he history of equitable decrees utilizing race criteria [in job discrimination and school segregation cases] fairly established the broad principle that race may play a legitimate role in remedial policies."[35] Affirmative action programs "are remedies designed to correct fundamental constitutional wrongs, which if permitted to persist threaten the very future existence of the nation."[36] Redressing unfair deprivation is no less consistent with the Constitution than is rewarding competence.

Obviously, the arguments put forward in defense of the Davis program overlapped. The outcome of the racial wrong for which compensation is due—the experience of being black in a racist society—may be seen in another context as a relevant criterion by which to distribute admission slots—the black experience provides the basis for a rapport between the black physician and patient. And, depending on whether that attribute is seen as a good in itself or as a means to a desirable social end, the black experience may be offered as a distributive or utilitarian consideration.

The conflict between Bakke's and the university's versions of the constitutional command of equal protection reflected the troubled state of equal protection doctrine. *Brown* v. *Board of Education* in 1954 had committed the nation to the comparatively simple task of abolishing school segregation as inherently unequal and hence unconstitutional. The courts and the nation have struggled since that decision with the more demanding choices of what types of equality should receive preferred status as public policy. An increasingly divided Court

arguing over the appropriate rationales underlying recent decisions involving racial and sexual discrimination testifies to the
complexity of this task.[37] The dissension over the substantive
theory of equal protection has become so acute that law professor Kenneth Karst wonders whether we may be approaching
the point of "maximum incoherence" in equal protection
analysis.[38]

Contemporary problems with equal protection can be traced
to Chief Justice Earl Warren's opinion for a unanimous Court in
Brown. *Brown* depended either on a theory of equal protection
as a shield against state actions stigmatizing a racial group as
inferior ("to separate them [black children] from others of similar age and qualifications solely because of their race generates a
feeling of inferiority as to their status in the community") or on
a notion of equal protection as an absolute ban on all forms of
racial discrimination ("where the state has undertaken to provide" an opportunity, it "must be made available to all on equal
terms").[39]

Both interpretations invoke strong precedents in their support. An 1873 decision defending the right of Louisiana to legislate a monopoly over New Orleans stockyards noted in passing
that legislation "which discriminated with gross injustice and
hardship against ["the newly emancipated negroes"] as a class,
was the evil to be remedied by" the equal protection clause.
"We doubt very much whether any action of a state not directed
by way of discrimination against the negroes as a class . . . will
ever be held to come within the purview of this provision."[40] By
1880, however, a shift of emphasis toward a broader antidiscrimination principle occurred. While *Strauder* v. *West Virginia* retained language supporting blacks' "right to exemption
from unfriendly legislation against them . . . implying inferiority in civil society," the Court nevertheless insisted that the
Fourteenth Amendment's "aim was against discrimination because of race or color."[41] This assertion of a universal antidiscrimination interpretation finds support in the language of
one of the Fourteenth Amendment's key legislative backers.
Senator George Boutwell of Massachusetts, explaining on the
floor of the Senate why he believed the *Slaughter-House Cases*

interpretation of the equal protection clause incorrect, argued that the sponsors of the amendment deliberately failed to include the phrase "race, color, or previous condition of servitude" in the Fourteenth Amendment as they did in the Fifteenth because "equality was an individual attribute that had no connection with class or race; the amendment extended the same rights to all."[42] This prohibition of all racial discrimination resurfaced in the *Japanese Relocation Cases* of 1943 and 1944 where the Court noted that "all legal restrictions which curtail the civil rights of a single racial group are immediately suspect."[43] The conflicting themes of universal protection and of a special concern for blacks and similar groups took on new life in the context of the sixties and seventies.

"The Equal Protection Clause is itself a classic paradox," Justice Rehnquist has written. Clearly, the Fourteenth Amendment could not have intended to outlaw all inequalities. Government rests on distinctions. The legislative process's "purpose is to draw lines in such a way that different people are treated differently."[44] If all inequalities are not unconstitutional or even unfair, then what fundamental aspects of American life fall within the command of equal protection? The Constitution provides few guidelines to resolve the problem of justified inequalities. Not only does the Constitution contain no fixed preference for equality over liberty, or liberty over equality, several passages in its original and amended forms reject ascription-based criteria, suggesting that certain types of equality and diversity are deemed compatible. The prohibition against bills of attainder in Article I, the outlawing of religious tests in Article VI, and the guarantee of due process to "any person" in the Fifth Amendment defend libertarian and egalitarian values at the same time. Several authors have noted a convergence in constitutional interpretation of the doctrines on equality and liberty. *Bolling* v. *Sharpe*, *Buckeley* v. *Valeo*, and *Trimble* v. *Gordon*'s rulings interpreting the due process clause of the Fifth Amendment in terms originally developed to give meaning to the equal protection clause of the Fourteenth Amendment appear to establish as a constitutional value the "equal exercise of personal liberty."[45] If this is so, fears of a disintegration of equal protection doctrine may be overly drawn. Problems in equal protection analysis may be more the product of increasingly complex understandings of the proper relationship between egalitarian and individualistic values than the result of a failure of imagination.

Nevertheless, the lack of firm guidance from constitutional doctrine contributed to a narrowing of the debate over affirmative action in *Bakke*. Much of the legal argument became a struggle over what "test" of judicial scrutiny should be applied to the Davis program. Should programs of affirmative action be obliged to withstand an examination which is lenient or demanding—or some middle-range variant? Need the university merely prove that its task force was a reasonable response to a legitimate state concern, or must it meet the more exacting standard of demonstrating a compelling state interest in the program?

This concern with the appropriate test is another facet of the problem of developing policies on equality. The need to distinguish between acceptable and unacceptable governmental discriminations among classes of individuals has prompted American law to develop the "antidiscrimination principle." It contains four propositions:[46] (1) Equal protection means equal treatment, the formalistic definition of equality as treating similar cases similarly. (2) The significance of similarities is based on judgments reflecting social and political attitudes; similarities lie in the "eye of the beholder." Therefore, a government may permissibly distinguish between mixed classes of similar and dissimilar things so long as it does not draw the lines in an arbitrary fashion. (3) Arbitrariness can not be assumed but must be tested and the courts are the authoritative arbitrators of disputes over the rationality of state-drawn lines. (4) Although the courts should generally defer to exercises of legislative will, they should apply stricter standards to legislative classifications affecting fundamental constitutional rights. The same standards of "color-blindness" (rejecting as generally irrelevant the ascription-based attributes of race, religion, and ethnicity) and universality (the precept that rules should be applied in an even-handed manner) that dominate the courtroom are applicable to the legislature.

The application of the principle to actual cases is more complex than the simple theory of equal protection might suggest. The principle forces the judge to engage in a complicated thought experiment: he must attempt to reconstruct the actual criteria creating the class, which might be very different from the stated ones. He must judge whether the actual governmental interest supporting the classification is a proper one. Finally, he must determine if the classification is sufficiently related to the legitimate purposes it is intended to serve. "Standards must therefore be set for determining how poor the relationship must be between criterion and purpose before it is deemed arbitrary."[47] Owen Fiss calls this testing of means and ends a "process of imagination" and rightly argues that it induces the judge to fall back upon norms of his "craft" as a guide for decision.[48]

One of those judicial norms counsels deference to legislative judgment. Hence, the judge's task is complicated not only by the "imaginative" exercise of reconstructing a statute's purpose but also by the task of determining whether the legislatively developed "fit" between criteria and purpose is allowable. The traditional response in cases not affecting fundamental rights or threatening racial groups has been a tolerant one. So long as the state demonstrates that the means it has selected are reasonably suited to accomplishing a legitimate (constitutional) end, the court is willing to permit broad measures of over- and under-inclusiveness. Should there be "room for debate and for an honest difference of opinion,"[49] the court will respect the legislature's judgment of the reasonableness of its actions. However, when a government practice adversely affects the exercise of a constitutional right, such as freedom of speech, or threatens to injure the status of a racial group, as the Jim Crow laws of the South did, the courts have not been so relaxed in their supervision. Apart from the Japanese-American internment and relocations cases of World War II, no state action adversely affecting a racial group has passed muster under the far sterner "strict" test.[50] So severe is this test that one author has christened it "strict in theory, fatal in fact."[51] Chief Justice Burger agrees: "[N]o state law has ever satisfied this seemingly insurmountable standard, and I doubt one ever will, for it demands nothing less than perfection."[52]

The stratification of equal protection doctrine into these two tests—one relatively toothless, the other a "kiss of death"—reflects another norm of the judicial craft. The antidiscrimination principle confines the promise of equal protection to the comparatively objective notion of equal treatment. This confinement is in part a product of the constitutional principle fostering containment of governmental power.[53] It also reflects a judicial concern with the containment of its own powers. Mindful of the political and popular reaction to judicial invalidation of New Deal legislation in the thirties, the courts have been sensitive to the propriety of intruding unnecessarily into legislative judgments. These doubts about the judiciary's role are also traceable to a tension between the practice of judicial review and the ideal of democratically accountable government.

In a political system that takes seriously its commitment to government "of" and "by" the people, the power of an independent, nonelected and life-tenured federal judiciary seems anomalous. Several sophisticated theories of jurisprudence have attempted to rationalize the apparent anomaly. Some point out that democracy is not found as a pure commodity in any part of the political system.[54] Others note that courts are deliberately isolated from the vicissitudes of ordinary majoritarian politics so that they can be sensitive to the long-term values of a constitutional order. "Their isolation and the marvelous mystery of time give courts the capacity to appeal to men's better nature, to call forth their aspirations, which may have been forgotten in the moment's hue and cry."[55] The process of accommodation and conflict among many interests that is the heart of the American political experiment seeks to protect the individual from group oppression while permitting the people to carry out their lawful wishes. But all would agree that courts should not intrude into the ordinary political process without a powerful justification. "Legislatures have the primary responsibility . . . for making critical choices."

When such choices must be made, the effort ought to be drawn from the legislature, as the most broadly representative, politically responsible institution of government, a focused judgment about the appropriate balance to be struck between competing values. Once the legislature has made such·a judgment, courts ought to be extremely hesitant to upset it, for if the values to which law gives expression are to change over time, the legislature's warrant for making the necessary decisions is a good deal stronger than that of the courts.[56]

Thus the Supreme Court's rulings on equal protection have been as much concerned with its own doubts about the limits of competent judicial lawmaking as they have been about the substantive principles giving the Constitution its life.

The political implications of applying one or the other standard of "fit" to the Davis program were important for reasons apart from the question of the court's role in American politics. If the court decided that the strictest standard should be applied, the university would carry the burden of justifying its special admissions program. Conversely, if the looser standard was invoked, Bakke would be obligated to prove that the Davis program was arbitrary or capricious. In practical terms, the selection of the appropriate test would determine the winner and loser. This debate affected not only the personal interests of the parties but also challenged presumptions about the responsibilities of the individual and the state in a healthy society. Crucial to the litigation was the issue of whether the strict test, developed to protect individuals against racially inspired injuries, should be applied to a program intended to remedy past racial injustices. The university insisted it should not. According to supporters of the Davis program, the constitutional prohibition of "invidious" racial discrimination is directed at something more than simple arbitrariness. "Invidious" connotes hostility or contempt, stigmatizing the individual as inferior because of his or her racial ancestry. The justification for invoking the strict test is to protect individuals from public insult because of their involuntary membership in racial groups.[57] Since whites are not stigmatized by preferential programs, they should not be protected by the "status harm" trigger of the strict scrutiny test. The state need demonstrate only a reasonable or substantial interest to defend this justifiable form of discrimination. The justice of a special solicitude for those suffering the stigma of caste and the loss of dignity or self-esteem outweighs the costs of whatever comparatively minor losses are suffered by white applicants such as Bakke.

Bakke's response invoked a different conception of the limiting principle of equal protection. He appealed to a simpler interpretation of the Fourteenth Amendment's intent and struck a different balance between social responsibility for rectifying past wrongs and the individual's claim to equal treatment. According to Bakke, antidiscrimination counsels neutrality; it protects every individual against discrimination regardless of his or her social or ethnic ancestry. Racial discrimination, no matter how well intentioned, is invidious. Stigma is a pertinent issue only when the question whether a classification inflicts a harm is debatable or not. The existence of a harm is not debatable here; Bakke suffered tangibly under the Davis admissions procedures.[58] Moreover, Bakke's loss was not insignificant. His application to Davis was based upon the reasonable expectation that the state would reward his personal merit and ignore the generally irrelevant characteristic of his skin color. Bakke's attorneys charged in their brief to the United States Supreme Court, "Are we to become involved in the testing of legal rights according to blood lines?" To do so would require abandoning "the commitment to a society protective of individual achievement" and replacing it "with a system of rights based upon racial or ethnic group membership."[59] Broader interests than Bakke's were at stake in the case, the attorneys continued. "[D]iscrimination on the basis of race is illegal, immoral, unconstitutional, inherently wrong and destructive of a democratic society."[60]

Rather than confront the powerful political and philosophical aspects of the dispute, the trial judge had concentrated on the narrow issue of quotas. Based on the evidence introduced by both sides in the trial, he concluded "that the medical school had in fact established [racially exclusionary] quotas for this so-called special program and carried that out in these admissions practices."[61] After canvassing the pertinent case law, the trial judge invoked the stricter of the two equal protection tests and held that "the use of a quota in favor of certain minority social or ethnic groups" violated the Fourteenth Amendment.[62] Without evidence of prior or continuing discrimination on its part, the university was not permitted to select its students on the basis of ethnic or racial backgrounds. Judge Manker's decision was not, however, a decisive victory for Bakke. The opinion refused to order Bakke's admittance, finding that Bakke had failed to prove he would have been admitted if the special admissions program had not existed. "The admission of students to the Medical School is so peculiarly a discretionary function of the school that the Court feels that it should not be interfered with by a Court, absent a showing of fraud, unfairness, bad faith, arbitrariness or capriciousness, none of which has been shown." [63] This mixture of successes and failures for both sides persuaded Bakke and the university to appeal to the Supreme Court of California, the next level in the judicial hierarchy.

Bakke's suit in the lower court had attracted little attention. The university's general counsel had been confident that Bakke's challenge would be easily defeated.[64] Others, even groups more organizationally committed to affirmative action, did not intervene. The West Coast office of the National Association for the Advancement of Colored People (NAACP), invited to participate in the original trial, declined to do so. Like the university's attorneys, the NAACP regional staff did not see Bakke's suit as a serious threat.[65] But the lower court's declaratory judgment against the Davis program and the California Supreme Court's decision to hear the appeal established the credibility of his challenge.

When the case was argued before the California Supreme Court, eight organizations offered amici briefs. The Anti-Defamation League and the American Federation of Teachers endorsed Bakke's attack on the Davis special admissions process. The National Lawyers Guild, the Society of American Law Teachers, the Mexican-American Legal Defense and Educational Fund, the Association of American Law Schools, the American Medical Student Association, and the Association of American Medical Colleges defended the university's position. Both sides urged the California Supreme Court to take a broader view of the case than had Judge Manker. Bakke argued that the burden of proving whether he would have been admitted in absence of the special program was the university's. Only the university had the data and expertise to determine how close he had been to being admitted. The university and its supporters challenged Judge Manker's depiction of the program as a quota.

The reservation of sixteen slots for special admittees was not a quota in the "usual sense of an absolute limit," the regents' attorneys wrote, but constituted "reasonable limits . . . placed upon . . . [the special admissions program's] scope."[66] Moreover, the racial classification was not an invidious one since it did not "exclude, disadvantage, insult, or stigmatize minorities" nor was it "designed to segregate the races."[67] The university also challenged Bakke's assertion that he would have been admitted if the special program had not existed. Bakke's 1973 admission rating (468 of 500 points) was "two points lower than any applicant accepted under the regular admissions program" that year. Thirty-five unadmitted applicants had higher scores. His score of 549 points out of 600 in 1974 was bested by thirty-two other unadmitted applicants.[68]

When the California Supreme Court accepted Bakke's challenge of the Davis program, the justices recognized the ramifications of the suit. As one of the most respected state supreme courts in the nation and one routinely at the forefront of judicial innovation, the California court knew that the nation would look to it to establish a persuasive and acceptable policy on the question of preference programs. The United States Supreme Court had already given indications that it wanted to address the question. That Court had held moot a 1974 case similar to Bakke's—*DeFunis* v. *Odegaard.* Justice William Brennan, in a dissent joined by Justices William O. Douglas and Thurgood Marshall, had warned in *DeFunis* that "[f]ew constitutional questions in recent history have stirred as much debate [as the issue of "reverse discrimination"], and they will not disappear. They must inevitably return to the federal courts and ultimately to this Court."[69]

Because of the traditional confidentiality shrouding the justices' deliberations, it is impossible to know what type of political maneuvering occurred in the California Supreme Court's conferences on *Bakke*. One can piece together some fragments of fact and speculate on the basis of clues in the opinions. Perhaps the most significant is the fact that the majority and dissenting opinions were written by the two most liberal and respected members of the Court.

Justice Stanley Mosk, author of the six-man majority opinion for the California Supreme Court, provided a rare glimpse into the deliberations of an appeals court in a television and newspaper interview one year after the *Bakke* decision was handed down. Although the attorneys for the university "put on a first-rate case and did . . . [their] best to justify a quota system," Mosk told the television interviewer, the court majority "had very little difficulty" in reaching a decision. If the university had presented evidence of past discriminatory action, the case might have turned out differently.

Under Title VII of the Civil Rights Act of 1964, minorities are entitled to a preferrence if they have been previously discriminated against in employment. You can analogize employment to school admission and argue that if they had previously been discriminated against in admission, they would be entitled to some kind of preference. . . . [However,] there was no evidence [that the university had discriminated against minorities] . . . and I honestly don't believe that the University of California has overtly discriminated. They've taken all comers. . . .

The court saw quite clearly that this was a case of racial discrimination, and it was our feeling that discrimination against a person of any race is just bad.[70]

The opinion written by Mosk for the majority commenced with the statement:

We conclude that the program, as administered by the University, violates the constitutional rights of non-minority applicants because it affords preference on the basis of race to persons who, by the University's own standards, are not as qualified for the study of medicine as non-minority applicants denied admission.[71]

In order to arrive at the conclusion that "the special admissions program is unconstitutional because it violates the rights guaranteed to the majority by the equal protection clause of the Fourteenth Amendment . . . ,"[72] the opinion addressed three related but analytically distinct questions: the rights of individuals, the logic and consistency of the rationale underlying the Davis program, and the value of merit.

The majority opinion fastened onto the language in *Shelley* v.

Kraemer in stating that "[t]he rights created by the first section of the Fourteenth Amendment are, by its terms, guaranteed to the individual. The rights established are personal rights."[73] From that axiom the court concluded that the race of the individual suffering a deprivation of equal protection was irrelevant to the issue of whether that deprivation was constitutional or not. The guarantee of equal protection required members of all races to be "subject to equivalent burdens" and to benefit from equivalent opportunities. The mandate of the Constitution is unequivocal: "The Equal Protection Clause commands the elimination of racial barriers, not their creation in order to satisfy our theory as to how society ought to be organized."[74]

Mosk then subjected the consistency and factual bases of the Davis program to a careful scrutiny and found that program wanting. The argument that "minority status in and of itself constitutes a substantive qualification for medical study" was a tautology; it "assumes the answer to the question at issue." There was no basis for assuming that minority physicians would be more sympathetic to or aware of the peculiar medical problems of minorities. Furthermore, programs such as Davis's might be "counterproductive." Not only are they racially divisive, destroying the prospects for racial harmony, but

. . . the principle that the Constitution sanctions racial discrimination against a race—any race—is a dangerous concept fraught with potential for misuses in situations which involve far less laudable objectives than are manifest in the present case.[75]

Perhaps the most crucial feature of the case for the majority was the role of merit: "The question we must decide is whether the rejection of better qualified applicants on racial grounds is constitutional." Mosk's answer was "no."

To uphold the University would call for the sacrifice of principle for the sake of dubious expediency and would represent a retreat in the struggle to assure that each man and woman shall be judged on the basis of individual merit alone.

Mosk was not insisting that universities are obliged to use such quantitative measures of ability as test scores or grade point averages. In fact, a university may properly use other indices of achievement such as recommendations, interviews, and an appraisal of the applicant's personal goals and the "needs of the profession and society." The opinion encouraged the use of "flexible admissions standards" and other devices such as remedial training and aggressive recruitment in order to provide meaningful access to the state's professional schools for minority individuals. But if a program was intended to aid disadvantaged applicants, then

[d]isadvantaged applicants of all races must be eligible for sympathetic consideration, and no applicant may be rejected because of his race, in favor of another who is less qualified, as measured by standards applied without regard to race.[76]

The Mosk opinion had the hallmarks of an opinion struggling to find a common ground upon which a majority could stand. It offered features attractive to the broad spectrum of political beliefs found on the court. The two California justices (Marshall McComb and William Clark, Jr.) who favored a conservative, restrained role for the court could accept the argument that legal precedents establishing a color-blind guarantee of equal protection to all individuals resolved the issue. The moderate and liberal justices might find compelling the questions about the consistency and fairness of the program. Mosk argued that his opinion "gives the university plenty of leeway." "It isn't race that is significant. It is the disadvantage one may have because of economic circumstances, language problems in the home, or cultural deficiencies."[77] To the extent the Davis program failed to meet its own standards, to the degree it overlooked the potential reservoir of nonminority applicants with the desire and ability to help the traditionally underserved minority community, or favored one element of disadvantagedness over another, the program could not justify the burdens it assigned to members of nonminority groups.

The lone dissenter to Mosk's majority opinion took a quite different approach. Justice Matthew Tobriner argued that the history and purpose of the Fourteenth Amendment was to free blacks and other minorities from past and continuing effects of state-fostered discrimination. The state had a compelling interest in breaking down the artificial barriers to achievement by redressing the injustices of the past with preferences for the present. It was unfortunate "that in many circumstances any remedy for the inequalities flowing from past discrimination will inevitably result in some detriment to nonminorities," but so long as

[the] court is convinced that differential racial treatment has been adopted in a good faith attempt to promote integration, it should uphold a benign [nonstigmatizing] racial classification so long as it is directly and reasonably related to the attainment of integration.[78]

Tobriner's dissent, longer than the majority opinion, saw integration as the paramount value promoted by the Fourteenth Amendment. More than equal educational opportunity must be given to those who have been disadvantaged in the past. "We've got to give them a special break."[79] And the court ought not impose its own policy preferences when constitutional values are not imperiled.

The majority are in serious error . . . in equating their own views of appropriate policy with constitutional commands. In this realm, it is the education authorities, not the courts, that are empowered to render policy statements.[80]

Many observers praised Tobriner's dissent as a more intellectually sophisticated response to the dilemmas posed by *Bakke*.[81] This ignores the fact that majority opinions are constrained by the need to compromise when presenting the views of a collectivity, a need for agreement that explains in part the majority opinion's neglect of the subtle complexities of equal protection doctrine. For example, Mosk was careful to state that the majority would accept the university's justifications as "compelling" for the sake of argument ("arguendo"), so that it could turn to the less politically divisive issue of whether the means selected achieve these ends.[82] Nevertheless, Mosk and Tobriner's debate did serve to restate many of the key issues and alternative policies. That so respected and highly regarded a body as the California Supreme Court should divide so drastically over the issue of racial preferences foretold the difficulties the United States Supreme Court would confront and represented in miniature the fundamental choices facing the nation.

The Antimonies of Equality

If the trial verdict had alerted the attentive legal community to *Bakke*'s importance, the announcement of the California Supreme Court's decision brought the case to serious national attention. Never before had a state's supreme court voided a university affirmative action program. The Supreme Court of Washington had upheld a state law school's preferential treatment of minorities in *DeFunis* v. *Odegaard*,[83] and the New York State Court of Appeals supported the idea of affirmative action in *Alevy* v. *Downstate Medical Center*.[84] Although some lower state and federal courts had ruled against minority preferences in public teacher employment,[85] and in college financial aid programs,[86] the declaration that quota-based affirmative action was unconstitutional was especially shocking coming from one of the most prestigious state supreme courts and from the most populous state.

Originally, a majority of the Board of Regents of the University of California opposed appealing the case. Some thought the decision was proper and did not want to risk its being overruled. Others feared that the more conservative federal court would uphold *Bakke*. They sought to "localize" the damage by isolating the holding to California.[87] After several civil rights organizations, and at least one University of California campus faculty, petitioned the regents *not* to appeal the case, fearful of spreading the "germ" of *Bakke*, the conservative members of the regents shifted their support in favor of an appeal.[88] On November 19, 1976, the regents voted to appeal to the United States Supreme Court.

The least charitable explanation of the regents' decision came from Ralph Smith, a representative of the National Conference of Black Lawyers and an assistant professor at the University of Pennsylvania Law School. Characterized by the university's general counsel, Donald Reidhaar, as his personal "nemesis,"[89] Smith charged that the regents "fundamentally disagree" with the purposes of minority admissions programs. This lack of commitment would prevent an effective defense of the Davis special admissions process. According to Smith, a university lawyer had admitted that the regents voted to appeal because the "university has nothing to lose."[90] Smith's allegations were supported by others. John Vasconcellos, chairperson of the California Assembly's subcommittee on postsecondary education, asserted that the university's handling of the case had been "less than competent."[91] Cruz Reynoso, a California appellate court justice, testified before Vasconcellos's subcommittee that the "university as a whole is antagonistic to minority programs."[92] California Assemblyperson Peter R. Chacon chastised the university for "racism." He asked, "What is the university's commitment to minority students? With *Bakke*, the university is turning away from the open door for minorities. The university is very, very racist."[93]

A more sympathetic explanation was offered by Bakke's counsel, Reynold Colvin. "This was a pocketbook issue as far as the university was concerned." If *Bakke* was allowed to stand, "the university would have to end its program. Remember, that this is not an entirely idealistic question. HEW demands achievement from schools in terms of the numbers of minorities in classrooms."[94] In a similar vein, the president of the University of California warned that the "*Bakke* case exists, and its consequences will not go away while we wait for some ideal case." President David S. Saxon argued that the case would deal a "crushing blow to the many minority students" hoping to gain "access to professional training." The special status and prestige of the California Supreme Court ensured that the effects of its decision would be felt "throughout the nation," exerting "a chilling effect on minority admissions programs" in every state. The regents had little choice whether to appeal or not. "Would not minority groups have protested strongly had the university declined to contest the initial suit? Had we not pursued the appeal, would not minority groups six months or a year from now protest strongly about our inability to admit more minority students?" Saxon concluded, "there is one more reason why the university is proceeding with its appeal . . . : We believe our admissions policies are legally and morally proper."[95]

Critics of the university's decision were not mollified. The Mexican-American Legal Defense and Educational Fund (MALDEF) joined with fifteen other organizations to petition the United States Supreme Court to deny *certiorari*, asking the Court not to review the lower court's decision. They argued that the necessary "case and controversy" was lacking because Bakke had no standing to challenge the Davis program since he would not have been admitted to the school even if there had been no special admissions program, and warned about the inadequacies of the trial record in so important a case. MALDEF suggested the case be returned to the California courts for further argument and the introduction of pertinent facts.[96]

While the case was pending before the federal Supreme Court, the dispute spilled out into the streets, onto the pages of the national press and scholarly journals, and into radio and television broadcasts. A "National Committee to Overcome the *Bakke* Decision" was formed to coordinate the activities of opponents to the California opinion. Mass rallies and protests were held.[97] When the student newspaper at the University of California, Berkeley, endorsed Bakke's position, angry students burned copies of the editorial on the steps to the newspaper office.[98] University supporters and critics presented their position in locally and nationally televised news programs.[99] Several conferences and debates on the topic were held. Howard University's Institute for the Study of Educational Policy established a clearing house to coordinate research and to disseminate findings on affirmative action. Articles recounting the pros and cons of Bakke's case appeared in the pages of *Harpers*, the *New Republic*, the *Atlantic Monthly*, *Time*, *Newsweek*, and in numerous other magazines. The Greater Washington (D.C.) Central Labor Union sent the Supreme Court a mailgram urging reversal of the California decision.[100]

Speakers for both sides recognized that the case posed dilemmas not easily solved. Writing in support of the Davis program, McGeorge Bundy nevertheless defended "the moral and intellectual standing of those who complain against special admissions."[101] Substantial numbers of blacks and other nonwhites opposed preferential treatment for minorities in college admissions and employment.[102] A poll sponsored by the *New York Times* and CBS News during the month oral arguments on *Bakke* were heard by the federal court indicated that forty-two percent of the blacks questioned opposed numerical preferences for qualified minority applicants to colleges and universities.[103] Such personal and group ambivalence over *Bakke* was a reflection of how the nation was torn by the issue of affirmative action. And this ambivalence pointed to a larger debate of which affirmative action occupied only a portion.

If affirmative action was a constitutional issue, it was "constitutional" in the fullest sense of that word: as the kind of problem which demands examination of the fundamental principles giving order and meaning to American politics. *Bakke* presented a conflict between the individual's claim to equal treatment by the state and the state's responsibility to foster some degree of equality among its citizens. As the word "constitutional" implies, this conflict was a fundamental one and reflected one aspect of the recurring dilemma of choosing from among mixtures of equality and liberty. The choice is not a simple one of liberty or equality, but a more challenging judgment of the proper mixture of libertarian and egalitarian values. The individual's *right* ("May I?") to equal treatment may be meaningless without the individual's *capacity* ("Can I?") to exercise that right. A government's efforts to guarantee capacities for some may obstruct the rights of others. It is against the backdrop of this broader concern that the debate over affirmative action becomes sensible.

Abraham Lincoln's words "a nation, conceived in liberty, and dedicated to the proposition that all men are created equal" are the most powerful summation of the American political creed. The two central ideals in American thought—liberty and equality—reflect a commitment to a democratic polity composed of free and equal citizens: free to express their individuality, equal in their status as worthy members of a common political community. Interestingly, however, while the concept of liberty received frequent attention in the original Constitution and in the Bill of Rights,[104] and although equality's claim on the American faith can be traced at least as far back as the opening proposition of the Declaration of Independence ("that all men are created equal"), commitment to the ideal of individual equality was not given constitutional status until the adoption of the

Fourteenth Amendment's "equal protection" clause. The fact that the notion of equality failed to become a part of the basic covenant of the American republic until 1868 suggests an irreducible sense of unease in American thinking on the topic of equality, an unease not unique to the American experience alone, but traceable to the paradoxical role played by equality in a democratic political and social order.

The problem of equality is decisive for all democracies. Founded on the premise that all men are in some important sense equal, democratic governments have as one obligation the promotion of equality among their citizens. Unfortunately, the ideal of equality is susceptible to a bewildering array of interpretations and understandings. One can distinguish the formal from the many ethical principles of equality. As a formal principle, equality requires no more than that similar cases be treated similarly and different cases be treated differently. As an ethical rule, equality may command a basic appreciation for the equal moral or legal worth of all individuals ("equal before God" or "equal before the law"), may require equal life chances or equal access to all significant social and political opportunities ("equal opportunity"), or may demand a fraternal equality of condition ("equal results"). As an ethical rule justifying the distribution of rights and opportunities then, equality is not the metaphorical equivalent of the mathematical concept of identity. Human beings are not fungible; equality does not demand that individuals be treated as if they were interchangeable. As a rule of human conduct, however, equality does demand that individuals be treated differently only with regard to relevant criteria.

The principle of *relevant differences* is the core of all substantive theories of equality. Each theory of what equality is, and therefore what American society ought to be, is an attempt to specify a meaning for equality general enough to be applied as a principle for action without being vacuous. The varying success of such attempts defines the possible alternatives for endorsement as public policy.

Answers to the question of which differences are relevant and which sorts of discrimination are invidious tend to take the form of an appeal to common human characteristics or an analysis of the nature of human relationships. The human char-acteristics approach minimizes the significance of differences among individuals by emphasizing common capacities or sta-tuses: men and women are equally to be regarded because of their shared moral or intellectual capacities, because of the in-trinsic worthiness of human beings, or because of their common status as children of God. As the basis for the precept of univer-salism—the axiom that rules should be applied in an even-handed manner—the appeal to human characteristics takes the form of the ideal of equality before the law.[105] In more modern terms, it supports the notion of equal citizenship.[106] As partici-pants in a common polity, all citizens may claim the respect ac-corded to peers. Not simply a "parity of esteem" but "a positive feeling of respect for all engaged in a common purpose" is their due.[107] The obligation of each citizen to respect the liberty and security of all is accompanied by the responsibility of all to en-sure that each member of the community is provided with the level of material goods necessary to secure his or her full status as a co-equal. Hence the theory of equal citizenship supports claims to equal social and economic rights as well as to equal political rights.

Despite its appeal, the common humanity tradition has an important shortcoming. While it successfully emphasizes the commonality among individuals, it fails to provide much guid-ance about the persistent differences distinguishing individuals and how to deal with those differences. The second tradition of egalitarian theory attempts to offer more useful instruction. This tradition emphasizes the nature of human relationships in order to explain justifiable inequalities. The selection of what ought to be relevant differences provides the basis for expecta-tions of equal status in all other spheres of human life.

In simplistic terms, the human relations tradition has evolved four justifications for treating individuals unequally. One justi-fication asserts that human beings are unequal in their *deserts*. "Deserts" imply some measure of real or potential performance. Thus differences in individual efforts and contributions ("ac-tual" performance) or in merit ("potential" performance) war-rant differences in treatment and results. The "desert" justification calls upon the justness of distributions which are the produce of competition—of a competitive assessment of actual contributions or of such indicators of individual promise as performance on professional school admissions tests. It might be called a "market" justification of inequalities.

A second justification rejects the competitive or marketplace metaphor underlying the deserts approach and emphasizes instead the claims of *needs*. Human beings are different in their needs, and justice dictates that when resources are scarce, those who are neediest have a prior claim to the resources. Where "market" equality stresses competitive performance, the "needs" justification focuses on personal deficiencies or wants. It would warrant unequal treatment in results because needs are unequal. Such justified inequalities might be labeled "fair shares."

Questions of *utility* underlie the third justification for inequality. The main concern here is to distribute opportunities and benefits in such a way as to maximize the general welfare of all. Considerations of what distributions are socially useful justify unequal shares. Some types of redistributive governmental programs, such as the progressive income tax, are defended because they prevent the broad disparities in economic power that divide some societies into a small but powerful elite of "haves" and a large mass of "have-nots." The inequalities of taxation promote an approximate economic equality not in order to satisfy legitimate needs or to respond to the claims of "desert" but rather to secure *social* peace, to secure the loyalties of the poor. Social utility therefore supports some kinds of unequal shares because they result in socially useful outcomes; it implies the existence of "useful" shares.

The final justification invokes the claim of *might*, defined as either physical force or according to some standard of political power. The right of a majority to rule in a democracy dedicated to equally weighed individual votes is a recognition of the claims of the greater number to win when policies are in dispute. The "might" justification is a pragmatic one and implies "political" shares.

These justifications need not conflict, but equalities of one type tend to create inequalities of another. The guarantee of an equal vote ("one man, one vote") overlooks the role played by intensity of convictions in politics. Should an apathetic majority of fifty-one percent overrule an intensely concerned minority of forty-nine percent? Intelligence, height, and strength are individual traits which have become identified as meritorious in some circumstances without violating common notions of justice or fairness. Should a family's earnings depend on the success of the breadwinner in an economic competition ("market equality") or should need dictate income ("fair shares")? "The question is not, Do you favor equality? It is, *Which* equality are you for, and what inequalities are you willing to accept as its costs?"[108] But the problem is more than one of trade-offs between types of equality. Just as important is the question of how much short-term inequality is tolerable in order to attain equality in the long term.

The problem of equality has yet another dimension: the value of equality struggles with the value of diversity. The tension is more complex than the common caricature of "equality versus liberty" portrays it. The real tension is between egalitarian values which respect diversity and those which challenge every diversity as an inequality and therefore as an injustice. In the language of John Rawls, both "liberal" and "democratic" conceptions of equality can tolerate enormous inequalities among individuals. So long as the "least advantaged members of society" benefit from the rewards granted to successful competitors, inequality of results may be socially efficient and morally justified.[109] A radical egalitarian such as Jerome Karabel, on the other hand, may reject any inequality, no matter how socially beneficial, since inequalities springing from natural endowments are viewed as inherently arbitrary.[110] No claim to a greater reward is merited if superior performance is the product of a capricious Nature.

The principal American response to the perplexing issues of equality and diversity has been "equal opportunity"—the principles of fair competition ("to afford all, an unfettered start, and a fair chance, in the race of life") and of careers open to talent ("to clear the paths of laudable pursuit to all").[111] Ideally, individual performance, not a system of statuses, would determine an individual's position in society. In the American tradition, equality has not meant a "uniform position in a common scale," but a "universal opportunity to move through a scale which traversed many levels. . . . The emphasis on unrestricted latitude as the essence of equality in turn involved a heavy emphasis upon liberty as an essential means for keeping the scale open and hence making equality a reality as well as a theoretical condition."[112]

Despite the centrality of the traditional equal opportunity formula to American beliefs, there is also a concern about the distribution of economic and social burdens and awards after the competition. The champions of equal results argue that if all individuals are created equal, then "equality of opportunity ought to lead to approximate equality of condition." A failure "to realize this goal reflects a deficiency (if not a positive error) in the existing social and economic arrangements."[113] Efforts to reconcile the centrifugal pressures of these ideals of equal opportunities and equal accomplishments have defined the debate on equality in the American tradition. Until recently, the attractions of equal opportunity have overshadowed the concerns about equal results. Universal suffrage, public education, and antagonism to blatant elite domination of the economic and political sectors promised that individual achievement would receive its due. The personal successes of upwardly mobile members of white ethnic groups such as the Irish, the Jews, and the Italians helped shift the divisions within American society away from those of ethnic background toward those of class distinction. These successes seemed to indicate that the important differences in America were not ones of ethnic ancestry but of economic status. However, in the late sixties and early seventies, this apparent national consensus on equality began to disintegrate.

The conviction that a color-blind policy would overcome the effects of racial discrimination had animated the civil rights movement at its beginning. Remove the stigma of public racism and the plight of the black would disappear. The passage of the Civil Rights Act in 1964 and the Voting Rights Act in 1965 seemed to accomplish this aim. Blacks had been assured of an equal right "to participate in the public sphere of the community."[114] At this stage, the civil rights movement was less a campaign in defense of the specific rights of blacks and other minorities than it was a crusade to realize the promise of American constitutional ideals. One civil rights leader explained, "The civil rights movement was and is essentially concerned with the structure of law and social justice; its goals were equality before the law and equality of educational opportunity. As a movement it was begun by people whose aim was not to aid the Negro as such but to bring American society into closer conformity with constitutional principle."[115] With the shift of the movement's attention from the specific problems of the South to the broader issue of equal rights in the nation, the character of the demands made by civil rights activists changed. A greater emphasis was placed on opportunities for material goods. Equal opportunity in employment and higher education coupled to a concern about the inequalities in income distribution among the races became a principal theme.[116] This concern was not novel; as President, John F. Kennedy had issued a call for "affirmative steps" by contractors on federal projects to recruit minorities and encourage their promotion in 1961.[117] His successor, Lyndon Johnson, strengthened federal affirmative action programs in 1965,[118] explaining in an address to the graduating class of Howard University on June 4, 1965, that "you do not take a person who, for years, has been hobbled by chains and liberate him, bring him up to the starting line of a race and then say, 'You are free to compete with all the others,' and still justly believe that you have been completely fair." The nation needed to move beyond equality "as a right and a theory" to "equality as a fact and equality as a result."[119] President Richard Nixon stiffened his predecessors' programs under the Department of Labor with the implementation of the Philadelphia Plan in 1969. The plan established specific goals and time tables for minority recruitment in the Philadelphia building trades.[120]

By the late sixties, it became clear that racially neutral programs of nondiscrimination might be insufficient to overcome the effects of prior and continuing discrimination. In an era of high unemployment and limited economic opportunities, the promise of advancement through personal achievement seemed to lose its magic. The "equal opportunity-antidiscrimination" programs of the early sixties had failed to bring about hoped-for changes in the economic and social status of minorities. The facts were overwhelming. According to the Bureau of the Census, the proportion of families with incomes below the poverty line was almost four times higher among black than among white families in 1969. The median school years completed by whites was 12.1 years in 1969; the median for blacks was 9.8 and for Latinos 9.6.[121] In 1974 the unemployment rate among nonwhites was double that of whites.[122] A study released by the Congressional Budget Office in 1977 reported that nonwhites suffered a seventy percent higher infant mortality rate and had six years shorter life expectancy than whites.[123] In such a world, the "openness" of the social system was seen as oppressive. Activist organizations formed and voiced demands for group reparations such as the "Black Manifesto" of 1969.[124] A controversy began in academic circles over the question whether race, economic class, or rural residence is the relevant factor that explains the disparities among the races. Some answered class,[125] others race,[126] still others suggested both.[127] It was against this backdrop of legal, philosophical, political, and scholarly controversy that the United States Supreme Court heard the university's appeal.

Indecision or Statesmanship?

Oral arguments on *Bakke* were heard on October 12, 1977, but eight months passed before the Supreme Court issued its decision. News accounts suggest that the justices had argued bitterly during their conferences on the case. "The Justices really agonized," an "inside observer" was reported to have commented.[128] Three drafts of the decision were sent to the printers only to be called back for revision. Reportedly, several members of the Court considered holding the case over until the next term because of their dissatisfaction with the case's record. However, fears about appearing foolish if the Court delayed its decision without powerful justification persuaded the justices to make

their positions known. "They are worried about the public perception of the Court if it failed to deal with *Bakke* now," an
unnamed source was quoted to say.[129]

On June 28, 1978, Justice Lewis Powell began his delivery of
the Supreme Court's judgment by stating:

We speak today with a notable lack of unanimity. I will try to explain
how we divided. It may not be self-evident.[130]

It wasn't.

A divided Court had ordered Bakke's admittance to the University of California, Davis Medical School but refused to ban
outright the use of race in admissions decisions. In an opinion
signed by four Justices—John Paul Stevens, Warren Burger, Potter Stewart, and William Rehnquist—Justice Stevens, the author, declined to address the equal protection issue, preferring
to rely on the "plain language" of Title VI to the 1964 Civil
Rights Act and its "broad prohibition against the exclusion
of any individual" from a public benefit on racial grounds.
Stevens's emphasis on Title VI was something of a surprise since
the 1964 act's pertinence had not been seriously argued in the
lower courts. Although Bakke had based his suit on Title VI
grounds, he had also invoked the California and federal consti-
tutions. Not until the Supreme Court requested supplemental
briefs on the Title VI question after oral arguments was its significance recognized. In the briefs offered, Title VI was usually
seen as an ancillary issue to the really important question of
the constitutional standard of equal protection. Nevertheless,
Stevens invoked this "perfectly clear" statute to order Bakke's
admittance, and by doing so, rejected the argument that only
stigmatizing racial exclusions were forbidden by the law.[131]

Justice William Brennan, writing for himself and for Justices
Thurgood Marshall, Byron White, and Harry Blackmun, argued that Title VI and the equal protection clause of the Fourteenth Amendment were functionally equivalent. "As applied to
the case before us, Title VI goes no further in prohibiting the use
of race than the Equal Protection Clause . . . itself."[132] Both
Title VI and the Fourteenth Amendment permit the use of
"color conscious" means to offset the debilitating effects of "so-

cial discrimination" against blacks and other similarly situated minorities.

[A] state government may adopt race-conscious programs if the purpose of such programs is to remove the disparate racial impact its actions might otherwise have and if there is reason to believe that the disparate impact is the product of past discrimination, whether its own or that of society at large.[133]

Accordingly, only government programs that "stigmatize—because they are drawn on the presumption that one race is inferior to another or because they put the weight of government behind racial hatred and separation—are invalid."[134] But Brennan recognized the potential dangers of affirmative action. Such programs, however lofty their intentions, cannot be used "'to stereotype and stigmatize politically powerless segments of society.'" Any preferential process singling out "those least well represented in the political process to bear the brunt" of an otherwise benign program was unconstitutional. Brennan was sensitive to "our deep belief that 'legal burdens should bear some relationship to individual responsibility or wrongdoing.'" To protect this important social value, affirmative action programs cannot be justified on the lenient test of reasonableness. They are obliged to show "an important and articulate purpose for [their] use." He concluded that "our review under the Fourteenth Amendment should be strict—not 'strict in theory and fatal in fact,' because it is stigma that causes fatality—but strict and searching nonetheless."[135]

In the decisive swing opinion, Justice Lewis Powell accepted Brennan's argument that Title VI restates the meaning of the equal protection clause, but held that since the Davis program "totally foreclosed" individuals like Bakke solely on the basis of race from the opportunity to compete in the special admissions program, it was unconstitutional: "When a classification denies an individual opportunities or benefits enjoyed by others solely because of his race or ethnic background, it must be regarded as suspect."[136] Powell, however, sought to establish a constitutional justification for less exclusionary affirmative action programs. "[U]niversities must be accorded the right to select those students who will contribute the most to the 'robust exchange of ideas.'" The First Amendment protects the "constitutional interest" of academic freedom which makes the search for "a diverse student body . . . a constitutionally permissible goal for an institution of higher education." Harvard College's admissions program, he maintained, is one example of such a permissible form of affirmative action.[137]

Supporters of both sides criticized Powell's attempt at "judicious" diplomacy. One defender of the university argued that Powell failed to provide a principled distinction between the operations of the constitutionally forbidden Davis program and the constitutionally permissible Harvard program. Both programs, Ronald Dworkin asserted, handicapped some marginal candidates on the basis of race. Since some individuals will be excluded on the basis of race if it is to be considered affirmatively, then Harvard's "bonus point" program was as constitutionally objectionable as Davis's.[138] Some Bakke supporters concurred. They too found the distinction between the two programs suspect, although for a somewhat different reason. William Bennett, executive officer of the National Humanities Center in North Carolina, and Terry Eastland, editorial writer for the *Greensboro Record*, claimed that Harvard's special admissions program would "produce much the same result as the invalidated Davis program, together with an encouragement to duplicity." Moreover, the Harvard program "bears no relation to the realities of admission to professional schools." They also deplored Powell's efforts to "soothe" the nation. "The Supreme Court does not have this function; its job is to assay what is just and right according to the Constitution and the laws of the land."[139]

Powell's opinion could be interpreted in a more defensible manner. It was not the diminished role played by race in the admissions process which made the Harvard program more palatable to Powell, but the type of competition found there. Powell might have been arguing that the values achieved by academic diversity were ones of experience and talents, not simply skin color and physiological features. A truly "competitive" system in Powell's sense would seek competition within the racial

class "black" as well as between the classes "black" and "white."
The middle-class black from Chicago's South Side would compete against the lower-class black from Chicago's 63rd and Cot-
tage Grove area. It is the experiences they possess as individuals
which would affect their claims to consideration under Powell's
diversity-merit standard. All those considerations that have traditionally served to distinguish among white candidates would
now serve to distinguish among black ones as well.

The announcement of the Court's decision on *Bakke* initiated
controversies within the nation's intellectual journals, and
sparked outraged attacks in newspapers, on television programs,
and on the floor of Congress. The black-owned and operated
Amsterdam News published a headline declaring "Bakke—We
Lost." The Reverend Jesse Jackson viewed the decision as a
"devastating blow to our civil-rights struggle." Congressman
Ron Dellums denounced it as a "racist decision by the Nixon
Court."[140] The Court's opinion was anticlimactic to some:
"This is a landmark case, but we don't know what it marks,"
said University of Chicago law professor Philip B. Kurland.[141] In
several respects the debate among the justices represented in
microcosm the fundamental choices and doubts confronting
the nation. The search for a fair accommodation between the
black's claim to the opportunities of modern life and redress of
past grievances and the white's claim to be treated as an individual labored under the familiar tension between theory and practice. All the justices endorsed the personal right to be judged in
accordance with one's individual attributes. The tragedy of
Bakke was that this apparent consensus over values could not
be carried over into practice. The vision of a race-blind society
authenticated conflicting policies like Stevens's "color-blind"
neutrality, Brennan's acceptance of racial group affiliation as a
proxy for individuals' claims of right, and Powell's less exclusionary but perhaps less effective compromise between the dictates of the merit principle and the demands of compensatory
justice.

CHAPTER II

THE IMPERATIVES OF
ORGANIZATIONAL SURVIVAL

Not all the organizations active in *Bakke* were experienced litigators. In fact, sixty-five percent of the 115 contacted had participated in fewer than five court cases during the preceding ten years.[1] Amici activity is increasing, but the use of litigation as a means to express policy positions is still an extraordinary occasion for most of these organizations. That they did intervene in *Bakke* underscored the special significance of the issue for them.

The reasons why *Bakke* was important differed for each. The issue raised by *Bakke* directly affected the interests of organizations such as the National Association for the Advancement of Colored People and the Polish-American Congress. It raised questions important to the long-term legal strategies of associations like the NAACP Legal Defense and Educational Fund and the Pacific Legal Foundation. It presented broad social problems which concerned, but were not central to, the purposes of organizations such as the American Public Health Association and the United Auto Workers. Organizations differed not only in their goals but also in the variety of strategies available to them, in their structures, and in their relationships with allies and opponents.

I have hypothesized that there is a direct relationship between an organization's purposes and its capacity to educate—its ability to encourage the exploration of new ideas and the discovery of new facts by its members on issues like those of affirmative action. The broader or more diverse the purposes an organization pursues, the greater is the likelihood that its members will learn; the narrower or more restricted the purposes, the less likely education will occur, although members' interests may be well protected. It would be expected, then, that in *Bakke* the more focused was the organizational purpose for intervening, the fewer would be the opportunities for mutual exchange and enlightenment among the members on affirmative action.

To test my hypothesis, I assigned the amici organizations to two sets of categories.[2] One distinguished among three kinds of advocacy goals or purposes—interest group, minority-defense, and public interest. *Interest groups* were organizations that sought to defend specific interests shared by all their members. *Minority-defense organizations* sought to protect more diversified interests, interests representing broad social and cultural bonds shared by the members but which did not necessarily benefit every member as an individual. *Public-interest advocates* entered *Bakke* in order to espouse principled positions they viewed as vital to the health of the entire nation, not to any specific individual or group. The second set of categories assessed the scope of debate over affirmative action within the organizations.[3] *Scope* stood for the breadth and variety of arguments and facts presented to the organization's members. It should therefore serve as an indicator of that aspect of education most likely to be affected by organizational purpose: the communication and exchange of knowledge and ideas. If Hypothesis I is correct, it is reasonable to presume that organizational purpose would determine the breadth and diversity (scope) of the organizational debate over *Bakke*. The more diversified and promotional purposes of public-interest advocacy organizations would encourage more education than the comparatively narrow purposes of interest groups. Minority-defense organizations would stand at some point between these two extremes.

At least in *Bakke*, the expected relationship between organization purpose and scope of debate did not exist. The more "business-like" (narrower or more focused) organizations were not necessarily the least "school-like." Interest-orientation and scope had no relationship.[4]

How can this apparent anomaly be explained? The answer lies, I believe, in the primacy of "survival" over "mission." The survival needs of many organizations took precedence over the goals they were formed to achieve. Fears about the loss of resources, the alienation of vital backers and allies, and the fragmentation of the organization were crucial.

The Politics of Self-Interest

Interest groups involved in *Bakke* pursued a variety of purposes, but, like all interest groups, they shared one characteristic—the pursuit of specific, member-directed benefits. Some, such as the University of Washington or the National Fund for Minority Engineering Students, sought to defend their own programs of affirmative action. Others, such as the Fraternal Order of Police or the American Subcontractors Association, wanted to protect their members from affirmative action challenges. All worked for benefits which were important to their members and which were divisible.[5]

The Equal Employment Advisory Council (EEAC) was one such organization. Formed in 1976 by equal employment enforcement officers working in private industry, the EEAC is committed by its members' personal beliefs and occupational interests to the principle of affirmative action. Officially, the organization seeks "to present the views of employers in the development and implementation of sound government policies and procedures pertaining to nondiscriminatory employment practices."[6] It does so by emphasizing amicus participation, attempting to educate courts and administrative agencies about the implications of their rulings on equal employment laws. More concerned with rationalizing or smoothing out inconsistencies in administrative regulations and judicial rulings than with advocating new interests or advancing new principles, the EEAC's primary commitment is to secure a stable and predictable regulatory environment for its members' business organizations.

Bakke posed special problems to the EEAC. The issue of quotas disrupted the general accord among the organization's members on the direction of antidiscrimination programs. Some felt that Davis had gone too far, others saw special admissions as reasonable, and others wondered if EEAC's interests were sufficiently affected by the case to justify involvement. "We all are human," confided one board member. "We all have our personal commitments that we would have liked to see endorsed by the Council."[7] The debate that followed ranged widely over all the concerns presented by the case, and therefore was "broad" in scope. It was facilitated by the fortuitous appearance of a one hundred forty-three page book compiled by the legal staff in 1977, outlining the controversy's political and legal background and detailing possible positions and strategies.[8] Despite, or perhaps because of, the breadth and intensity of discussions, it took a year for the board of directors to decide to enter the case.

The debate on *Bakke* was not confined to the board. The Case Selection Committee, the EEAC subunit charged with advising the board which cases warranted the organization's involvement, met on at least four occasions to discuss *Bakke*. At the outset, the committee agreed that the EEAC must intervene. The case promised to produce important new rules affecting equal employment litigation and regulation, and the failure to present the EEAC's views might handicap future efforts to mold the development of equal employment law. But, like the board, the members of the committee disagreed whether to support the regents or to distinguish affirmative action from "reverse discrimination." A committee member recalled the thrust of the debate. "[Douglas] McDowell and [Robert] Williams [the EEAC staff counsels] told us that *Bakke* was too important to ignore. We could agree on that. But should we endorse quotas— that we couldn't agree on. Some of us recognized that 'goals,' 'quotas,' 'targets,' whatever you call them, are pretty much the same when an employer has to make a hiring decision. There were others, however, who argued that to endorse California would open us up to discrimination cases because we didn't create our own voluntary programs."[9]

The members were also actively engaged in the deliberations. In two meetings—one in the Midwest in October 1976, another in Washington, D.C., in March 1977—the executive director and the council president briefed the membership on the case. An EEAC member who attended both meetings characterized them as "consultative."

Q. How was *Bakke* raised at the Midwest Meeting?

A. The executive director placed it on the agenda, and we discussed it as new business.

Q. Was there much debate?

A. It depends on what you mean. All of us are conversant with the case law and regulations on quotas. That's what we are paid for. So *Bakke* was not something totally new to us. We talked about it at the meeting, but we spent more time asking questions of the staff than we did arguing what we should do.

Q. What kinds of questions?

A. What a case about university admissions had to do with employment? Was the case a good one to make policy in? What did the parties argue in the lower courts?

Q. Was there any agreement on what you should do?

A. Yes and no. Yes, we agreed that we should offer a brief. No, we weren't sure what brief. By the way, the discussion was not confined to the meeting room. I remember the most interesting talk occurred after the meeting, during luncheon and dinner breaks.

Q. What happened then?

A. We talked long and intensely about the real issues—should quotas be allowed when there is no prior finding of culpability. I don't remember anything new that came up in the discussion, but we did explore old ground carefully. One man warned that we would all be slapped with EEOC [Equal Employment Opportunity Commission] writs if we weren't careful.[10]

During the break between the October and March meetings, he received notice through the EEAC newsletter that a brief was being written.

Q. Did you have any opportunity to stipulate what would be in the brief?

A. I wrote a letter to [Kenneth] McGuiness, the chief counsel, and urged that we support Davis.

Q. Did McGuiness reply?
A. I got a pleasant, noncommital reply.
Q. What happened at the Washington meeting?
A. The board decided to authorize a brief. We voted to endorse the brief's position.
Q. Was there agreement or disagreement at Washington?
A. The brief was a safe one. It stood by the association's special interests in making affirmative action regulations consistent.[11]

Recurrent in this and other interviews was an appreciation for the role played by the staff attorneys in the organization's deliberations. As in many other organizations, the legal staff was an active participant in the debate over *Bakke*. Unlike the situation in many organizations, the EEAC's legal staff took a position of studied neutrality on the case's merits but insisted on the necessity of intervening. "Our task is to develop ideas and arguments and alert the board to promising cases or hearings," explained Douglas McDowell. "If we become too involved in advocating a particular position, we would lose our credibility. While I might state a position, I try to separate my personal from my professional opinions."[12] An EEAC director agreed. "The staff does not attempt to lead. It helps us lead. They try not to embarrass us by getting into cases where where we have no cause to be or to state as recommendations purely personal opinions."[13]

The EEAC attorneys recommended to the board that the brief be tied directly to the organization's formal purposes—the shared concern over inconsistencies in equal employment law. The recommendation offered what appeared to be a statesmanlike compromise. "It stated what we as an organization had to say and no more," said the director.[14] By emphasizing the material interests of the members, their concern with consistency among affirmative action regulations, instead of the divisive symbolic issue—the differing views on what type of affirmative action was good policy—the brief offered a common ground on which all the members could stand.

The brief implored the Supreme Court "that, whatever conclusion the Court reaches, full consideration be given to the implication of the case for private employment affirmative action programs." The nondiscrimination laws passed in the 1960s and the affirmative action regulations promulgated under executive orders subjected employers to bewildering and contradictory demands. The employer faced Title VII liability or the loss of government contracts for failure to implement an affirmative action program and was open to suits by whites for "reverse discrimination" if the program was effective. Should the Court find voluntary quota programs unconstitutional, it would be unfair and poor public policy to permit reverse discrimination plaintiffs to sue private businesses for their good faith effort to increase minority employment. The brief urged the Court "to make it clear that any remedy should be *prospective* only, and limited to injunctions against further implementation of the program." [15]

In contrast with the EEAC's struggle to develop a brief, another interest group, the National Association of Minority Contractors, experienced little difficulty in preparing its position on *Bakke*. The organization is composed of black contractors and subcontractors who seek to improve their opportunities in the construction industry. Responding to the historic exclusion of nonwhites from that industry, the association campaigns for affirmative action legislation and pressures governmental agencies to include affirmative action stipulations in their construction plans.

This association seldom acts as an amicus. Its resources are devoted to more traditional forms of lobbying such as appearances before congressional committees and testimony at agency hearings. Successes in these arenas diminish the attractiveness of amicus participation as an organizational tactic. However, the organization is willing to litigate when a propitious situation appears. It has brought suit under Executive Order 11246, which mandates affirmative recruitment of minorities by federal contractors, and under the Public Works Employment Act of 1977, which set aside ten percent of its funding for minority business. [16] Nevertheless, the organization is wary of becoming entangled in court proceedings because of its limited legal expertise and resources.

One of the association's affiliates, the Minority Contractors

Association of Northern California, alerted the national headquarters to *Bakke*. Coverage of the case by California news
media and promptings from friends in the state's civil rights community had warned the affiliate about *Bakke*'s potential repercussions on black hopes for a greater share of the construction
trade. Acting under an explicit mandate to intervene at its discretion in cases affecting members' interests and after virtually
no discussion, the board of directors authorized the submission
of an amicus brief.[17]

The contractors' brief was a calculated appeal to the conservative justices on the Court. While it urged the Supreme Court
to overturn the California decision, its principal efforts were directed at defending the "permissibility [of the Davis program]
as an act of legislative or executive competence." Constitutional
principle and precedent counsel a restrained role for the Court
when assessing other governmental branches' efforts to overcome racial discrimination. The Court should defer to the special competence of the regents when they authorized affirmative
action programs.[18] This was not the appropriate occasion for judicial overruling of an administrative decision.

The brief was as narrow in its discussion of the issues posed
by *Bakke* as was the EEAC's, despite the lack of dissension in
the association. By employing the issue of judicial deference,
only one small aspect of the general controversy, the association's attorneys avoided duplicating the arguments of others
while minimizing their own expenditure of organizational resources and personal efforts. Although the brief was firmly
backed by the organization, it was not intended to record all of
the factors prompting its composition.

The association was not afraid to endorse the Davis program
partly because it saw its members' interests as directly and obviously affected and partly because those interests were in harmony. The National Association of Minority Contractors is
comprised of individuals in the class of "favored groups" under
existing affirmative action programs, those who receive substantial material benefits from such programs. The EEAC, on
the other hand, represents individuals from several racial backgrounds who occupy executive-level niches in the complex ecol-

ogy of the modern business and industrial firm. As such, they respond to a host of organizational expectations and bureaucratic pressures to which the members of the National Association of Minority Contractors are not subject. Self-employed, the typical member of the latter association saw *Bakke* as threatening his income-earning capacity. The pressures to which he was subject were those associated with the responsibilities of an independent businessman and family head. As one member said, "Speaking for myself and for most of my fellows, *Bakke* touched our pocketbooks. It represented a threat to our livelihood and, in the long run, to the sort of society I hope my child will live in." Because of the coincidence of personal belief with material interests, there was no stimulus for a broad debate about the principles of affirmative action. (The contractors' association was coded as "narrow" in the scope of its debate.) The decision to participate in *Bakke* was facilitated by the conjunction of economic interests with social aspirations for the family.

Some organizations had other specific interests to protect. For example, the Council on Legal Education Opportunity (CLEO) participated in *Bakke* because it feared challenges to its own special admissions program if *Bakke* were upheld. The interest it pursued was organizational rather than individual.

During the sixties, a clamor arose for greater minority access to the nation's policy-making process. CLEO was the organized legal profession's response to this demand. After examining proposals to increase minority presence in the legal profession, the American Bar Association, the Association of American Law Schools, the National Bar Association (composed of black lawyers), and the Law School Admission Council (which designs and administers the Law School Admissions Test)[19] had established a "council on legal educational opportunity" to encourage "economically and educationally disadvantaged students" to enter law school.[20] They hoped that, as the doors of law schools were opened to those traditionally excluded, the doors to political power and influence would also swing open. This was the theme of a 1977 letter to the American Bar Association (ABA): "There is an acute need for equal access not only to our system of justice, but also to the decision-making process in this country. . . . [T]he role of 'Law' in the decision-making process in the United States' democratic form of government . . . is the crucial thread woven into American institutions. Since law has such an important role in society, those who draw up, enforce and interpret laws play key roles in the functioning of government."[21]

To meet its goal of increasing minority access to law schools, CLEO sponsors regional summer institutes—intensive six-week courses in legal analysis, writing, and research—for selected college students from minority and poor backgrounds. While "it is not sufficient, nor is it a requirement to be a member of a minority group" in order to receive CLEO assistance,[22] the great majority of the youths assisted by CLEO are minorities. In 1976, for example, only nine of the 560 students enrolled in CLEO-sponsored programs were non-Spanish-surnamed whites, and these were largely from Appalachia.[23] If successful graduates of the summer program win admission to a law school, they receive financial aid from CLEO to help defray living expenses. Participating law schools customarily waive tuition charges or provide grants and loans to pay for the students' educational costs. By 1977, 2,188 CLEO program graduates had attended law school.[24]

Unlike the EEAC or the National Association of Minority Contractors, CLEO is comprised of representatives from other organizations, not private individuals. Its thirteen-member governing board establishes policy for CLEO and monitors its programs. The board members are appointed by the five sponsoring organizations, except for three student representatives designated by the American Bar Association, the National Bar Association, and La Raza National Lawyers Association. As a coalition of interests, CLEO is accountable both to its sponsoring organizations and to the students it assists through the summer institutes and by providing financial aid. This multiple accountability has its advantages and liabilities.

The chief advantage is the assurance of support from powerful organizations when CLEO is attacked. For instance, although CLEO had attracted more than one million dollars from private foundations during its first years, it had to turn to the federal government in 1970 for financial assistance. The 1972 Educational Amendments to the Higher Education Act of 1965 guaranteed CLEO an annual appropriation of one million dollars,[25] but the appropriation was threatened by President Ford's 1974 and 1975 budget-cutting campaigns. Ford's Office of Management and Budget sought to reduce summer institute participation from two hundred to forty in 1974 and attempted to delete CLEO's entire grant in 1975. On both occasions friends in the legislature and CLEO's sponsoring organizations were able to guarantee funding through last minute supplementary appropriations bills. Well-placed friends like the American Bar Association are valuable assets in budgetary wars.

The liabilities of being an interest coalition include the potential for disruptions should the council's sponsors disagree on policy. CLEO is understandably reluctant to become embroiled in political controversies and has never lobbied Congress, except in support of its own funding, nor entered law suits, except for two occasions: *DeFunis* v. *Odegaard* and *Bakke*.

CLEO's staff and leaders saw *DeFunis* and *Bakke* as threats to the central objectives of the organization. The organization refused to identify itself as "a proponent of outright preferential admission to members of disadvantaged groups," but it feared that a Bakke victory might cripple its programs. As the champion of "more flexible admissions practices and policies on the part of law schools for economically and educationally disadvantaged students, including the right to consider race as an admission factor,"[26] CLEO had an interest in preserving affirmative action programs. Virtually all the graduates from its summer institutes are admitted to law school through special admission processes.[27] Further, as a federally funded program granting preferential treatment to minorities, CLEO feared it would be vulnerable to charges of "reverse discrimination" if Bakke won. Thus, "while we are primarily an educational body," the associate director of CLEO explained, "we will use the amicus process when a constitutional issue is laid at our door."[28]

The decision to submit a brief in *Bakke* was made by the governing council after a short but intense discussion. As a student member recounted, "we [the board] were very careful to explore all the possibilities. We were less concerned about what to say than we were how to say it. We didn't want to be perceived as being overly political in our involvement." Discussion was facilitated by the fact that CLEO had already participated in *DeFunis*. Although there was a discussion of the philosophical and social concepts of the case (CLEO was coded as a "medium" scope organization), the key questions were more tactical than substantive. Was a case dealing with medical school admissions sufficiently relevant to the organization's purpose to justify participating in it? Was it wise to endorse the Davis program explicitly?

Representatives of four of the five sponsoring organizations pressed for outright endorsement of Davis. Representatives from the American Bar Association counseled a more cautious approach. Some members of Congress might use CLEO's support of "quota" programs as a weapon against CLEO in the next appropriations hearings, they warned. Since members of the American Bar Association were divided over the issue of affirmative action, it might be unwise to undermine ABA support for CLEO by identifying the organization with Davis. The ABA representatives' fears were well founded. Another federally funded program was to receive unpleasant publicity for its involvement in *Bakke*—the Legal Services Corporation (see Chapter 3). And the ABA itself offered a brief which, in the words of its president, "opposes racial quotas" yet defended "race and economic and educational background as relevant factors in selecting from among qualified candidates for admission."[29] Even this relatively timid statement was challenged by members of the ABA's House of Delegates at the August 1977 meeting. An attempt to pass a resolution repudiating the brief failed, but that failure owed less to widespread support of the brief's arguments than to many delegates' reluctance to embarrass the organization by so public a rejection of an already filed brief.[30] The ABA's leadership also successfully appealed to a 1972 House of Delegates policy statement encouraging programs "having as their purpose the admission to law school and ultimately to the legal profession of greater numbers of interested but disadvantaged members of minority groups who are capable of successful completion of law school."[31]

The arguments within CLEO for caution and equivocation won. Declining offers from other amici to co-sponsor briefs in order to retain control of its brief in its own hands, CLEO concentrated on its special interests and experience. It hoped to provide the Court with a provocative view of minority-admission realities without antagonizing its allies or detractors.[32] The little non-amicus lobbying CLEO undertook was low-keyed and cautious. In a memorandum to U.S. Assistant Attorney General for Civil Rights Drew Days, the executive director of CLEO at the time, Alfred Slocum, urged the Justice Department to ask the Supreme Court to reverse and remand the case "on the grounds that the new Administration would like an opportunity to review the matter in its entirety and then make a recommendation to Congress designed to still the debate by exercising the guiding hand given to Congress by the Fourteenth Amendment itself."[33] But even these attempts at behind the scenes lobbying were more scholarly than partisan in their tone.

The brief filed in *Bakke* faithfully reflected CLEO's concerns and communicated effectively the commitments of the organization and its supporters. The brief began by challenging the unfounded "suggestion . . . that racial exclusion through standardized testing because of its 'racially neutral' character can be justified as the 'fault' of the victims."[34] CLEO warned against an excessive reliance on brute numbers as an admission screening device. Actual classroom performance in CLEO's summer institutes, not the Law School Admissions Test nor undergraduate grade point averages, was a better "means of determining legal aptitude, at least with regard to minority applicants."[35] CLEO's success with students who had completed law school but who would not have gained entrance if traditional criteria were used persuaded it that alternative means of predicting minority success were necessary and desirable.

The CLEO brief did not simply make an empirical argument, it also cited its genesis as a justification for granting preferences to disadvantaged law school applicants. The passage of the Civil Rights Act of 1964 indicated that "Congress has explored the social utility of racial integration and established a public policy in favor of such." More important, the enactment of the 1972 and the 1974 amendments to the Higher Education Act of 1965 established clear congressional endorsement of the CLEO program. Calling upon the tradition of judicial deference to "the guiding hand of Congressional leadership in enforcing the Fourteenth Amendment," CLEO asked the Court not to undermine legislative efforts to open higher education to the victims of racial and ethnic prejudice.[36]

In contrast to the *Bakke* brief, with its emphasis on CLEO's experiences and successes both with minority students and with the legislature, the brief submitted by CLEO in *DeFunis* had taken a far more legalistic and technical approach; only two of its twenty-five pages concentrated on the achievements of CLEO-sponsored students. The *Bakke* brief committed twenty of its forty-eight pages to the role played by CLEO in affirmative action programs. The contrast represents a deliberate shift in tactics: the "me-too" nature of the *DeFunis* brief, repeating as it did the legal pros and cons of the parties' briefs, was later seen as a missed opportunity to reveal the uniqueness of CLEO's position. "We have the hierarchical support of the legal profession," stated the current executive director of CLEO, "and are funded by the federal government. Support like this is an uncommon commodity where affirmative action programs are at stake."[37] CLEO is unique in another, somewhat different, way. As a board member who taught at a Western law school argued, "CLEO is a one-of-a-kind operation. We are the reality about which other groups can only hypothesize. We get blacks into and through law schools. Our successes put a lie to Bakke's allegations of 'unqualified admittees.'"[38]

The appeal of the CLEO arguments resided not only in the organization's success rate but also, and perhaps more significantly to its supporters, in its embodiment of the traditional, liberal belief in combating discrimination through remedial education. The most frequently cited alternatives to numbers-oriented special admissions programs in briefs submitted in support of Bakke were remedial programs like CLEO's. "Subsidized summer institutes for disadvantaged college students who aspire to be admitted to medical school should be made available to enable such students to actualize their potentialities and to compete successfully with other aspirants," the American Jewish Congress responded to arguments that preferential programs were the only effective means to increase minority access to professional education.[39] In the same vein the American Federation of Teachers declared its support for "remedial programs" which grant "each individual, no matter his racial or ethnic background, the same opportunity to reach that level of achievement which he is able to attain by virtue of his own intrinsic ability."[40]

The belief in the power of remedial education to overcome educational disadvantages had been a unifying tenet of the civil rights movement of the fifties and sixties. Its continued vitality despite the emotions and interests raised by *Bakke* can be attributed to its appeal to individualized justice. Remedial programs need not be racially exclusive. CLEO itself sponsors a small number of disadvantaged whites in its programs. Disadvantage, not racial identity, serves as the core of the idea; the needs of individuals provide the focus, not the abstract rights of racial groups to "fair shares" in the legal or medical professions. The minority students are helped not because of past wrongs to their racial group but because their true abilities ("to actualize their potentials") can not properly be assessed through conventional means. The appeal is to the merit of the minority applicant, not to the "guilt" of white society. Performance in the summer institutes, not LSAT scores or undergraduate grade point averages, provides the measure of individual talents. CLEO's successes reaffirmed to many Bakke supporters the social value of advancement by merit and the continued relevance of the American belief in self-improvement through education.

CLEO's brief tapped into that immense reservoir of good will so many Americans cherish for the notion of individual achievement through education. By clothing itself in this ideal, CLEO developed a brief acceptable to its sponsoring clienteles. At the same time, the brief reflected the debate within CLEO, a debate which had ranged relatively widely over abstract and concrete issues but which coalesced around the specific interest of the organization—preserving CLEO's educational mission. The robustness of the debate may indeed have been facilitated by the specificity of the interest. Commitment to CLEO's purposes may have made more abstract debates about the broader issues posed by *Bakke* appear less menacing. And, as in the EEAC, the clarity of the material interests served by the organization offered an alternative basis for accord when the members' conflicting personal opinions about the larger issues threatened organizational harmony.

Commitment to goals did not always broaden discussions of *Bakke*. As the National Association of Minority Contractors illustrated, sometimes preexisting commitments and personal arguments about the broader social issues make discussion appear unnecessary and therefore irrelevant. The National Fund for Minority Engineering Students was another example of an organization where specific interest group purposes did not liberate debate. But the fund did not have an organizational interest corresponding to that of the National Association of Minority Contractors' members. Unlike the latter, the fund's leaders and staff were not defenders and recipients of preferential treatment. Like CLEO, the fund is rather a coalition of interested organizations and individuals committed to expanding minority educational opportunities.

The National Fund for Minority Engineering Students (NFMES) is a non-profit corporation founded in October 1974 "to increase the participation of underrepresented disadvantaged minorities (including Blacks, Puerto Ricans, Mexican-Americans, and American Indians) in the engineering profession by enabling members of such minorities to acquire an engineering education."[41] It devotes its efforts to providing scholarship money, special training, and recruitment drives for minority students, and to lobbying engineering schools to establish special programs for minority applicants. The fund owes its origin to J. Stanford Smith, then chairman of the International Paper Company. Alarmed by the scant numbers of minority engineers graduating from the nation's colleges and universities each year, Smith warned the profession that "a formula for tragedy" was being concocted in America's lecture halls. The failure to attract sufficient numbers of minorities into engineering was resulting in "angry charges of discrimination with regard to upward mobility in industry." Before long "a lot of minority people are going to feel that they have been had." The fault, Smith was quick to add, could not be laid simply to racial prejudice; the problem lay in the paucity of trained, minority college graduates: "There just aren't enough minority men and women who have taken the college training to qualify for professional and engineering work. . . . To put the challenge bluntly, unless we can start producing not 400 but 4,000 to 6,000 minority engineers within the decade, industry will not achieve its goals of equality, and the nation is going to face social problems of unmanageable dimensions."[42] His solution was two-fold: to attract minority students to engineering school and to provide them with financial aid.

Two engineering professional associations and a private foundation answered Smith's call to action. The Engineers' Council for Professional Development, a federation of sixteen professional societies of engineers that develops and accredits college and technical school engineering programs, established as its goal a fifteen-fold increase in minority engineers by 1985. In May 1973 the National Academy of Engineers, an affiliate of the prestigious National Academy of Sciences, sponsored a symposium on minority opportunities in engineering. It also co-sponsored the creation of the National Advisory Council for Minorities in Engineering. At the same time, the Alfred P. Sloan Foundation financed a task force representing professional societies, universities, scholarship programs, and industry charged with analyzing the causes of minority underrepresentation in engineering and recommending remedies for the problem. The task force reported that the "single most important barrier . . . to increasing minority participation in engineering" was "the lack of adequate financial aid." It recommended "the establishment of a single national organization to raise and distribute essential new funds for financial aid to minority engineering college students."[43] The National Fund for Minority Engineering Students is this national organization.[44]

The fund has always attracted substantial contributions from

private individuals, foundations, and large industrial corporations. Its 1978 budget exceeded 2.5 million dollars, eighty per
cent of which came from private industry.[45] Its success can
be attributed to the presence on its board of trustees of the
chairmen of American Can Company, General Electric, General
Motors, IBM, Standard Oil of California, and United States
Steel Corporation; the presidents of DuPont and of International Harvester; and the executive vice president of American
Telephone and Telegraph. To this imposing array of American
business leaders are added the names of major figures in the academic world and from organizations like the National Urban
League.

The curious blend of trustees' backgrounds—public and private, educational and business—would suggest that their discussions on *Bakke* would be wide-ranging and subtle. Occupy-
ing leadership posts in major American firms or professional
posts in prestigious university engineering departments, they
promised to be intelligent, articulate, and insightful. The discussion within the fund over *Bakke* was, nonetheless, virtually
nonexistent. Members of the law firm of Ginsburg, Feldman
and Bress (the fund's counsel), initiated the move to intervene in
Bakke. Most of the trustees deferred to the advice of their legal
counsel and the fund's executive office rather than aggressively
questioning the fund's interest in the controversy. As one trustee
explained, "The president came well-prepared. Our comrades
from the black groups and the colleges were vocal in their support of a brief. Some of the rest of us were hesitant—the Fund is
an educational group, not a political one. We were persuaded to
okay a brief when the legal report showed how threatening
the California decision was to our operations."[46] Despite the
breadth of their background, most trustees were willing to see
only the legal aspects of *Bakke*—which rule of constitutional
interpretation best defended the fund's goals. This emphasis on
the issue of what the Constitution "said" to the exclusion of
broader questions of political, social, and philosophical significance, made the NFMES debate "narrow" in scope.

The first half of the fund's brief concentrated on the area of its
special expertise and concern, engineers and engineering. The

brief sought to distinguish the fund's program from Davis's; still it feared the probable consequences of the Supreme Court's affirmance of the lower courts' decisions.

Because the NFMES scholarship funds are generated solely to assist minority engineering students, and must be used to supplement rather than to replace existing scholarship funds, the NFMES program does not "have the effect of depriving persons who were not members of a minority group of benefits they would otherwise have enjoyed." . . . Similarly, the lack of access to a specific source of financial aid assistance "cannot be regarded with the absolute denial of a professional education" [quoting the California Supreme Court decision].[47]

Nevertheless, the fund contended, forbidding racially based quota programs placed its goals "in grave danger of atrophying."

Even though we can distinguish the NFMES effort from the University of California's special admission program, affirmance of the opinion below would almost surely prevent NFMES from achieving its objectives. Even if the Court decided the case on the narrowest possible grounds, there would be a period of uncertainty during which university administrators and corporate donors might understandably be cautious about contributing to or working with any programs that used race as a selection criterion.[48]

Alternatives to racially based programs were not pertinent to the fund's objectives. Its task is not solely to provide student aid; it also seeks to stimulate universities to recruit more minority engineering students. The fund does this by joining self-interest to principle: the scholarships are awarded to students through the engineering schools, encouraging these schools to seek out minority engineering prospects. A race-neutral program of assistance would not serve to meet these objectives, since "the engineering profession has traditionally attracted people from low socio-economic background, with the exception of minorities. Thus, the fundamental concerns that NFMES addresses are racial concerns, not cultural or economic concerns." The fund concluded that "there are no 'racially neutral means' of reducing the underrepresentation of minorities in engineering schools and in the engineering profession."[49]

Up to this point, the brief tracked the organization's purposes well. Late in the brief, however, the argument moved beyond the specific interest of NFMES to a broader argument. After reviewing the history of discriminatory laws and practices excluding minorities from the engineering profession, the brief invoked judicial precedents and legislative actions endorsing voluntary affirmative action efforts. While recognizing Bakke's plight, it insisted that the greatest personal harm has been inflicted on the minority victims of discrimination. The greatest good was served by upholding "the voluntary desegregation of education institutions and of the professions."[50]

Although not a dramatic shift, the movement from a specific organizational to a broader social perspective in the brief reflected the personal judgments of the brief writers, not the fund's trustees. Lee Marks and Martha Jane Shay of Ginsburg, Feldman and Bress recalled that they had hoped to strengthen Davis's position in the controversy by enlarging the number and types of organizations explicitly supporting its program.[51] This decision dismayed some trustees, who had been assured that the brief would not stray from the defense of the fund's objectives. It surprised one trustee that the prestige of the organization had become a "pawn" in a contest implicating values far broader than those with which the fund was identified.[52] But briefs purporting to represent the well-considered views of an organization while in fact reflecting the values of a self-selected few were not uncommon in *Bakke*.

The Politics of Small Differences

The interest groups' experiences in *Bakke* illustrated some of the reasons why organizational purposes failed to affect the scope of organizational debate. Discussions in the Equal Employment Advisory Council were wide-ranging as a result of the nonorganizational demands made by its members. The National Association of Minority Contractors' discussions were narrowed by the fortuitous conjunction of organizational and personal interests. Debates within the Council on Legal Education Opportunity were diversified, prompted in part by the mutual recognition of the goals to be achieved, and in part by the moderating influence of a varied set of clienteles. On the other hand, the National Fund for Minority Engineering Students lacked the broad discussions that CLEO exhibited. Its trustees deferred to the expertise of the organization's legal advisors, and, ironically, the advisors infused the brief with nonorganizational values and perspectives.

In every instance except the National Association of Minority Contractors, the power of the organization's interest in survival was clear. The conflict within the Equal Employment Advisory Council was moderated by the adept use of the organization's common concern with inconsistent affirmative action regulations. The Council on Legal Education Opportunity was alert to the implications of too explicit an endorsement of Davis-like quota programs. Hesitant about antagonizing members of sponsoring organizations like the American Bar Association or unnecessarily endangering its funding from Congress, CLEO decided to root its brief in the traditional American commitment to remedial education. The National Fund for Minority Engineering Students accepted its legal experts' counsel that *Bakke* should be treated as a narrow question of legal interpretation. Unfortunately, interviews with the fund's directors did not reveal the basis for this deference. Like leaders of so many other organizations, NFMES's trustees may have feared the potential divisiveness of an internal debate over affirmative action and may have been willing to delegate the decision to their attorneys as a way to save the organization from what might be a dangerous confrontation. Only in fortunate associations like the Minority Contractors, in which personal beliefs and material interests of the members were compatible, did the survival interest not appear.

Interest groups were not the only organizations susceptible to these concerns. Many minority-defense organizations were also affected by the ameliorating influences of nonorganizational pressures and interests.[53] The Children's Defense Fund, as the organizer of a "coalition" brief, felt obliged not to explore new ideas or evidence in the case. Its brief attempted to exert the pressure and prestige of numbers on the Court, not to break new ground in the law. As Steven Berzon, the organizer of the twenty-two organizations that endorsed the Children's Defense Fund's brief, explained, the brief presented the views of "real groups, groups peopled by real members. . . . Professional groups like the ACLU [American Civil Liberties Union] and the legal defense funds may produce legally impressive briefs, but their presence is discounted by the Court since they are only doing their jobs. 'Real groups,' like the Young Women's Christian Association, mainline, 'establishment' types, may alert the Justices to the broader social values in the case."[54] Others hoped that the sense of solidarity conveyed by coalition briefs would attract the Court's attention.[55] However, the larger the coalition or the more powerful the organizations sponsoring it, the more difficult it was to maintain consensus on a single position. As was the case for CLEO, coalition briefs were usually obligated to respond to diverse clienteles and therefore to moderate their stands.

The problems posed by coalition briefs were especially acute for the minority-defense organizations active in *Bakke*. Minority-defense organizations are advocates for a host of values and interests that loosely tie groups like the Japanese American Citizens Political League or the Polish-American Congress into a social whole. The NAACP is a minority-defense organization committed to fostering the social goals of its members and of blacks generally. It is the cultural and social ties binding its members, not economic interdependence, which direct the organization's goals. Charged to serve the interests and values of a cultural group, they pursued goals both more specific than the exhortatory ones pressed by public-interest advocates and more diffuse than the individual member-oriented goals of interest groups. Minority-defense organizations were therefore coalitions of individuals bound by similar but not identical interests and concerns. And they suffered the common plight of such coalitions in so divisive a controversy as *Bakke*.

One especially clear instance of this problem was provided by the legal defense funds active in *Bakke*. Their proliferation in the last fifty years attests to the increasing emphasis placed on litigation in American politics. Since the establishment of the NAACP Legal Defense and Educational Fund, Inc., in 1939, defense funds have been organized to protect the rights of non-union workers (National Right to Work Legal Defense Fund), to represent politically and economically conservative causes (Pacific Legal Foundation, Mid-American Legal Foundation), and to guard the legal rights and interests of the country's racial and ethnic minorities (Mexican-American Legal Defense and Educational Fund, Puerto Rican Legal Defense and Education Fund, Italian-American Foundation).

In a different context, James Q. Wilson has suggested that the most intense competition occurs not between ideological opponents but among allies sharing common goals and values. "Associations that oppose one another typically do not compete with one another. That is, if two associations have goals that are mutually exclusive . . . they rarely, if ever, compete with one another for members and funds from the same list of prospects. Where competition does exist, it is in part because the two associations are not in opposition with respect to their objectives and therefore appeal to similar or identical contributors."[56] The John Birch Society and the Americans for Democratic Action obviously do not compete for the same set of backers. It is organizations like the NAACP and the Mexican-American Legal Defense Fund, who share a dedication to representing the minority communities, that most directly compete for sympathetic donors and supporters. Nor is the competition for dollars the only example of the politics of small differences. Organizations cherish their autonomy because independence seems to affirm the worthiness of their existence. The claim that an organization is the independent "voice" of a body of individuals makes even small differences among organizations seem significant.

Organizational purposes in *Bakke* were poor predictors of the scope of intraorganizational debates because organizational objectives were often molded or frustrated by a set of secondary organizational needs. Organizations must continue to exist if they are to accomplish their goals; therefore survival may become a legitimate concern of the organization. If Wilson is right, threats to survival come largely from successful allies, not from ideological opponents. In *Bakke* all but one legal defense fund sponsored coalition briefs with non–legal defense organizations of the same ethnic or racial backgound which did not compete for the same contributions. The Mexican-American Legal Defense Fund organized a brief representing, among others, the League of United Latin American Citizens, the National Council of La Raza, and the Association of Mexican American Educators. The Puerto Rican Legal Defense Fund joined with a New York Puerto Rican community group, Aspira of America. The Native American Rights Fund served as the unnamed sponsor of a coalition brief joined by the American Indian Bar Association, the Native American Student Union of the University of California at Davis, and four other American Indian organizations. The Italian-American Foundation played a less active role as an endorser of a coalition brief led by the American Jewish Committee and the American Jewish Congress.[57] In all but the latter case, the legal defense funds did not feel threatened by coalition with like-minded organizations. The Mexican-American Legal Defense Fund could cooperate with the League of United Latin American Citizens because each offered its own distinctive services. The legal defense fund provided expert legal counsel; the League of United Latin American Citizens provided the opportunity for social interactions as well as organized political action such as electioneering and lobbying municipal, state, and federal legislatures. Their tasks were distinctive enough to minimize competition for the same resources.

The archetypical legal defense fund, the NAACP Legal Defense and Educational Fund, Inc.,[58] can claim primacy not only in terms of longevity but also in its importance. During the seven Supreme Court terms of 1958 through 1965, the fund "controlled about two-thirds of the race relations cases" heard on appeal.[59] It successfully argued most of the historic civil rights cases: *Shelley* v. *Kraemer* (striking down racially restrictive covenants among private homeowners); *Brown* v. *Board of Education* (overturning the *Plessy* v. *Ferguson* "separate-but-equal" rule); *Alexander* v. *Holmes County Board of Education* (discarding the "all deliberate speed" doctrine of *Brown* and ordering immediate integration of public schools); *Griggs* v. *Duke Power Company* (interpreting Title VII of the 1964 Civil Rights Act to require tests failing a disproportionate percentage of black and other minorities to be directly job-related); *Furman* v. *Georgia* (ruling capital punishment unconstitutional in certain circumstances); and *Keyes* v. *School District #1, Denver* (extending the desegregation requirement of *Brown* to northern school systems).

The fund was formed in 1939 by the National Association for the Advancement of Colored People in part to circumvent the income tax restrictions placed on lobbying organizations and in part to develop a self-financing, full-time legal program devoted to civil rights litigation. The Internal Revenue Service (IRS) regulations prohibiting nonprofit organizations from receiving tax exemptions when a substantial portion of their activity is devoted to lobbying stimulated the NAACP leaders, like the leaders of other groups, to establish a coordinate group freed of the onus of lobbying and thus able to attract contributions that qualified as charitable deductions. Hence, an ironic consequence of the IRS's attempt to confine the tax status of conventional lobbying groups was to foster the formation of advocacy organizations devoted to pursuing political ends through the supposedly nonpolitical processes of law.

During its first fifteen years, the fund worked closely with the NAACP, sharing their offices in New York and some administrative arrangements. Then, pressured by Southern congressmen upset with the successes of the fund, and especially with its victory in *Brown*, the IRS ordered the fund to dissolve its relationship with the parent group or lose its tax-exempt status.[60] In 1957, consequently, the two organizations went their separate ways. The fund's physical separation from the association is now accompanied by differences in organizational objectives, interests, and styles.

The fund prefers a cautious approach to litigation where "all the technical and professional preparation in a civil rights case . . . is done thoroughly even though the case seems clearly just. . . . [Thurgood] Marshall [the first director-counsel of the fund] felt you ought to attend to that and not just go in and say: Look, somebody's been denied his rights; make it all well."[61] The NAACP is less reluctant to litigate boldly in defense of its causes. Lacking the legal resources and staff of the fund, the association places a premium on the swift resolutions of cases and carries on battles it has lost in the courts by appealing to the legislature to rewrite the laws—an approach denied to the fund by its tax-exempt status. To some extent, then, the differences in styles are a reflection of the differences in roles played by each organization. The fund is a civil rights law office; the NAACP is closer to conventional understandings of an advocacy organization, lobbying the legislative and executive branches as well as the courts.

As Wilson predicted, the similarities between the organizations stimulate a search for distinctive roles and goals. Each seeks its own special niche in the ecology of advocacy organizations. The statements of their interests as amici prefacing each one's brief in *Bakke* expressed these subtle differences. The NAACP described itself as a "non-profit membership association representing the interests of approximately 500,000 members . . . throughout the United States."[62] The fund, on the other hand, called itself "a non-profit corporation . . . formed to assist black persons to secure their constitutional rights by the prosecution of lawsuits . . . rendering legal services gratuitously to black persons suffering injustice by reason of racial discrimination."[63] One emphasized its mission as a membership organization, the other characterized itself as a champion of the civil rights of blacks.

These differences in style and the competition for common financial sources intensified during the retrenchment by foundations and private contributors in the late seventies. At the 1979 annual convention, the NAACP membership voted to strip the fund of all rights to use the "NAACP" label. "The LDF wrongfully has been collecting money off our name," a NAACP board member stated to the delegates at the convention. "The only reason we didn't bring this dispute to the public before is that we didn't want to show that there was a crack in the civil rights movement. But these people have treated us with so much disrespect—with so much treachery. This treachery we should not tolerate any longer."[64]

Disturbed by the fact that contributions intended for the NAACP were going to the fund because of the confusion over names, the membership ordered its directors to take whatever action deemed appropriate "to withdraw and revoke permission previously granted to the NAACP Legal Defense and Educational Fund for the use of the initials 'NAACP' in its name, publication, publicity, activities and solicitations."[65] Representatives from both the NAACP and the fund feared that a confrontation in court over the issue was "unavoidable."[66] It was. In 1983 a Washington, D.C., federal district judge ordered the fund to remove the acronym "NAACP" from its name.[67] In an era of tight finances, the contest for dollars and identity has helped to transform civil rights allies into financial antagonists.

Like all other legal defense funds, the Legal Defense and Educational Fund, Inc. has no "members" in the strict sense—only contributors. In 1978 while *Bakke* was pending before the United States Supreme Court, the fund raised 4.5 million dollars through mail campaigns and from foundations, corporations, and unions. Several hundreds of thousands were donated by black social organizations like the Shriners and the Daughters of the Eastern Star.[68] Perhaps the most visible source of funding is the "Committee of 100," a voluntary support group which sponsors annual appeals for the fund. Members of the committee include persons active in the fields of entertainment, letters, politics, and the arts. Leonard Bernstein, Jacob Javits, Archibald Macleish, Walter Mondale, Carl Rowan, and Robert Penn Warren served on a recent committee. The fund takes great pride in the diversity of its financial backers and takes an even greater pride in the fact that its "support is so broadly based that no contributor can tell us what to do and carry out a credible threat if we refuse. Contributors have cut off support when they have disagreed, and we have continued to do what we believe in."[69]

Some critics charge that, in the words of Harvard Law School professor Derrick Bell, the "strain of harmonizing the contributor-sensitive ideology of leadership with the representational interests of black clients" has created a "penthouse plantation" attitude among the legal staff, and that the views of contributors, more than the needs of clients, determine fund policy. The fund responds, "'There may be financial contributors to reckon with who may ask that certain cases be brought and others not. . . . but within broad limits lawyers seem to be free to pursue their own ideas of right, not influenced a great deal with regard to particulars by the constituencies they have chosen or which have chosen them, and affected little or not at all by contributors. This, of course, is not so free-wheeling as it may sound because lawyer, client, related organizations, and contributors usually share a common social outlook.'"[70]

The fund would seem to be the type of organization equipped with the resources and independence to prompt a broad discussion of *Bakke*. Yet its directors dealt briefly with that case, largely because *DeFunis* v. *Odegaard*, the case preceding *Bakke* in which a state law school's special admissions program was challenged, had already stimulated an intense and wide-ranging debate on affirmative action. The fund's directors had hammered out a policy on the issue after an exhausting series of board meetings. According to Charles Stephen Ralston, staff attorney for the fund, they had been worried that not to file an amicus brief in *DeFunis* would demonstrate an unhealthy sense of equivocation in the fund's litigation strategy. On the other hand, the issue of affirmative action evoked a set of conflicting values and principles which thwarted an easy resolution. Like many other organizations, the fund feared that an endorsement of quotas, a shibboleth for its many Jewish supporters, would be interpreted as a retreat from its commitment to a society free of race-consciousness. Such a signal could weaken the integrity of its claims to be speaking for racial justice. Moreover, the fund had learned during the long struggle over school desegregation that court decisions, especially on highly controversial topics, are seldom automatically translated into changes in citizen behavior. To press the Court to state a position in so difficult a case might not be in the interests of either side if that position was untenable.[71] The eventual decision by the directors to support the University of Washington was therefore the product of a broad debate implicating many aspects of the controversy over the means of countering racial discrimination.[72]

The brief submitted in *Bakke* was not subjected to so intense a scrutiny because the organization could rely on this existing policy, which seemed to mandate the director-counsel and his legal staff to support special admissions but did not specify a form or a particular approach for the brief.[73] The lack of supervision by the board, however, cannot be interpreted as an evasion of its responsibilities. The NAACP Legal Defense Fund did answer to a board (unlike, for example, the National Fund for Minority Engineering Students), one which numbered among its members some of the most prominent lawyers of this generation: Ramsey Clark, William K. Coblentz, Marion Wright Edelman, Walter Gellhorn, Nicholas deB. Katzenbach, Louis H. Pollak, and William T. Coleman. Despite having the ability and interest to monitor staff activities, the board deferred to its staff's expertise. The considerable freedom the staff enjoyed in its conduct of litigation was rooted in the board members' perception of it as trustworthy. The staff had earned this trust by responding to the interests and concerns of the directors. That the board has never had to overrule staff on a policy decision demonstrates the strength of this trusting relationship and the astuteness of the director-counsels (Thurgood Marshall and Jack Greenberg), who have kept the fund healthy while breaking new ground in civil rights. Additionally in this case, the presence of an explicit policy on the issue, one molded by the intense earlier discussion, guided the staff.

Of the fifty-one briefs presented to the Court by amici organizations, most were satisfied to tread familiar ground or to rework, if in a more sophisticated and elaborate manner, arguments first developed in *DeFunis*. Few aspired to or achieved any degree of originality in their arguments. The American Jewish Congress's *Bakke* brief, for example, was a polished and expanded version of its *DeFunis* brief. The NAACP Legal Defense Fund's brief was an exception. Unlike its *DeFunis* brief—a short (twelve-page) review of the pertinent case law dealing with the equal protection clause of the Constitution and Title VI of the Civil Rights Act of 1964,[74] the fund's *Bakke* brief was a long, careful analysis of the "clear and unequivocal" history of the Fourteenth Amendment. It attempted to demonstrate "that the framers intended [the Fourteenth Amendment] to legitimate and allow implementation of race-specific remedial measures where a substantial need for such programs was evident."[75]

A serendipitous process produced the brief. Originally, the

members of the fund's legal staff had no intention of intervening in *Bakke*. Although allies and clients in the civil rights establish-ment pressured them to participate, two fund lawyers ex-plained, "We had nothing to contribute. The university's and other groups' briefs were quite competent to deal with the issues." [76] However, an interest in history intervened: a staff member recalled the 1866 veto of the Freedman's Bureau by President Andrew Johnson and realized that Johnson was "intel-lectually incapable" of the arguments in the veto. "I guessed that Johnson had drawn his arguments from the Congressional debate on the statute. I turned to those debates to find the meat of his message." [77] It became clear during the staff's ensuing dis-cussions that the debates shed new light on the original intent of the Fourteenth Amendment. Enthusiastic at the prospect of contributing something new to the arguments over *Bakke*, the fund's attorneys decided to pursue a legislative history ap-proach. The happy coincidence of browsing through the aged pages of the *Congressional Globe* and the discussions on a *Bakke* position led to a provocative insight on the Fourteenth Amendment.

The LDF brief began with the premise that the Fourteenth Amendment prohibited only racial classifications that stigma-tized members of a racial or ethnic group as inferior. It argued that the same Congress which approved the Freedman's Bureau, with its provision of educational help to blacks and not whites, also endorsed the Fourteenth Amendment.

The Freedman's Bureau Act of 1866, the Reconstruction measure which probably contained the most race-specific remedial legislation, was considered simultaneously in Congress with the Fourteenth Amendment . . . On several occasions the Act was debated in one House at the same time the Amendment was being debated in the other. . . . Moreover, the same legislators who comprised the two-thirds majority necessary to override President Johnson's second veto of the Freedman's Bureau Act of 1866 also composed the two-thirds majority who approved the Fourteenth Amendment.

They maintained that therefore

[t]he propriety of race-conscious remedies was a matter squarely con-sidered by the Congress which fashioned the Fourteenth Amendment,

and that Congress believed such remedial programs [were] not merely permissible but necessary.[78]

The legislative debate over the Freedman's Bureau and other race-conscious programs was similar to the contemporary debate over "affirmative discrimination." The same concern about denying benefits to whites that are available to blacks and the strictures of the principle of compensatory justice which require a definite victim and a definite offender were raised in the thirty-ninth Congress's floor discussions of the act that established the bureau. These concerns were "repeatedly and overwhelmingly rejected over a hundred years ago, and insofar as respondent's [Bakke's] arguments in this case assume the Fourteenth Amendment is founded upon such a theory, these arguments do not withstand analysis." Moreover, given the harsh history of racial discrimination in the medical profession and in California's public education system, and the special health problems of the minority community, the state had a pressing interest in ameliorating these wrongs. Davis's special admissions program was consonant with the equal protection clause's intent.[79]

Although this exegesis of the Fourteenth Amendment's intentions was an original and persuasive effort, historical arguments made in legal briefs are inevitably the products of advocacy, not disinterested scholarship. A historian responsible for researching and writing the NAACP's arguments in *Brown* v. *Board of Education* admitted, "We produced a piece of highly selective and carefully prepared law-office history. It presented, indeed, a great deal of perfectly valid constitutional history. But it also manipulated history in the best tradition of American advocacy, carefully marshalling every possible scrap of evidence in favor of the desired interpretation and just as carefully doctoring all the evidence to the contrary, either by suppressing it when that seemed plausible, or by distorting it when suppression was not possible."[80] Thus in *Bakke* the Anti-Defamation League cited the same passages from the Congressional debate over the Freedman's Bureau that the Legal Defense Fund had used, but for a contrary purpose—to support the League's assertion that equal protection was intended to forbid all race-conscious public programs.[81]

Historical arguments about the intent of the Fourteenth
Amendment's framers may also prove irrelevant to a decision.
In *Brown*, for instance, the Supreme Court held segregated public education unconstitutional because of the current status of
public education and the modern understanding of the dictates
of the equal protection clause.

> In approaching this problem of the constitutionality of segregation in
> public schools, we cannot turn the clock back to 1868 when the
> Amendment was adopted, or even to 1896 when *Plessy* v. *Ferguson*
> was written. We must consider public education in the light of its full
> development and its present place in American life throughout the na-
> tion. Only in this way can it be determined if segregation in public
> schools deprives these plaintiffs of the equal protection of the laws.[82]

In a similar manner, whatever the original understanding of the
Fourteenth Amendment's supporters, it is arguable whether
contemporary American law and politics need be controlled by
the concerns or preferences of the nineteenth century. So, many
Bakke supporters asserted that the equal protection clause is an
expanding guarantee and protects all individuals from unequal
treatment without regard to racial or ethnic ancestry.[83]

Other minority organizations who defended the Davis program were convinced that the fund's brief justified blacks' claim
to preferences while threatening the claims put forward by Chicanos, Asian-Americans, and Puerto Ricans. The logical extension of the argument that the Fourteenth Amendment permitted
preference programs for blacks as an exception to its otherwise
color-blind mandate was that only blacks are to be accorded the
extra protection. Other groups, similarly situated but lacking
the special status that the condition of slavery had established,
were not to receive this special exemption. Some might well be
constitutionally denied preferences in state-funded programs.

However, the fund did not extend its argument so far. Indeed,
it defended the propriety of extending the exemption to other
minority groups, by citing language in an 1873 case suggesting
that blacks were not to be held the only group deserving special
status.[84] Nevertheless, other organizations, such as the Mexican-
American Legal Defense Fund, concerned that the LDF could
not adequately represent all minority viewpoints, sought to

present their own versions of minority rights and equal protection.

During the sixties, when the NAACP Legal Defense Fund initiated its poverty law program, it was inundated with cases from the Mexican-American community. Unable to cope with the volume of cases, Jack Greenberg, of the NAACP Legal Defense Fund, and representatives from the Chicano community approached the Ford Foundation to fund a legal defense association for Mexican Americans. Some staff and board directors from the NAACP fund continue to sit on the board of the Mexican-American Legal Defense and Educational Fund (MALDEF)—notably Jack Greenberg—but the two organizations are structurally and legally separate. MALDEF seeks to protect the "civil rights of Mexican-Americans through litigation and education."[85] As a "privately funded civil rights firm" and the representative of America's second largest minority group,[86] it provides the same kinds of legal assistance to Chicanos that the NAACP Legal Defense Fund provides to the black community.

MALDEF was one of the few amici organizations active in *Bakke* from the outset. Like the NAACP Legal Defense Fund's board, MALDEF's directors had established the organization's position on affirmative action during the *DeFunis* controversy, but, unlike the former fund, MALDEF's staff attorneys did not initially hesitate to intervene in *Bakke*. They offered a brief to the California Supreme Court which called attention to the special plight of the Spanish-speaking community. Chicanos suffered not only the deprivation and discrimination accorded an unassimilated ethnic group, they argued, but labored under the additional burden of a language handicap. "Even in small towns the barrio tends to be isolated from the rest of the community. This cultural isolation has fostered retention of the Spanish language and the Chicano culture."[87]

The brief sought to substantiate Davis's argument that the need for better medical care in minority communities justified the pressing state interest in increasing medically trained individuals from these communities.

Chicano physicians clearly constitute a vital component of meaningful health delivery in the Chicano community. There are over 4,000,000 Chicanos now living in California, comprising 18.5% of California's population. Most, if not all, of these people either are monolingual in Spanish or communicate with greater facility in Spanish. Yet there are no more than a scattering of Chicano doctors [at most 250] to meet the needs of these patients.

After summarizing the history of discrimination against Chicanos in California's public school system and questioning the predictive value of traditional entry criteria for graduate education, the MALDEF California brief concluded,

California clearly has a compelling governmental interest in implementing affirmative programs which will break the chain of discrimination and accord qualified minorities their rights to higher education and entry into professional careers. The Davis medical school's program clearly promotes this overriding state interest and should be upheld.[88]

MALDEF failed to dissuade the regents from appealing or the United States Supreme Court from granting *certiorari*.[89] They therefore formed a coalition brief with ten other organizations and a California state legislator.[90] Like the brief submitted to the California court, MALDEF's brief filed in the United States Supreme Court insisted on the unique character of Chicano problems in California and the country generally and amassed statistics substantiating the gross disparities between "the Anglo majority" and Chicano income levels, educational opportunities, employment achievements, housing availability, and imprisonment rate.[91] It noted that, although segregation of blacks in California's public schools was outlawed in 1880, segregation of Asians and Indians was not repealed until 1947. Mexican-Americans comprised eighteen percent of the California population to blacks' 7.6 percent, but 2.2 percent of the physicians in the state were black compared to only one percent who were Mexican-Americans. MALDEF was not arguing that Chicanos were more disadvantaged than blacks, only that they were at least as disadvantaged.[92]

This effort to distinguish the plight of Chicanos from that of blacks was calculated. MALDEF's attorneys felt that most policy makers lumped the many minority communities into one monolithic entity and tended to identify the problems of blacks with the problems of all minorities, failing to see the different problems, and different sources of the same problems, that afflict each minority group. A brief detailing the special afflictions suffered by Mexican-Americans was necessary to alert the Supreme Court about the important differences between Chicanos and blacks.

Members of MALDEF's legal staff offered another reason for the distinctive MALDEF brief—the need to protect organizational autonomy and identity. Coalition action in litigation, as in legislative lobbying or general politicking, is a variable thing. Minority-defense organizations and their clienteles were battered by the centrifugal needs for effective collaboration and for organizational identity. They felt that the psychic benefits in stating "we" did it were marginal compared with the satisfaction in saying "I" did it. The diminished sense of accomplishment and the necessity of accommodating to the interests of others seldom made coalition action worth the time or investment of energies. As Jack Greenberg, the current director-counsel of the NAACP Legal Defense Fund, has explained, "[a] lot of organizations think that if you all put your names on the brief or get together as a coalition, it's somehow a better case. To us [the LDF] that seems a waste of energy, and it creates an association with issues and their development over which you have no control."[93]

Organizations were not the only ones affected by the contending forces of collaboration and identity. The struggle for civil rights and racial justice often places blacks and other minorities in competitive rather than cooperative relationships. Ralph Kramer, in a study of antipoverty programs, argued that there is a strain in relations between Chicanos and blacks, due partially to "the difference in their social goals," and partially the Chicano community's sense of "cultural superiority and distinctiveness." The latter is reflected in the words of a Chicano college student: "We're not like the Negroes. They want to be white men because they have no history to be proud of. My ancestors came from one of the most civilized nations in the world."[94] The strain results also from a fierce competition for the same jobs and benefits between the two groups. Economic and political rivalry reveals itself in black suspicions "that Hispanics consider themselves whites and will dump blacks once they use them to climb higher on the totem pole."[95] Despite recent efforts to forge a black-Hispanic alliance,[96] many blacks are upset by the specter of illegal aliens from Mexico usurping "black jobs" at a time of high black unemployment.[97]

Black reluctance to join with other minorities is not only a product of concerns about competition. As the largest and most politically well organized minority group in the nation, blacks are increasingly exercising power on the local and national levels. Coalitions are apt to decrease, not increase, the comparative influence at their command. The unspecified rewards of coalition pale in comparison with the hard specie of program benefits such as those offered by the Comprehensive Education and Training Act (CETA) or revenue sharing.

Groups representing Asian-Americans and American Indians were active in *Bakke*, using their amici briefs to substantiate their unique claims to redress for prior and continuing discrimination. The Asian American Bar Association of the Greater Bay Area wrote that "Asian Americans, as a racial group, continue to bear the social and economic scars of a century of de jure and de facto discrimination." The association's "paramount concern" was "whether the growing Asian American community . . . will receive adequate legal representation." A successful attack on medical school programs threatened special admissions to all state-supported professional schools.[98] Representatives of the American Indian community made similar arguments. "[We] wish only to point out that historically there have been few American Indians in medical, legal and other professions." Invoking the special status accorded Indian tribes by Article I, Section 8 of the federal Constitution, Indian advocates insisted that "the legal status of American Indians . . . with respect to special admissions is vastly different than the status of non-Indian persons."[99] Within the Hispanic community, Puerto Rican spokespersons offered a separate brief in order to distinguish their problems from those of Chicanos.

The Puerto Rican Legal Defense and Education Fund, established in 1970 to provide legal and educational services similar to those which the LDF and MALDEF provide their clienteles, filed an amicus brief in *Bakke*. Although the legal staff questioned the contribution its brief would make, the symbolic value of being associated with the "right" side of the controversy outweighed the expenditure of resources required. The organization also saw *Bakke* as an opportunity to introduce itself to the Supreme Court as a major civil rights legal program. "We plan to be frequently before the Court in defense of Puerto Rican civil rights. This seemed to be a good chance to make ourselves known to it."[100] Most important, the Puerto Rican Legal Defense Fund was concerned that the special problems of Puerto Ricans would be overlooked if it did not present its own case.

The Puerto Rican Legal Defense Fund had joined the MALDEF coalition brief in *DeFunis* and had co-sponsored the National Urban League brief's petition to the Supreme Court not to grant *certiorari* in *Bakke*. "But we felt we had been lost in the shuffle in the development of those briefs. There were organizational problems—lack of control over the brief, little opportunity to have input into it—, but the major concern was to emphasize the distinctiveness of Puerto Rican problems and how they differed from those of Mexican-Americans."[101] The fund hoped to add a new dimension to the arguments presented by others by statistical documentation of the plight of Puerto Ricans. But such evidence was not available; most research had used the broader category "Hispanic" as the data base, and not until two years later did the United States Department of Labor release a study reporting that "when Puerto Ricans were compared with whites, blacks, and other Latinos such as Mexican-Americans, the Puerto Ricans consistently rank lowest on the ladder" of affluence.[102]

The Puerto Rican Legal Defense Fund's attorneys were confronted with two alternatives, neither of which was attractive, one of which was unpalatable. The unpalatable alternative was to publicize the competition within the Hispanic community for government benefits such as bilingual programs or employment training. The safer course was to write a standard legal analysis of the case. The Puerto Rican Legal Defense Fund chose this safer course. Its brief differed from those filed by most other organizations only in the presence of its name on the cover.

Most nonwhite minorities insisted on the vital differences among themselves, yet they, in effect, endorsed the concept of a "monolithic white majority"[103]—that whites constituted a sufficiently homogeneous and advantaged class not to require or deserve special care or protection. The Black Law Students Union of Yale University Law School insisted that "America's [nonwhite and Spanish] minorities are not similarly situated with the Anglocentric, white middle-class majority."[104] The coalition brief headed by the National Council of Churches dismissed the claims of disadvantaged whites in this instance because the "class of white applicants for admission to Davis Medical School . . . have 'none of the traditional indicia of suspectness.'"[105] The Board of Governors of Rutgers University felt that "whites continue to enjoy an artificially superior position that represents the final legacy of chattel slavery."[106]

Several minority-defense organizations representing white ethnic groups, such as the Italian-American Foundation and the Polish-American Congress, contended that such assertions were fallacious and injurious. They were apprehensive about affirmative action programs and about the belief that "official minorities"[107] (blacks, Hispanics, Asian-Americans, and American Indians) deserve special protection through the imposition of quotas.[108] Since white ethnics have only recently entered the middle class and thus been able to lay claim to the privileges and opportunities accorded that status, they are likely to carry a disproportionate share of the burden for redressing the racial balance. The marginal Slavic-American or Italian-American, burdened with economic and social disadvantages, will likely be the candidate forced to compete for medical school admission with the special minority student admittee. The burden of preferences for redress has been placed on their shoulders, not on those of students of English ancestry and from well-educated and financially secure families. Justice Brennan acknowledged this potential injustice in a 1977 case involving racial gerrymandering: "the most 'discrete and insular' of whites often will be called upon to bear the immediate, direct costs of benign discrimination."[109] Struggling with the lingering effects of discrimination against their own heritages, white ethnic students were confronted with the additional obstacle of competing with individuals from legally preferred minority groups.

Representatives of white ethnic groups seldom claimed that they had suffered the same degree of victimization as blacks. "Because of the unsavory role slavery has played in the history of our country, it was only natural for all of us to have our attention centered by the problems which flowed from this most fundamental form of discrimination," wrote the Polish-American Congress.

Nevertheless, this Court, Congress, the Executive and our national leaders have repeatedly stated . . . that our national policy, with regard to discrimination in general, forbids more than racial discrimination. Color, religion, sex and national origin are equally paramount and today we have quite properly added age and the handicapped.[110]

They added that substantial numbers of their own people have suffered disadvantages comparable to those suffered by blacks and other nonwhite minorities. An investigation conducted by the United States Department of Labor and its Office of Federal Contract Compliance concluded that:

[M]embers of various religious and ethnic groups, primarily but not exclusively of Eastern, Middle, and Southern European ancestry, such as Jews, Catholics, Italians, Greeks, and Slavic groups, continue to be excluded from executive middle management, and other job levels, because of discrimination based on their religious and/or national origin.[111]

If the nation's obligations to rectify past wrongs justify preference programs, then individuals of all races and nationalities who have suffered discrimination have legitimate claims to special assistance.

Most defense organizations of white ethnics were satisfied to plead the cause of all individual victims of discrimination, regardless of their racial or ethnic affiliations. The Order Sons of Italy said they "would be offended by any program which deals

with them on a group basis rather than as individual human beings, and consider that such treatment would bring with it the
stigma of inferiority."[112] The American Jewish Congress and the
American Jewish Committee attacked the idea of "a 'proper'
proportion of representation of each group in each program or
calling" and expressed apprehension that the "acceptance" of
such an idea "would profoundly damage the fabric of our society."[113] However, at least two white ethnic defense organizations asserted claims of their own for "shares" in quota
programs.

Although the Italian-American Foundation and the Polish
American Affairs Council joined the American Jewish Committee's coalition brief in *Bakke,* both did so because of time and
resource restraints. They would have preferred to present their
own briefs and to argue for upgrading "quota" programs to include Polish-American and Italian-American students.[114] The
Italian-American Foundation did not reject group-based rationales and quota-oriented affirmative action programs, but
was only concerned that not all qualified groups were receiving
preferential consideration. As its national chairman wrote in a
special "Op-Ed" article for the *New York Times,* "We're more
in favor of affirmative action than blacks are—because we
are yet to benefit from it, and we need it badly. The fact is
that Americans of Eastern and Southern European stock . . .
are about as under-represented in higher education as are
blacks."[115] Such a response might not be unexpected, given the
powerful inducements for white ethnics to stake out their claims
to the nation's resources. Nathan Glazer, writing on "the white
ethnic . . . reaction" to "affirmative discrimination," wondered
how long white ethnic groups would emphasize their similarities with other white Americans:

What the rise of a distinctive black political movement meant was that
inevitably the question had to be raised, "Are we indeed like other
Americans, only more so?" or—another form of the question—"Is it
to our *interest* to emphasize this kind of identity rather than a separate
identity as ethnics? If we are like all other Americans, then we bear the
responsbility for slavery, exploitation, and imperialism. If we are,
however, Poles, Italians, Jews, and the like, we have our own history of

being exploited to refer to in protecting our position and extending it." [116]

Organizations like the Italian-American Foundation and the Polish American Affairs Council chose the latter course. As the legal counsel for the Polish American Affairs Council explained, "We would approve a 'sixteen slot' quota at Davis Medical School if the selection pool was appropriately expanded to insure that all groups are adequately represented in the professions." [117]

Arguments like these were founded less on principles than on pragmatics. The Italian-American Foundation, for example, is a nonprofit foundation established in 1976 as "an advocate for things Italian-American." [118] In 1978 its board of directors included Joseph Alioto, former mayor of San Francisco; Jack Valenti, a special assistant to the late President Lyndon Johnson and current president of the Motion Picture Association of America; and John Volpe, former governor of Massachusetts and secretary of transportation of the United States. Persons of such prominence were unlikely to reject the powerful American creed of individual merit. Rather, their acceptance of a "fair share" for all groups argument was guided by practical considerations. If the only way to ensure reasonably open opportunities for Italian-Americans to enter state-supported professional schools was to secure "favored group" status for them, then they would play the new "'group rights' game" and assert their claims. [119]

The concern among many minority-defense organizations to distinguish the special claims of their clients from those championed by other organizations was expected since minority-defense organizations *defend* minorities. What was significant in *Bakke* was the importance placed by such organizations on the differences between them and like-minded associations. An amicus brief was often more than a statement of political, legal, or philosophical principle. Many organizations used their briefs as weapons in a political struggle. The brief promised to provide recognition for the organization, and in the equation of American politics, recognition equals access, which may equal success. The actual differences among the briefs submitted by the minority-defense organizations ranged from none, e.g., the

Puerto Rican Legal Defense Fund and the Mexican-American Legal Defense Fund, to moderate, e.g., the LDF and the Mexican American Legal Defense Fund. These were small differences when compared with the positions taken by most organizations representing white ethnics or Jews. But small differences still made a difference.

The need to be distinctive was not confined to minority-defense organizations. Interest groups like the American Federation of Teachers and public-interest advocacy organizations like the Young Americans for Freedom also sought to establish their status as spokespersons for special clienteles. The pursuit of secondary objectives—especially organizational identity—overshadowed the primary purposes of these associations.

The Politics of the Public Interests

Public-interest advocacy organizations championed general social and political principles in *Bakke*. Their efforts were not directed at the promotion of the material or cultural interests of their members but at the advancement or preservation of what they perceived as socially important values. Unlike the interest group or the minority-defense organization, the public-interest advocate has no minority group constituency as such and thus seeks the general goal of preserving or reforming a good society, rather than the protection of the interests of members or clients.

Of course, most organizations in *Bakke*—interest group, minority, or public-interest—sought to champion the general good or the public welfare. What was distinctive about the public-interest advocates was commitment to such ideas as their principal or sole concern. In the language of political economy, the benefits such groups pursue are "indivisible" and therefore available to all, regardless of their organizational affiliations; the "collective good" they work for cannot be, and is not, distributed to their own members only. The American Jewish Congress and the NAACP pursue goods they regard as socially beneficial; still, their primary commitment is to the condition of Jews and blacks respectively. A public-interest advocacy organization like the American Civil Liberties Union is dedicated to a more abstract constituency—the Bill of Rights.

The use of the term "public interest" is fraught with difficulties. The concept has an irreducible "mushiness" or ambiguity that partly results from public cynicism. The "public interest" is a powerful touchstone in American politics, evoking
images of disinterested champions of the general good who
speak not for personal aggrandizement but for principles and
values that transcend the dictates of "petty politics." Paradoxically, the notion of a "public interest" is disparaged both as an
unattainable fantasy and as a cynical subterfuge that conceals
the machinations of private interests. John Calhoun aptly sum-
marized this latter theme: "Instead of being the united opinion
of the whole community, [the public interest] is usually nothing
more than the voice of the strongest interest or combination of
interests; and not infrequently a small but energetic and active
portion of the people." [120] In a similar vein, Alexander Hamilton
suggested that "a judicious estimate of our true interests, un-
perplexed and unbiased by considerations not connected with
the public good . . . is a thing more ardently to be wished than
seriously to be expected." [121]

Efforts to develop a defensible understanding of the public interest tend to founder on the rocks of ambiguity or over varying
contentions of what ought to be in the general good. [122] Most
often, the "public interest" is defined by exclusion, in terms of
what it is not. In the American thinking about the concept that
commenced with James Madison, it is differentiated from the
private interest or "faction," the latter defined as "a number
of citizens, whether amounting to a majority or minority of
the whole, who are united and actuated by some common
impulse of passion, or of interest, adverse to the rights of other
citizens, or to the permanent and aggregate interests of the
community." [123]

Unfortunately, apart from the perplexing circularity of defining the public interest as the "permanent and aggregate interests
of the community," attempts to define public interest as exclusive of private interests do not recognize either the role private values play as vehicles for public values or the possibility
that there may be several public interests, often conflicting in
their dictates. So there may be a public interest in preserving the
cleanliness of our environment and a public interest in encour-

aging industrial development and employment opportunities. Just as with the values of liberty, equality, and human community, so the concept of a public interest may be ambiguous because of its abstracted relationship to the pragmatic values of daily social and political life.

Nonetheless, the idea of public interest should not be too quickly discarded. At one level, it respects the fact that some individuals do act in concert for reasons other than the pursuit of narrow self-interests. "The reality of the common interest is suggested by the demonstrated capacity of the community to survive."[124] At an even more fundamental level, the notion of the public interest retains a set of valued meanings that are not easily discarded. In classical democratic theory, the public interest connotes both what is on balance good for the polity, and values that are or should be attractive to the citizens of a nation. The promise of a conciliation of the general good with individual interest invests the words "public interest" with emotional and intellectual power.

One might expect debates within public-interest advocacy organizations to be broad in their scope. Their dedication to broad principles should prompt a receptivity to new ideas in a situation where existing principles offer little direct guidance, as well as compel a search for what can in fact be done. However, like the interest groups and minority-defense organizations, the public-interest advocates demonstrated no consistent affinity to broad or narrow scope of debate.

A possible explanation may be prior experience in a similar case. *DeFunis* v. *Odegaard* had posed many of the same problems as *Bakke* had, and organizations active in *DeFunis* might have established positions which foreclosed the need for broad debate in *Bakke*. Forty-six amici organizations in *Bakke* had been amici or litigants in *DeFunis*. But involvement in *DeFunis* did not ordain a narrowing in scope. Previous experience in *DeFunis* seemed to increase, not decrease, the chance of a broad debate on the issues.[125] Of the forty-five participants in *DeFunis* studied, twenty-one demonstrated broad scope while twenty-four exhibited narrow scope. Five of the nine public-interest veterans of affirmative action cases conducted debates with broad scope, contrasted with three of nine veteran interest groups and thirteen of twenty-seven veteran minority-defense organizations. Forty-seven percent of the *DeFunis* organizations displayed a broad scope, compared to only twenty-six percent of those not veterans of *DeFunis*. Perhaps these organizations' frequent participation in affirmative action cases reflected the strength of their concerns about, and the continually troublesome nature of the dispute over, special programs for minorities. For many, the discussion within the organization broadened rather than narrowed as the issue reappeared in new cases such as *Bakke*.

Unfortunately, there was only anecdotal material available to test whether organizations active in both cases broadened or narrowed the scope of their debates from *DeFunis* to *Bakke*. Most organizations, like the American Jewish Committee,[126] apparently did neither, suggesting that the same factors affecting scope during *Bakke* were present during *DeFunis*. However, some organizations, such as the National Education Association, broadened their debates.[127] On the other hand, the American Civil Liberties Union narrowed its debate.

The American Civil Liberties Union (ACLU) illustrates how prior involvement in an issue can affect organizational purpose.[128] The ACLU's experience was exceptional. Most *DeFunis* organizations appeared to have broadened or maintained the scope of their debates. The fact that one of the most prestigious private organizations in the United States, one strongly committed to the ideal of a public interest, narrowed its scope may teach us how organizations reduce conflict by reducing the opportunities for discussion and learning.

The American Civil Liberties Union is the nation's oldest and largest advocacy group committed to the defense of civil rights and liberties. Founded in 1917 as the National Civil Liberties Bureau to defend conscientious objectors, it assumed its present name in 1920 and began its campaign to secure the fundamental individual rights it perceives to be guaranteed by the Bill of Rights. By 1976 the ACLU had 250,000 members, and its national office had a budget of $1.6 million and assets of over half a million dollars. It was supported by forty-nine affiliates in forty-seven states with 325 local chapters. It could enlist the legal services of more than 5,000 "cooperating attorneys."[129]

The ACLU is devoted "to protecting the fundamental civil

rights of the people of the United States."[130] In pursuit of that
end, it has become the most frequent private litigant in cases before the Supreme Court.[131] The organization does not see itself
as the protector of specific individuals so much as a nonpartisan
defender of civil rights and liberties. Evoking Herbert Jacob's
distinction between policy making and norm enforcement as
litigation strategies, Stephen Halpern suggests that the ACLU is
more concerned with establishing new rules to guide future action than with settling the specific evidentiary issues in a case.[132]
As a consequence, the ACLU prefers to champion cases that are
likely to influence the development of constitutional doctrines.

From 1950 through the late sixties, the local affiliates exerted
considerable control over litigation. They decided whether to
intervene in a case and what kind of and how much aid to provide. National ACLU assistance included direct sponsorship of a
test case, advice on strategies, recommendations of attorneys
who might render their services without fee, or participation as
an amicus. Since 1970, however, the national legal office in New
York has asserted its independent judgment on those questions.
It is no longer simply the appellate arm for the grassroots ACLU
programs, or only a supplemental legal resource for the weaker
affiliates. Bolstered by its own independent funding from foundations and the national membership, the national headquarters, based in New York and Washington, files its own briefs in
hundreds of cases a year.[133] The national board, once composed
only of a small elitist group, primarily lawyers, now has a majority membership of nonlawyers representing the affiliates.

At one time the ACLU was devoted almost exclusively to litigational forms of influence. However, responding to the criticism that this concentration forced it into a defensive position,
a "shield" rather than an aggressive champion of the "traditional rights of free expression and thought,"[134] the ACLU now
emphasizes more traditional types of lobbying. It was active in
the legislative campaign conducted by the Leadership Conference on Civil Rights that led to the Civil Rights Act of 1964 and
the Voting Rights Act of 1965; it was a principal backer of
the Legal Services Corporation; and it helped defeat Senate Bill
1 in 1976, a proposed revision of the federal criminal code

which, critics charged, threatened important First Amendment freedoms.

Despite these new directions in ACLU thinking and action, the organization has continued to emphasize litigation. Litigation fulfills an important organizational need by providing a highly visible forum for its role as a nonpartisan spokesperson for the unorganized, the powerless, and the unpopular. The courtroom drama of an ACLU attorney defending a young child who refuses to salute the flag on religious grounds confronting the local prosecutor representing the force of community pressures for conformity exerts more appeal to contributors than the low-key, day-to-day lobbying necessary to ensure passage of major legislation. Its litigation activity has also achieved important victories. The ACLU is known for its successful sponsorship of, or participation as amicus in, cases dealing with unlawful search and seizure (*Mapp* v. *Ohio*); the right to counsel for the poor (*Gideon* v. *Wainwright*); the constitutionality of the death penalty (*Furman* v. *Georgia*); and the freedoms of speech (*Roth* v. *U.S.*), association (*DeJonge* v. *Oregon*), and religion (*W. Virginia Board of Education* v. *Barnette*). It was also instrumental in the fight to declare racial covenants unconstitutional (*Shelley* v. *Kraemer*) and to overturn the "separate but equal" rule (*Brown* v. *Board of Education*). Every organization values success, and a small association organized to represent broad public interests rather than more discrete individual or group interests is happy to find evidence that its efforts are worthwhile. The lack of more concrete indicators of effectiveness ensures that judicial endorsement of policy positions will be important to the organization. "The only real satisfaction we get," stated a senior member of the ACLU, "is seeing our names in the paper and hearing our voices when the [Supreme Court] justices speak." [135]

The preface to the ACLU brief in *Bakke* spoke of a decade of intense and vigorous debate culminating in membership support for racially sensitive special admissions programs. [136] However, the national legal staff and individuals active in the decisions to offer briefs in *DeFunis* and *Bakke* conceded that the brief's language evoked an illusory sense of agreement. The battle within the organization over affirmative action was fought during *De-Funis*, and the losers in that conflict remained quiet in *Bakke*.

During the late sixties, at the same time that other organizations such as the NAACP and the American Jewish Congress were struggling to develop a stand on the issue of affirmative action, the governing bodies of the ACLU began their attempts to reach accord. The specific issue was not raised at the biennial meetings attended by representatives of the organization's affiliates and national board members. The conventions endorsed the concept of affirmative action, but the leaders were reluctant to place as potentially disruptive a controversy as "quotas" on the agenda. The issue did appear in articles and letters published in the Union's major publications, *Civil Liberties Review*[137] and the newsletter *Civil Liberties*. A debate between national board members Frank Askin and Carl Cohen, published after the ACLU submitted a brief in *DeFunis*, illustrates the range of arguments presented to the organization.

Favoring preferential admissions, Frank Askin, then the corporate secretary of the ACLU and now one of the general counsels, contended that the only hope for "eliminating racial inequality in a racist world" was to compensate blacks as a group for the injuries they have sustained as a group. "Is it a necessary libertarian principle that, despite all the years of slavery and discrimination against them as a group, black people must now work their way into the American mainstream one by one?" Askin's support of special admissions programs entailed more than the principle of compensatory justice—since the injury to each has been an injury to all, redress to all properly serves to redress each. He also cited the justifications of preventing social unrest ("the alienation of these minority groups from the system of justice went hand-in-hand with the scarcity of lawyers drawn from them") and extending political pluralism ("we realized that the scarcity of black lawyers also helped to explain the relatively small number of blacks elected to public office"). To use racial classifications to assist the victims of racial discrimination did not raise the same moral and social qualms as the use of race to stigmatize minorities as inferior. "We are talking about a situation in which institutions dominated by members of the racial majority decide, as a short-term expedient, to favor the minority in an effort to foster racial harmony, to promote racial integration, and to eliminate racial stigma." Fears about the abuse of such programs are therefore misplaced, Askin concluded.[138]

Carl Cohen's reply concentrated on the dangers attending the well-intentioned use of "unsavory means" to accomplish "honorable ends." A professor of philosophy, Cohen addressed a set of problems not dealt with by Askin. While lauding the ends "reverse racial preferences" were intended to achieve, Cohen worried that the "qualities of the means will inevitably penetrate" and pervert the ends: "If the instrument is ugly, we must expect the product to share that ugliness." The Fourteenth Amendment guarantees that race "will be irrelevant to one's entitlements under law." To abridge that guarantee in the name of an objective so honorable as the remission of racial inequities might jeopardize the ethical basis for the equal protection of the laws. "Civil libertarians," he wrote, "are well-advised to be cautious in belittling the force of the equal protection clause when it serves their purposes to do so. Others, whose purposes are as compelling to them as ours are to us, will find that practice very convenient, to our distress." Cohen's doubts extended beyond the question of ethical propriety. He also voiced a concern over whether preference programs attained their intended objectives. The use of race in the highly competitive context of medical school admissions could well be seen as the "paradigm of unfairness" and might "excite ill will and envy" in the heart of a "plain person." The racial animosity produced might cause many to conclude that the minority doctor or lawyer had gained his or her position by virtue of race and not effort or merit. Consequently, there may be a lack of trust in and respect for his or her professional abilities.[139]

It is difficult to reconstruct an intraorganizational conflict years later. The passage of time can cloud participants' memories and can subject these memories to the subtle influences of changing attitudes. Nevertheless, reports from individuals active on both sides of the controversy and contemporary letters to the editors of ACLU publications suggest that the Askin-Cohen debate encapsulated the character of the debate within the organization. The issue of affirmative action struck at the heart of the principles most cherished by the association. The ACLU stresses individualism as its primary value. It takes seriously the words "Congress shall make *no* law . . ." affecting the freedoms of expression and belief. The absolute insistence on individual autonomy creates problems whenever individual rights conflict. The issue of affirmative action was one such conflict, pairing the individual right to be free of racial discriminations against the right to the realistic opportunity to compete for social benefits. The question posed a challenge to the organization's mission as a defender of the weak and the unpopular against the coercive force of government; it posed the subtle problem of reconciling two rights, not protecting a right from a wrong.

The ACLU never fully resolved the problem. In 1970 its board of directors endorsed the use of specialized standards and methods for evaluating the abilities and potentials of members of disadvantaged groups and called for the institution of "massive compensatory programs for educationally deprived students."[140] The policy statement expressed a conception of affirmative action acceptable to almost all camps in the controversy; it carefully side-stepped the problem of quotas for minorities. But this policy declaration masked the intensity and extent of the discussion within the organization. Discussions on the topic at board meetings and within the chapters became acrimonious —in the salty language of one board member, "it was a bitch." Questions of general policy swiftly translated into aspersions on the character of the speakers, and "racist" epithets were sometimes voiced. Fearing continued disruption, several chapters, such as the Chicago chapter, refused to address the question further, silently agreeing to disagree. At the national board, the prospect of continued confrontation prompted members to postpone discussion during the late sixties and early seventies.

By 1973, when the *DeFunis* case arrived at the Supreme Court, the ACLU had still come to no definite conclusions on affirmative action. The general counsels and the national office's legal staff pressed vigorously for board approval of ACLU participation in the case. At this point, individual informants differ

in their recollections of what occurred. Some, such as Aryeh
Neier, then the executive director of the ACLU, report extensive
debate by the board. On the other hand, E. Richard Larson, the
staff head of the ACLU's *Bakke* task force, maintains that the
decision to defend the University of Washington Law School
program was "rammed through two board meetings," a bare
majority of the national board "grudgingly" approving the idea
of a brief.[141] But two of the key antagonists in the *DeFunis* controversy, Askin and Cohen, say that the decision was neither extensively debated nor "rammed through." They characterized
the discussion as a brief one followed by a quick but narrow victory for the University of Washington position.

Approval of intervention into *DeFunis* was facilitated by two
factors. One was the justifying language for ACLU involvement
available in prior board statements. In the absence of a mandate
from the members on the issue, the governing board was persuaded to endorse the Washington program on the limited
grounds of the constitutionality of state agencies applying different measures of aptitude and ability to members of different
racial groups. A prior board statement had seemed to settle this
question.

In order to achieve genuine equality of educational opportunity colleges should apply, in respect to persons who are members of disadvantaged groups and who previously have been denied opportunity
for equal educational advantage, standards and methods of evaluating
applicants different from those used with other applicants, as long as
these standards and methods are reasonably designed to increase
equality of educational opportunity.[142]

The noncompetitive nature of the admissions process was deliberately played down in the *DeFunis* brief. The ACLU addressed
solely the propriety of the use of "culturally biased" quantitative measures such as the Law School Admissions Test when
assessing minority applicants' potential.[143] The issue whether
minority applicants should be evaluated by placing them in a
separate, racially segregated admissions track was ignored.

The second factor influencing the ACLU board's decision was
the attraction of filing a coalition brief with several traditional
allies. The legal staff worked to sponsor a brief with Hispanic

organizations like the Mexican-American and the Puerto Rican legal defense funds. A coalition brief eased fears among some board members that a failure to support preferences would damage relations with important allies. Other board members were reassured of the brief's appropriateness by this display of solidarity among like-minded organizations.

Despite, or perhaps because of, the low-key nature of the *DeFunis* argument, official ACLU policy on the issue of quota-oriented admissions programs remained ambiguous in the years between *DeFunis* and *Bakke*. The organization publicly reiterated its repudiation of the "separate but equal" doctrine and affirmatively supported compensatory programs in education and "'target' ratios and timetables" in employment.[144] At the same time, the ACLU retained language in its official policy guide opposing the determination of a "teacher's access to school employment" on the basis of "race, sex, ethnic origin, creed, or political affiliation" and the maintenance of "separate admission requirement for men and women."[145]

In 1977 the ACLU voluntarily implemented an affirmative action plan requiring it to employ "within three years of the adoption of this . . . plan . . . at least 20% minorities and at least 50% women at every level of employment." The plan was elaborate and specific in its requirements. Current statistical breakdowns of employees' racial and sexual backgrounds and income levels were mandated. Failure to realize its goals automatically freed $2,000 for more intensive recruitment effort. Special funds for expanded recruiting announcements and for reimbursing minority and women applicants for travel expenses were also provided.[146] The ACLU board of directors thus imposed a quota program on the organization itself.

The board's decision to implement this stringent plan coincided with the legal staff's decision to submit a brief in *Bakke* supporting the concept of a two-track admissions process. Both decisions symbolized a significant shift in organizational policy. While a commitment to equality of result had been implicit in previous ACLU litigation such as *Brown* v. *Board of Education*, that commitment was limited and seemed reconcilable with the dominant civil liberties theme. In *Bakke*, however, the defender of individuality appeared to be transformed into a promoter of substantive equality.

Although the decision to impose a quota program on the ACLU itself had stimulated vigorous dissent among the board members,[147] the *Bakke* brief was received quietly. In fact, the outline of the brief's position was presented to the board only a month before it was due to be filed. In a memorandum addressed to "Interested ACLU Folks"[148] from the member of the legal staff acting as head of the *Bakke* task force, the ACLU's leadership first heard the brief's two primary themes: the special admission program was an effective device securing the "individual equality necessary to enjoyment of individual liberty in a democratic society," and the program was entirely compatible with the equal protection requirements of the Fourteenth Amendment.[149]

The ACLU's *DeFunis* brief had focused on the narrow issue of differential evaluation for minority applicants; the *Bakke* brief argued that justice, not expediency, was the fundamental justification for preferential programs. Quoting a contemporary philosopher, John Rawls, the brief admonished that "'inequalities of wealth and authority are just only if they result in compensating benefits for everyone and, in particular, for the least advantaged members of society. . . . [I]t may be expedient but it is not just that some should have less in order that others may prosper. But there is no injustice in the greater benefits earned by a few provided that the situation of persons not so fortunate is thereby improved.'"[150] In their own words, the authors of the ACLU brief went on to argue that, since those who attend state-supported medical schools receive greater benefits than those who do not, it is just that the state apportion the opportunity on the basis of improving the lot of other members of society. Since minority populations have traditionally been underserved by the medical profession, and since minority physicians are more likely to return to minority communities, the dictates of justice permit granting admissions on the basis of racial identity to individuals otherwise qualified to attend medical school.[151]

The brief was careful not to endorse the extreme argument for affirmative action, warning against the "premise" that equality meant the guarantee of "the same homes, the same jobs, the same educational attainments, the same happiness." Instead, it argued that, quoting A. D. Lindsay, "not all men ought to be treated as if they had equal capacities, but as if they were equally to count."[152] Individual liberty could only be achieved by securing racial equality. "By extending to members of traditionally disadvantaged minorities opportunities that otherwise would be denied to them, the University of California is promoting the ideal that all individuals are equally to count in our society."[153] As the "Interested ACLU Folks" memorandum put it, the "compelling individual rights in *Bakke*" were the "rights of minorities" to graduate school opportunities.[154] Frank Askin explained later to a reporter, "the Court may see some merit in the fact that with sixty years of experience representing the cause of civil liberties, the ACLU has come to the conclusion that Allan Bakke's civil liberties were not infringed."[155]

A former legal staff member likened the national office's efforts in *Bakke* to a "coup." "Askin, Larson, [board chairman Norman] Dorsen, and [acting legal director Joel] Gora did not even query the board. They feared that some directors would object to the brief's cast—its pro-quota stance. Why antagonize people and perhaps lose the opportunity to make a statement in so important a case?"[156] Larson agreed with the substance of his colleague's remarks although he denied that there was a "conspiracy." "*DeFunis* has settled the question of ACLU policy" on affirmative action. "All we had to do was put that policy on paper." When asked how could so settled a policy exist when the board had never issued a statement on the question, Larson replied, "That wasn't the way we [the national office] saw it. The ACLU is committed to defend the rights of the weak—that wasn't Bakke."[157] Frank Askin was more direct. "We did not contact the board because we are paid to make the decisions on the law—this was not a policy decision in the normal sense of the word. *Bakke* was a legal, not a policy, decision."[158] Apparently, most of the board agreed with Askin.

Unlike the debate during the *DeFunis* period or the controversies in the intervening years on other matters, *Bakke* created relatively little conflict within the ACLU board. Dissenters to the brief made only weak-hearted efforts to raise the issue at board meetings. "The numbers just weren't there," one director replied when asked why she had not forced the issue. "The sentiment of the board was that the question was best left to the lawyers. We were afraid to reopen old arguments and old wounds." [159] Buffeted by challenges and counterchallenges over affirmative action and engulfed by a tide of court suits on the issue, the board appeared to grow weary of the problem. Some board members admitted that a growing familiarity with the idea of affirmative action helped dispel some of their suspicions about quotas. "The more I thought about it, the clearer the tie between benign quotas and equal opportunity became for me." [160] Others were influenced by the ACLU's ambiguity concerning so important a matter. In both cases, board members were willing to leave the final decision with the legal staff, and the legal staff was more interested in pursuing its plans for future litigation than it was in seeking agreement within the association. Unlike the EEAC's attorneys, the ACLU's were concerned with accomplishing a policy objective, not with drawing a clear line between internal "winners" and "losers." [161]

Most members did not learn of ACLU involvement until after the brief was filed. In the July 1977 issue of *Civil Liberties*, Frank Askin explained the union's support of the university. The article downplayed the more difficult aspects of the case, suggesting that the Davis program was intended to aid "'disadvantaged' applicants, all of whom turned out to be minority members." It ignored the criticism, from organizations such as the American Jewish Congress, that the program intentionally aided only disadvantaged minority applicants. The article reflected the brief's endorsement of short-term quotas and quoted its conclusion that "[n]o other asserted claim of right surpasses the wholly justified demand of the nation's discrete and insular minorities for access to the American mainstream from which they have so long been excluded." [162] To some extent, then, the brief and its presentation in an issue of the organization's newspaper, *Civil Liberties*, to ACLU members seem to have been designed not only to convince the Supreme Court about the fairness of the Davis program but also to persuade the organization's affiliates that their commitment to individual freedom was best served by the brief's position.

Membership reaction to the brief was muted. It is difficult to determine the degree and extent of member dissatisfaction with it since the membership was riven at the same time by the ACLU defense of the "Nazi Free Speech" march in Skokie, Illinois. Estimates of membership defection over that issue ranged from two thousand to forty thousand, and income from membership renewals dropped fifteen percent from the previous year.[163] By comparison, membership concern over the *Bakke* brief seemed minimal; one member of the national office in New York believed only fifty to one hundred letters of resignation were received condemning the *Bakke* policy compared to more than four thousand letters opposing the defense of the Nazis.[164] ACLU staffers reported that resignations were greatest among the newest members; there had been little erosion among old members. Approximately forty percent of the ACLU's constituents were Jewish in 1974,[165] and many may have found the positions of the traditional Jewish organizations on Skokie and *Bakke* more appealing. But membership dissatisfaction need not have been translated automatically into membership defection. Many members may simply not have known the ACLU's position in *Bakke* until well after the submission of the ACLU's brief. Despite efforts by both supporters and opponents of the policy favoring preferential or compensatory admissions programs to disseminate the major features of the controversy through the organization's media, most members were still unaware of the official policy on the issue. For many, the turmoil over the Skokie Nazi defense effectively masked the controversy over *Bakke*.[166]

The ACLU lacked the kinds of material incentives which elicited support for interest groups such as the EEAC or the National Association of Minority Contractors. Conventional wisdom warns about the instability of organizations founded, like the ACLU, on symbolic and promotional awards.[167] Yet, on the whole, it retained its members' allegiance.

The role played by the nature of the tie between the ACLU and its members was significant. Many members in organizations such as the ACLU have little interest in the day-to-day policies the organizations pursue; they maintain involvement because of the historical stances taken by those organizations.[168] In its members' minds, the ACLU represented the unorganized, the weak, and the unpopular. Its stalwart defense of First Amendment liberties and its commitment to carving out new realms of personal rights attracted individuals who wished to be associated with its special vision of American society. The symbolic power of the organization formed resilient ties among its members, holding their allegiances even in the face of widespread internal disagreement over specific policies. The ACLU members who disapproved the organization's posture on affirmative action may have continued their affiliation because of such a passionate commitment to the traditional policies espoused by the association. The absence of competing or equivalent organizations for dissatisfied members to join was another factor. The ACLU is in a "monopoly" position for some valued functions because few or no effective alternatives exist. Many members contributed because of their conviction that the nation needed to maintain an organization like the ACLU, one prepared to argue the cause of the unpopular when such causes are threatened by systematic efforts to silence them. The need to keep the ACLU healthy for such emergencies outweighed any member dissatisfaction with policy stances in less dire times.

These strengths of symbolic membership were accompanied by corresponding weaknesses. Symbolic membership is vulnerable to changes in fashions. "The ebb and flow of supporting sentiments" in society for the values and purposes espoused by an action-organization like the ACLU can cause mass defections when the organization pursues a policy which challenges an important facet of its legitimizing belief system.[169] The dramatic loss of membership resulting from the defense of the rights of Skokie Nazis might be attributed to this process; some individuals attracted to the ACLU because of its condemnation of the Vietnam War, its early call for the impeachment of Richard Nixon, and its legal defense of individuals such as Angela Davis and Benjamin Spock failed to realize that the same organizational principles could provide protection for the rights of such disreputable groups as the American Nazi Party and the Ku Klux Klan. Confronted with the unfashionable defense of groups like these, marginal members fled the organization.[170]

The Problem with Purpose

In several ways, the ACLU's experience with *Bakke* demonstrated why organizational purpose did not affect the scope of organizational debate. Many board members in the ACLU and other organizations like the National Fund for Minority Engineering Students were willing to accept the premise that *Bakke* was merely a legal rather than a broader political or social issue, and therefore within the purview of the professional legal staff. Further, the concern about ally expectations expressed by some ACLU directors and by the Council on Legal Education Opportunity suggested the significance of extraorganizational factors. The ACLU's concern that litigation in this case was necessary to reassure ACLU contributors of the ACLU's distinctive role in American politics was similar to that of the legal defense funds' concern with the maintenance needs of their organizations. Finally, the enormous publicity and ensuing dialogue generated by the national media's treatment of the issue no doubt superseded intraorganizational debates. The competing influences of strategic and tactical organizational concerns and the peculiarities of the case itself thus weakened the relevance of "purpose" to "scope." At least in *Bakke*, the differing perspectives, resources, and pressures among organizations determined the kind of decision-making process they were to exhibit.

If any organizational interest was paramount in *Bakke*, it was an interest in the organization's continued well-being. The avoidance of confrontation in the ACLU indicated a concern that renewed debate on the issue might severely disrupt the organization's working majority on equal-protection issues. By accepting the legal staff's decision as the organization's policy, rather than reopening the dispute among board members and within the membership of affiliates, the ACLU illustrated how considerations of organizational stability and harmony can overrule one of the programmatic purposes of the association, the nurturing of a constituency informed about civil liberties issues. The status of the organization as an "end"—as a valued thing in itself—was more important than its status as a means to accomplish other ends.

It is possible to expand the meaning of organizational "purpose" to include these extra- and intraorganizational concerns. The consequences of such a redefinition are not attractive. More ambiguity, not less, would result, and thereby lessen the value of the idea of a "purpose." Nor is redefinition necessarily desirable. Hypothesis I could be construed to mean that the breadth or narrowness of an organization's perception of its purposes will affect the extent of the ideas and issues legitimately within the range of the organization's decision making. In a less controversial context, it may not be untenable for purpose to mold scope in the manner suggested by the hypothesis.

The invalidation of Hypothesis I in *Bakke* does serve a useful function. The prospects for education seemed to be greater in organizations like the Equal Employment Advisory Council, the Council on Legal Education Opportunity, and in some legal defense organizations. The ACLU demonstrated some of the features of an enlightening debate in the years preceding *Bakke*. In each case, these organizations encouraged membership participation while seeking to create broad agreement. Hypotheses II and III, with their respective emphases on the intensity of conflict and the nature of participation, would therefore seem promising predictors of litigation as a form of political education for an organization's members.

CHAPTER III

THE OLIGARCHIC IMPULSE

The tendency for groups to divide into the leader and the led has long perplexed social theorists. Is the tendency "natural," arising from the intrinsic dynamic of social relationships, or is it "artificial," the forceful imposition of the will of a self-selected few? The classical answer insisted on the division between aristocracy and oligarchy, and sought to preserve the legitimacy of rule by a natural elite—an elite comprised of the virtuous and wise—against the corruptive rule by the wealthy few.[1] A similar concern animates modern thinking. For example, many contemporary social theorists differentiate between "power": obedience produced through physical force; and "authority": "a competence based upon skill, learning, talent, ability, or some similar attribute."[2]

For centuries, the accepted and therefore acceptable bases of aristocratic regimes were provided by religion and social status. By the late nineteenth century, however, it was no longer sufficient to state, as John Adams did, that "there must be in every society of men, superiors and inferiors, because God has laid in the Constitution and course of nature, the foundations of the distinction."[3] Social theorists and political commentators had shifted their emphases from attributional to structural factors.

And the notion of authority as a distinctive form of rule was threatened by a new skepticism.

With the publication of *Political Parties* in 1915, Robert Michels inaugurated the modern theory of the oligarchic group.[4] The product of his investigations of large political parties in prewar Germany, *Political Parties* proclaimed an "iron law of oligarchy," the discovery that even the most democratic and egalitarian-principled organizations are characterized by bureaucratic hierarchy and authoritarian control. Taking his cue from Weber's description of the dynamics of "legal-rational" or bureaucratic administration, Michels constructed a theory of oligarchic behavior which concentrated on the distinction in the roles and resources available to leaders and followers.

According to Michels, the technical necessities of organizational governance makes the direct rule of the members "mechanically" impossible. As a result of the complexity and fluidity of modern group life and because of the division of labor necessary to cope with that complexity and fluidity, it is difficult for the members to participate in organizational activities. As the size and purposes of an organization expand, the members relinquish their prerogatives over day-to-day policy making to the executive leaders and staff. The putative incompetence of the mass to act without leaders justifies the transfer of authority from members to the staff.

The thrust toward oligarchy results not only from the members' inadequacies; the context of and opportunities afforded to leaders are also important. Access to and direct control over the apparatus of organization—membership lists, office files, organization circulars and publications—vest the leaders with advantages unmatched by the members. The control of organizational resources and opportunities in turn fosters managerial skills and technical knowledge of the "ins and outs" of the organizational process which further strengthen the leaders in the organizational policy process. Moreover, the grant of authority and discretion to the leaders to perform the routine tasks of governance produces opportunities to expand and develop that discretion. Challenged to attain group objectives, the leader seeks to enlarge the membership base of the organization; as the resource base expands, there is a corresponding decrease in the opportunities for meaningful member participation. The transformation of the party from a small band of dedicated activists into a mass association provides the leader with even greater opportunities to enhance his or her authority. As Michels remarked, "It is easier to dominate a mass than a small audience."[5]

The differences in roles and resources between leaders and members also lead to differences in the perception of the interests at stake in organizational action. The demands of organizational life place leaders in a different context from the members, and differences in milieus of action generate corresponding differences in the interests of the leaders and the followers. The differences are deeper than those Burke recounted in his "Bristol Address." Leaders are not torn solely between a devotion to presenting their constituents' views and the need to exercise their independent judgment. The status and monetary rewards of leadership instill in the leaders and staff personal interests in maintaining their organizational roles and authorities distinct from the general interests the association was officially formed to serve. According to Michels, this transformation of personal interests leads to the displacement of the original organizational interests. The growth of oligarchical elites within the organization will impose a conservatism on the association since the leaders' stake in maintaining the status quo overshadows the members' interests in the organization as a movement for social change.

Michels concluded his analysis by drawing a parallel between political associations and "fighting groups." The difficulties confronting political parties, and especially socialist parties in a capitalist society, compel them to exhibit the "efficient" structure of oligarchies; they are forced into dependence on the few in order to accomplish efficiently and effectively their tasks.[6] In the words of Carl Friedrich, the "inevitable preponderance of the leader [in the political party] is the result of the same forces which produce monocratic leadership in government; for the party is almost constantly in the position of a nation at war."[7]

That Michels accepted the inevitability of oligarchy does not imply that he was happy with it. Like Weber, who feared the stifling effects of the "iron cage" of bureaucracy, where the "individual bureaucrat cannot squirm out of the apparatus in which he is harnessed,"[8] Michels was disturbed by the oligarchic tendencies of "legal-rational" forms of administration. He feared that organization will destroy democracy, transforming democratic participation into oligarchic domination: "He who says organization, says tendency toward oligarchy. . . . The machinery of organization . . . completely inverts the position of the leader in respect to the masses. . . . Wherever organization is stronger, we observe a smaller degree of applied democracy."[9]

Michels's thesis that the growth of oligarchic elites fosters organizational conservatism has been tested by a battery of empirical studies. These studies conclude that homogeneous organizations which depend on unsuccessful, single-goal strategies are vulnerable to mass defections by their memberships, leaving the organization in the hands of the most radical members.[10] As Rudwick and Meier's research on the contrasting fates of the NAACP and the Congress on Racial Equality suggest, when an organization's purposes become obsolescent, its leaders are as likely to become radical as they are to become conservative.[11] Nor is bureaucratization alone the culprit; Pratt and others have argued that organizations characterized by growing bureaucracies do not inevitably become conservative in their aims. The AFL-CIO, the National Council of Churches, and the NAACP have all become more bureaucratic at the very same time as they have pursued increasingly liberal and reformist objectives.[12] Apparently, the "iron law of oligarchy" is less ferrous than it is plastic.

Other studies question the inevitability of oligarchy on different grounds. Lipset, Trow, and Coleman's analysis of the International Typographical Union[13] persuaded one critic of Michels's work that "certain components in the oligarchical concept and certain alleged effects of oligarchy may not be applicable to the American scene."[14] Recognition of the commonality of interests among the leaders and members, the norm of opposition, and a tradition of rapid turnover of elected officials may offset the oligarchical tendencies in large organizations.[15]

Despite these shortcomings, Michels did graphically delineate a bothersome aspect of organizational membership in a mass society. In all organized bodies of men and women, control of the direction and content of policy making is increasingly vested in the hands of a small number. Members' passivity or indifference, the growing imbalance in information capacities between leaders and followers, and the complexity of organized action in a turbulent world in furthering the concentration of day-to-day power are matters best decided case-by-case. But the fact that the concentration seems to be growing, often without the conscious approval of group members, is a feature of contemporary organizational life.

An *oligarchic* theory of organizational behavior emphasizes the advantage of the leaders and the relative impotence of members. However, there is an alternative way of depicting organizational behavior, one concentrating on the mutual obligations of leaders and members. A *democratic* theory emphasizes the ideal of "self-government" and the values of member participation in the organizational policy-making process.

"Democracy" is a much abused word in political discourse. It is subjected to a variety of contentious usages, parading under the multihued garbs of "people's democracy" (the rule of the communist party in the putative interests of the proletarian majority), "social democracy" (the massive intervention of the popularly elected government into the national economy so as to redistribute economic and thus, it is hoped, social opportunities), "liberal democracy" (popularly elected, limited government committed to the protection of political rights and liberties), and "democratic republicanism" (the American constitutional variant of "liberal democracy," emphasizing a structured system of complex checks and balances, federated power, and separation of governmental functions). The common theme in all these usages is the identification of the legitimate source of power with "the people," a concept translated in the American experience to government that entails the "consent of the governed." [16] Democracy becomes an expression of the ideal of *self-government*, the notion that the citizen ought to have the opportunity to participate in public policy making.

Although the pedigree of the idea of "democracy" can be

traced as far back as the Athenian city-state of the classical period, the concerns that animated the *polis* of Periclean Athens are markedly different from those characterizing current debate on the meaning of democracy. The tradition in political philosophy that commenced with Plato and Aristotle views democracy as a synonym for the rule of the "mob," the rule by right of the massed might of the proletariat, which is capable of tyrannizing society and which in turn is itself tyrannized by base emotions and nameless fears. That tradition still dominated American thinking through the founding of the republic, influencing the theorists of 1787 to devise a means to screen, buffer, and refine popular opinion so as to produce, in Tocqueville's words, an "enlightened self-interest" among the majority. More recently, however, the growing complexities of the modern nation-state have recast the debate into one concerned with the role of minorities in politics, and the fears about majority tyranny have given way to worries about the rule of elites. "Government is always government by the few," write two respected political scientists of our era, "whether in the name of the few, the one, or the many." [17]

Democracy, it would seem, requires at a minimum that each citizen has the reasonable expectation of being treated as a being of equal worth. On the other hand, the division of labor characterizing society gives rise to the need for leadership, thereby providing the conditions fostering elites and oligarchies. The problem of modern democracy lies in accommodating the horizontal pressures toward equal power among its citizens and the vertical pressures toward leadership and authority.

Since World War II, political scientists and sociologists have sought to determine how effectively the American political system has dealt with these double imperatives, equality and authority. Perhaps responding to a need to distinguish American "democracy" from its cold war competitors, specifically, the multiplying "people's democracies" of the communist world, academicians such as Robert Dahl and Nelson Polsby offer pluralism—"the thinking man's democracy"—as the American solution to the problem. Carol Greenwald summarizes one pluralist position: "[Pluralism] . . . tries to reconcile the existence of a large, modern, heterogeneous technocratic society with democratic notions of individual self-development through participation in civic decisions that affect the quality of one's life. . . . The pluralists have tried to accommodate the notion that participation in public decisions furthers such public values as human dignity, equality, and liberty with recognition of the fact that millions of Americans can not be intimately involved in billions of specialized, technical, public policy decisions." [18]

As an empirical theory, pluralism explains American politics in terms of the behavior of democratic elites through which individual citizens are able to make their voices heard in the public arena. The elite system is characterized by fluidity and competitiveness. Different issues attract different sets of elites and require those seeking to influence policy to expend different resources in order to be powerful. Political power becomes "situational and mercurial." [19] American politics is "fractured into congeries of hundreds of small, special interest groups, with incompletely overlapping memberships, widely differing power bases, and a multitude of techniques for exercising influence on decisions salient to them." [20] These differing powers ensure that no one group will be victorious in all policy areas; they encourage a rapid turnover of elites and therefore a continual circulation of personnel. Finite resources and multiple actors force elites to modulate their demands, to accommodate to the interests of others, and to negotiate with one another according to the generally accepted norms of political behavior. [21] Most important, the citizens can choose from among competing elites and make their preferences known through the electoral process. To the pluralists, the question of democratic participation "is not so much whether citizens are active but whether they have the opportunity to exert control through activity when they wish to do so." [22]

The pluralist paradigm translates democracy into a procedural methodology; it describes a way of proceeding, not a substantive outcome. Insofar as the idea of democracy would seem to require that men and women make the decisions that affect their lives, the pluralists emphasize the "due process" of politics, the acceptance of elemental "rules of the game" that guide the competition and ensure sufficiently aggrieved individuals access to the political struggle. Unable to agree on where to go, on what goals to achieve, we attempt to do things by agreed-upon procedures, hoping that doing things the "right" ("generally accepted") way will lead us to the "right" ("generally acceptable") ends.

Despite charges that pluralist explanations are conservatively biased and empirically misguided, since they condemn mass participatory political movements as extremist and fail to account for those excluded from and victimized by the interest group process,[23] the pluralist approach does attempt to evade entrapment by the "middle-of-the-road fallacy"—the assumption that since all political systems are founded on elite governance, there is little distinction between democracy and oligarchy.[24] The pluralist approach places a premium on the activities of leadership and cautions us to examine carefully the relationship between leaders and followers. The leader as entrepreneur, soliciting support and therefore made responsible to his or her constituents, becomes the hallmark of American social science's image of politics. Democracy, in this perspective, becomes identified with the controls followers place on leaders and with those factors that prompt responsive leaders in the absence of the imposition of controls.

A democratic politics, then, does not deny the importance of leadership; in fact, more than any other form of public action, it requires leadership of a special kind—responsible and responsive. The American solution, as stated in the Constitution and articulated in the pages of the *Federalist Papers*, to the problem of democratic leadership relies on a circulation of power, distributing authority in turn and jointly among elites. Democracy becomes polyarchy, government by many minorities.[25] As such, the American search for democratic mechanisms of government offers the hope of an alternative to other approaches to the question of democratic governance. Democratic leadership need not be reduced to the rule of the majority or the rule of the few in the interests or name of the majority. And the effort to realize that hope rests on the efficacy of the formal devices of popular control as exercised through the direct vote of the citizenship (referenda) and their representation by elected officials and of the informal process of private group articulation of aggregated individual interests.

If leaders are the key actors in a polyarchic or pluralist democracy, then their capacity to "represent" their followers and be controlled by them becomes critical. Yet most commentators on organizational politics emphasize an organization's reliance on small staffs and executive leaders. Most organizations speak "through the voices (and deliberations) of a very few."[26] Consequently, "in only a few areas of political life is the discrepancy between formal juridical guarantees of democratic procedure and the actual practice of oligarchic rule so marked as in private or voluntary organizations . . . [A]lmost all such groups are characterized internally by the rule of one party oligarchy."[27]

It seems we have come full circle. The "democratic" alternative to "oligarchic" tendencies threatens to founder on the harsh realities of organizational life. Even in the most democratic organizations—those most committed to the protection of minority views and composed of competitive elites—the professional staff's control over policy initiatives and its ability to frame the issues coming before the members invest it with an important source of power and hence of control.

An easy response to the recognition of staff influence in organizational policy making is to see the whole issue of democratic forms of governance as mistaken when applied to organizations. The relative homogeneity of philosophical and issue preferences characterizing most organizations when contrasted with the more heterogeneous nature of more complex democratic forms make comparisons difficult. "Since the organization is the total of its membership and since its goals are the common goals of its members," writes Grant McConnell, "limitation of its power is not only undemocratic but also irrational."[28] In a similar vein, V. L. Allen deplores the presumption "that a voluntary society must provide for membership participation and install the checks and brakes on authority in the manner undertaken by the State in order to achieve and maintain democracy. This contention is misleading, for a voluntary society is not a State within a State; nor does it operate on the same scale or undertake the same functions." Lacking "the supreme coercive power" and therefore the consequent "necessity of preventing the use of that power contrary to the interests of the community," voluntary societies "have no means of enforcing their regulations other than by persuasion and sound common sense." Allen goes on to state that "it is the voluntary nature of organizations within a State which is essential for the preservation of democracy within those organizations." Thus, voluntary associations should be judged solely in terms of the ends and goods they achieve for their members, not as exercises "in self-government."[29]

Both McConnell's and Allen's doubts about the democratic capacity of organizations are belied by the character of oligarchy itself. We cannot assess whether the "ends and goods" oligarchic associations attain are those which its members desire or approve. As Michels pointed out, the bureaucratization of organizations encourages the substitution of its staff's for its members' interests. Moreover, the fact is that democratic organizations *can* be distinguished from oligarchic organizations in terms of the leaders' commitment to active participation by their members and of the kinds of conflict tolerated within the organizations.

The Choice: "Oligarchic" or "Democratic"

Political education requires the right types of conflict and participation. Conflict which nourishes discovery and participation which fosters responsibility encourage the mutuality, sensitivity to consequences, and principled action which define education. Did the amici organizations active in *Bakke* encourage nourishing conflict and responsible participation among their members?

Some did and others did not. The amici organizations in *Bakke* characterized by high levels of personalized conflicts, where differing sides were intransigent in their positions and hostile to criticism, were polarized and not amenable to discussion or debate. Those organizations where conflict was less personalized—less "intense" in its hostility—tended to be more receptive to the presentation of differing ideas or new facts. These findings confirm Hypothesis II and the expectation that "good faith" conflict—conflicts in an atmosphere where disagreements are tolerated and dissent respected—facilitates education.

Hypothesis III emphasized the role of leadership in affecting the nature of membership participation in organizational decision making. Democratic organizations are those in which the leaders involve the members in the pursuit of organizational values. Structurally, such organizations take seriously the mechanisms of elected officers, annual meetings, and direct membership vote on policy to insure leadership accountability and responsiveness. Oligarchic organizations, on the other hand, may display the same structures of accountability, but treat them as obstacles to be overcome rather than legitimate devices to extract leadership fidelity to the members' needs and opinions. Informally, leaders act upon and are in turn acted upon by the members in democratic organizations. In oligarchic organizations, the important decisions are made in private councils attended by the professional staff and some leaders; members ratify rather than participate in policy making.[30]

Fifty-three of the one hundred fifteen *Bakke* amici organizations contacted were oligarchic. That is to say, a small number within each association made the decision whether to intervene and on which side of the controversy. They were characterized by a process of "domination"—the outright victory of one internal group over another—or by the avoidance of confrontation. The maintenance of the members' willing participation in the organization—the problem of organizational cohesion—was not always an important consideration.

Forty-seven amici organizations were democratic in their policy processes in *Bakke*. These organizations were characteristically concerned with encouraging membership involvement in developing the organizational position on affirmative action. While internal confrontations over *Bakke* produced little effort to establish a common ground for agreement or consensus in oligarchic organizations, democratic organizations valued and sought broad-based agreement. Figure 1 illustrates the indicators distinguishing oligarchic from democratic organizations in *Bakke*.

FIGURE 1 Indicators of Democratic versus Oligarchic Decision Making

	Democratic	Oligarchic
Broad membership input in policy process *before* brief was filed	Yes	No
Dissent encouraged; supportive atmosphere for disagreement over issue	Yes	No
Competitive elites offered alternative solutions to the problem of affirmative action	Yes	Seldom
Preexisting membership mandate on issues of quotas and affirmative action	Occasionally	No
Leadership and staff sought consensus among internal groups; compromise a valued objective	Often	No

The term "oligarchic" should not invoke the image of conspiratorial maneuvering by secret elites to thwart the majoritarian will of the association's members. Often the decision by leaders to pursue a policy line without eliciting the members' approval was the result of insufficient time to appeal to the members for an explicit mandate. Their reluctance to stimulate organizational deliberations was sometimes a pragmatic adjustment to the realities of resource and time limitations. Other leaders avoided informing their followers because they feared that the organization would be so riven by disagreement that discussion about the causes compelling intervention into the controversy would be so hurried or simplistic that no policy statement would be produced. In practice, then, the leaders of amici organizations manifesting oligarchic processes struck a different balance between the mobilizing and articulating functions of their craft than did the leaders of democratic organizations. Whereas democratic leaders emphasized the responsiveness as well as the responsible portion of the leadership equation, oligarchic leaders saw themselves obliged to the responsible portion alone. Commitments to the needs of allies and clienteles, concerns over protecting organizational resources in order to insure continued organizational survival, and the concerted pressure of personal preferences all served to induce oligarchic patterns of organizational action.

It is also important to distinguish membership indifference

from the leadership's unilateral decision not to encourage membership participation. Democratic policy making does not require that the members participate in the day-to-day process of decision making nor does it entail a larger obligation on the member's part than to vote. To demand more than that of a member is to demonstrate that the commitment to democracy outweighs the commitment to personal liberty. Moreover, on many issues an association's members will be silent because they have no opinion. When not confronted by the leader-stimulated demand to participate, some members operate on the expectation that the leader will do what is needed. The members' inability or unwillingness to inform themselves on the matter or their trust that their leaders would represent their best interests was one of the most powerful factors contributing to the development of oligarchic organizational processes in *Bakke*.

Distinctions between "oligarchic" and "democratic" organizations are necessarily one of degree. No organization ever exhibits "a sharply defined 'mass' who merely obey and an equally definite 'minority' who always command."[31] The delegation or usurpation of control is never complete. The option of "exit" or defection from the organization by dissatisfied members exercises a powerful restraint on the level of oligarchic behavior any organization will manifest.[32]

Even granting these cautionary caveats, an analysis of the amici organizations in *Bakke* says something definite about oligarchy and democracy in private associations. Surprisingly, Michels's emphasis on the role of bureaucratization as a factor in the transformation of an organization from "democratic" into "oligarchic" was not borne out by the experiences of the *Bakke* advocacy groups. The degree of organizational complexity of bureaucracy—the ratio of the number of paid or voluntary staff to the number of members—did *not* predict the level or caliber of membership participation in *Bakke* amici organizations. The correlation between staff size and membership participation was low (theta = −.02).[33] However, the quality of leadership style, more difficult to assess, was highly predictive. Those organizations whose leaders perceived themselves as representative rather than dominant scored highest in membership participation.[34] Organizations demonstrating "democratic" leadership styles were also characterized by low intensity of conflict.[35]

The data on membership participation do not include the fifteen amici organizations which were neither democratic nor oligarchic, but *managerial*, serving clients, not members. More akin to the modern business firm in their structure than to other forms of private association, managerial organizations were composed of self-perpetuating boards of directors and large professional staffs. They solicited funds from contributors, not members, and survived to the extent they could "sell" their positions in the litigation market. The absence of a membership did not insulate managerial organizations from conflict. Dependent on the support of clients and contributors, they were obligated to act in ways similar to but not identical with those of the more numerous mass-membership associations. Many managerial organizations, like the other amici, actively solicited responses from their "members," although members in this context were extraorganizational clients or contributors.[36] Like all the amici, managerial organizations were pressured to afford some opportunity for discussion and dissent or assent to their policies. Some managerial organizations, such as the Council on Legal Education Opportunity, did provide this opportunity while others, like the Legal Services Corporation, did not.

What caused some organizations to behave in an oligarchic fashion in *Bakke* while others behaved in a democratic fashion? That an organization was oligarchic in *Bakke* does not imply that it will be oligarchic in all situations; organizational behavior no doubt varies from issue to issue, dependent on time and resources available and the nature of each controversy, and including the external and internal demands and pressures concentrated on an organization in the context of a particular issue.

Leadership style best explained organizational behavior in *Bakke*, but why did some leaders choose an oligarchic style while others preferred a democratic one? What were the "issue-specific" conditions prompting the selection of one style over another in *Bakke*? Did the members' demands or needs affect these choices? If the opportunity for dissent arose, did opposition develop and how was it handled? These questions are not easily answered by referring to tabulations of data; they require the application of theory to facts.

A second set of questions also deserves attention: How did *Bakke* amici organizations survive the controversy? What factors contributed to the persistence of organizations that were internally divided? Not all organizations were beset by conflicts. Thirty-five percent of those interviewed claimed that their organizations suffered little or no conflict over *Bakke*.[37] It is necessary to understand why some organizations had conflicts while others did not in order to learn how and why these conflicts were accommodated.

Oligarchic Leadership and the Promise of Efficiency

Apart from the mechanisms Michels identified as promoting the "oligarchization" of large organizations, there were six major reasons why some organizations manifested an oligarchic style of decision making in *Bakke*. Two have already been discussed. In the first, the case of the National Fund for Minority Engineering Students, the board acquiesced to its legal staff's putative expertise, a consequence of the board members' willingness to view *Bakke* as a narrow, technical problem in the law. (See Chapter 2). Although NFMES was a managerial rather than a true oligarchic organization, it illustrates well one dilemma many oligarchic organizations confronted. The greater an organization's reliance on its staff's expertise, the greater the power of the staff to dictate or guide organizational activities and positions. The American Civil Liberties Union's experience in *Bakke* depicted the problems of staff domination. Despite an intense debate within the organization in the years preceding the case, the actual decision as to how to proceed was made by a small elite composed of executive leaders and staff attorneys. Membership participation was not encouraged.

Four other reasons were important in explaining why fifty-seven organizations were oligarchic in *Bakke*. In some organizations, like the University of Pennsylvania, the issue of affirmative action became enmeshed in a continuing struggle for control of the institution; some leaders were prompted to take unilateral action in order to defend what they perceived as their legitimate decision-making prerogatives. Sometimes the imperative of maintaining control was used to justify the failure to consult members within the organization. Organizations like the American Federation of Teachers were dominated by the personal beliefs of their executive leaders. The personal commitments of some leaders led them to restrict membership participation in the preparation of the brief. Others, like the National Legal Aid and Defender Association, were obliged to make hasty decisions because of time and resource restraints; time pressures and technical limitations obstructed the leaders' efforts to be accountable as well as prudential. Finally, many organizations suffered a kind of blindness in *Bakke*. They were so sensitive to the views of one set of constituents that they overlooked or ignored the needs or fears of another set. The Legal Services Corporation, a "managerial" organization, best illustrates this type of "oligarchic" approach.

A Tale of Two Schools

The University of Pennsylvania had not offered a brief in *De-Funis* v. *Odegaard*. Its decision to do so in *Bakke* was the result of two men's efforts: Stephen Burbank, the university's legal counsel, and Louis Pollak, dean of the university law school. Burbank was concerned with the case's implications for Pennsylvania's professional schools. Since Pennsylvania received federal moneys for many of its programs, it could be vulnerable to "reverse discrimination" suits if *Bakke* was upheld on Title VI grounds. Pollak's concerns were broader. Long active in the civil rights movement, he feared the damage a pro-Bakke decision might inflict on recently won civil rights gains.[38]

Burbank and Pollak persuaded university president Martin Meyerson to approve a brief defending faculty autonomy in making admissions decisions. Traditionally, the brief argued, decisions about admissions have been made by educational institutions and their faculties. *Bakke* endangered this autonomy and threatened to substitute judicial inexperience for the educators' special competence in determining how and by what standards applicants should be admitted to professional schools. Academic freedom, not the guarantee of equal protection, was at the heart of the argument.

Meyerson approached the presidents of the other "Ivy League" universities in order to form an "Ivy League" coalition brief. After discussing the idea at the February 1977 meeting of the Council of Ivy Presidents, Harvard and Columbia agreed to join.[39] Disagreements among trustees and faculties prevented endorsement of the brief by Princeton, Dartmouth, Yale and Cornell.[40] Stanford University was also invited to participate and decided to do so, in part because its interest in *Bakke* was not altogether abstract.[41] Bakke had considered suing Stanford, finally choosing Davis because it was more vulnerable to a suit, given its status as a state agency.[42]

Like many other amici briefs, the four universities' brief was a committee effort. The universities' legal counsels circulated among themselves several outlines of suggested arguments. Columbia University Law School professor Albert Rosenthal based a first draft on these recommended approaches. Dean Pollak of Pennsylvania then edited the Rosenthal draft and presented it to a meeting of the attorneys for the four universities who completed the editing. The universities differed substantially in their boards' and presidents' involvement in the brief approval process. At Stanford, the president and board delegated preparation of the brief to the university's attorneys.[43] At Harvard and Pennsylvania, the trustees deferred to the judgment of their respective presidents. Only at Columbia was there substantial participation in the brief approval process by the trustees and faculty.

Although authorized to approve the brief, the Columbia president invited participation by his trustees. The discussions among the trustees were intense and continued over a period of several meetings. Some trustees insisted that Bakke was morally right; others defended the Davis program as a justified corrective to societal patterns of discrimination. Whether Columbia ought to intervene at all, given the probable reactions of alumni and donors, became an important issue. Finally the trustees agreed to suspend discussion until they could read a draft of the proposed brief. When the draft was circulated, several expressed astonishment at its departure from the originally promised "neutral" stance to a positive endorsement of "quotas."[44] At this point, members of the Columbia faculty were consulted informally by both partisans and opponents of a strong pro-Davis brief in order to generate faculty support for their respective positions. This appeal to faculty leaders, such as the vice-chairperson of the faculty senate and the chairpersons of the educational policy, admissions, and affirmative action senate committees, not only developed support within the faculty for both sides, but alerted the campus community that a brief was being developed. The presence of faculty, alumni, and student trustees on the board ensured some representation of these diverse viewpoints during the board's deliberations.

The conflict among the trustees threatened to end in a stalemate, thereby preventing any brief bearing Columbia's name from being filed with the Supreme Court. Columbia's general counsel, Mason Harding, was able to shepherd a compromise version of the final brief through the board of trustees.[45] This brief softened the earlier version's support for quotas and emphasized instead the special needs of private universities for preferential programs like those established at Harvard, a concise description of which was appended to the brief. Harvard's program eschewed quotas, employing race as one of many meritorious considerations in developing a diversified student body.

Columbia sought willing and informed clearance of the policies espoused in the brief carrying its name; the University of Pennsylvania was less prudent. Its board of trustees gave control over the brief to President Meyerson, and Meyerson in turn granted Pollak and Burbank considerable leeway in their handling of it. According to Robert Lucid, chairman of the University Council Steering Committee, Meyerson ignored pleas that representatives of the faculty be allowed to review the final draft, despite the fact that the brief was "the kind of thing the University community might want to talk about."[46] Faculty critics caustically pointed out the irony of excluding them from deliberating on a brief which championed the faculty's right to adopt policies it deemed necessary for the proper functioning of higher education.[47]

Both the campus newspaper and the faculty senate served as forums for attacks on Meyerson. Not all the attacks were directed at the brief's position; most demands were for faculty participation in the brief approval process rather than disagreements with the brief's substance. "We are a contentious lot to begin with," one member of the University of Pennsylvania Academic Senate stated, underscoring the tradition of faculty activism at Penn, "and our anger over the President's handling of the issue of faculty involvement was more an expression about *how* the brief was written rather than why or for what purposes."[48] The *Bakke* controversy was one in a long series of disputes over the faculty's role in university governance. What many perceived to be a lack of "political touch," an inability to soothe the faculty's ruffled feathers, further exacerbated the already unhappy relations between the administration and the faculty and helped foster disenchantment with Meyerson's competence as a leader. The disenchantment resulted in an unanimous vote of "no confidence" when the question of extending Meyerson's contract as president arose in the faculty senate in 1978.[49] Meyerson retired as president during the 1979–1980 academic year.

Meyerson's reluctance to invite faculty participation was in part the product of a need to defend the administration's prerogatives to establish policy for the university as an institution. The brief's authors had recognized the potential for conflict over the issue of who properly spoke for the university, and had hoped to defuse it by stating in the brief's opening footnote that it "speaks for our institutions as such—not for faculty members collectively or individually."[50] Pennsylvania's experience suggested that the issue was not the simple one of institutional authority but the far more complex question of the proper procedures to be taken in extraordinary situations.

The faculty insisted that the university's formal clearance procedures were inadequate to legitimate this specific policy, thus distinguishing between routine matters of administration and extraordinary situations like *Bakke* where an institution "speaks" in defense of a vision of the "good society." In the faculty's view, the brief was not an ordinary policy expression reflecting the administrative or financial competence of the executive leadership but rather an educational judgment about what factors win "admission" to the community of scholarship, a judgment traditionally made by the faculty. The debate at Pennsylvania could thus be traced to a paradox that underlies all universities— they are at once utilitarian organizations based on contractual agreements between employers (board of trustees) and employees (educational and support staffs) and expressive communities of individuals bound together by associational and promotional incentives.[51] The relationship of the members to the organizational leaders at Pennsylvania was one marked by a willingness to acquiesce on "routine" administrative questions and a determination to be consulted on matters affecting the central purposes of the university, education and scholarship.

Columbia had forestalled an organizational crisis by ensuring scrutiny of the university's position by its board of trustees and by informal consultations with its faculty. The university community's vicarious participation through the board's deliberations on the subject deflected much of the criticism that at Pennsylvania served as a catalyst for faculty indignation over the *Bakke* brief. The same brief that was received with outrage on Pennsylvania's campus in the end met with indifference at Columbia.

The contrasts between the tales of Columbia's and Pennsylvania's involvement in the amicus process suggest that the problem of organizational governance is one of harmonizing diverse interests in such a manner as not to immobilize efforts on key public policy issues. Columbia University's story suggests that the problem is solvable; Pennsylvania's indicates that ignoring the problem is not always a healthy way of containing intraorganizational conflict. The contrasts between the two universities are also instructive about whether their members— trustees, faculty, students, and perhaps alumni—"learned" in *Bakke*.

Ironically, universities may be the *least* likely organizations to learn something new in situations like *Bakke*. Their members may already be aware of the arguments (and the facts) implicated in the controversy since universities house many of the major proponents and opponents of affirmative action. *Bakke* may have provided a pretext and context for the espousal of already formed opinions. However, one need only recall the lack of sophistication among the Davis Medical School faculty when it developed its preference program. Not all the members of a university are equally equipped for or attentive to the subtleties of this controversy.

The brief submitted by Pennsylvania and Columbia was "educational" in at least one respect. Justice Powell invoked it as the basis for his justification of preferences as a part of a university's search for diversity. Whether the brief's authorizing and authoring processes were illuminating for the universities' members is another matter. Columbia's trustees participated in an ongoing debate over *Bakke* and were subjected to a panoply of ideas and arguments. Other members of the campus were implicated in a less direct fashion. The trustees, faculty, and students at Pennsylvania were not involved until after the brief was filed in the Supreme Court. The differences between the two schools' experiences were less those of substance than of form; differences in opportunities, not outcomes. While some respondents at Columbia felt that they had "learned," most at both Columbia and Pennsylvania stated that they had already formed their opinions before the debate. But Meyerson's persistent refusal to engage other members of the Pennsylvania campus community in the decision-making process did have adverse effects on the education of the community.

One element of political education is the creation of a supportive atmosphere for action—the communication of ideas and facts in such a manner that the "student" gains the confidence that he or she can act, can make a difference. "Learning" that occurs *after* the submission of a brief will tend to thwart rather than facilitate action. When confronted with the accomplished fact of a brief, few critics in organizations similar to the University of Pennsylvania, such as the American Bar Association and the National Legal Aid and Defender Association, campaigned for a retraction of the brief. In these organizations, *Bakke* did not teach the members.

The contrasting experiences of Columbia and Pennsylvania suggest that consensus-evoking procedures need not always produce stalemate. They also indicate that "oligarchical" efforts to prevent conflict may undermine the associational attractions of organizational membership, as it threatened to do in the case of the American Federation of Teachers.

Disunity in the Union

The American Federation of Teachers' (AFT) actions in *Bakke* reflected one man's efforts to mold an organization's policy-making process to ensure an outcome he preferred. The AFT's brief was therefore more an instrument of an individual's perception of the requirements of a civilized society than the outcome of a collective deliberative process. It was a more accurate portrayal of the intensity of that individual commitment than a measure of membership agreement on the appropriate solution to a difficult issue.[52]

The AFT represents 450,000 elementary, secondary, and college teachers organized in two thousand local unions, chiefly in the nation's urban areas. Organized in 1916, the AFT has long been the most militant of the teachers' unions, but it only became a national force when Albert Shanker ascended to the presidency in 1974 from presidency of the New York affiliate. Under his leadership, the union has built up a national constituency through a series of bargaining victories throughout the country. Two-thirds of the union's members were from New York in 1973, sixty percent lived in other states in 1978.[53]

The AFT has been a prominent advocate of civil rights. The national union ousted segregated locals during the 1960s and provided funding and manpower to help establish the "freedom schools" in Prince Edward County, Virginia, when public schools were closed in order to evade integration. Shanker's challenge of preferential programs was in part an expression of this concern for civil rights. He feared that special admissions programs "perpetuate racism by reinforcing the view that one group possesses lower abilities and therefore requires lower standards for [college] admission."[54]

AFT advocacy of civil rights has not been unqualified. It has been tempered by an appreciation of the interests of its members. It was to protect these interests that Shanker successfully influenced the American Federation of Labor–Congress of Industrial Organizations (AFL-CIO) to offer a brief in *DeFunis* cautioning the Court about the undesirable consequences of quota-based employment programs. In *Bakke*, Shanker was concerned that a pro-Davis decision might adversely affect the careers of his predominantly white New York City constituency.[55] The concern was not wholly hypothetical. In September of 1977, HEW's Office of Civil Rights ordered the New York City board of education to assign teachers to schools according to race in order to correct imbalances in placement and to encourage the hiring and promotion of more minority teachers. It threatened to withhold thirty-five million dollars in federal aid if its orders were not obeyed. Shanker joined with the school district in a suit challenging the hiring plan; a federal court eventually issued an injunction against the civil rights office's efforts on a procedural technicality.

The AFT is accustomed to appearing before the courts as an amicus curiae. Lawrence Poltrock, general counsel of the AFT, characterized the union's use of the amicus process as "quite typical, not at all exceptional."[56] Generally the AFT's local chapters alert the national staff to pending litigation affecting the union's interests; in *Bakke*, the California chapter brought the case to the Washington office's attention. At the insistence of Shanker and members from the "Unity Committee"—Shanker's supporters in the national union—the executive committee instructed its legal counsel to prepare briefs opposing the use of racial quotas in college admissions for submission to the California Supreme Court in 1975 and to the United States Supreme Court in 1977.[57]

The briefs submitted to the California and the United States supreme courts were similar. Both opened with statements affirming the AFT's dedication to the ideals of equal educational opportunity and nondiscrimination. Both appealed to that understanding of equality which takes its bearings from the premise that "all men stand equal before the law." Both accepted a conception of equality which drew upon the judicial norm admonishing the judge to ignore "certain irrelevant characteristics of the litigants—their race, wealth, . . ."[58] Finally, both briefs presented an unusual argument: insofar as the special admissions program at Davis offered "special favors" to minorities suffering educational or economic disadvantages, minorities were forced to compete among themselves for the limited number of special admissions slots available to them. They were thus persuaded not to attempt to compete for the larger number of slots available through the regular admissions process. The AFT briefs interpreted the practical consequences of the two-track admissions process as creating the "old quota system in disguise, placing a maximum on the number of minority group applicants who would be admitted."[59]

While there were many similarities, including a great deal of identical wording between the two briefs, the brief written for the federal court took a different tack from that prepared for the California court when the question of alternatives to special admissions programs arose. The brief submitted to the California Supreme Court dwelled on the advantages of instituting "open enrollment" programs to admit all minimally qualified medical school applicants to first-year standing. Alternatively, a special admissions program designed to aid all applicants suffering economic or educational disadvantages without regard to race or ethnic origins would also prove constitutionally and socially acceptable, it urged.[60]

The brief drafted for the federal Supreme Court followed a different line. While repeating the California brief's open enrollment and nonracial special admissions proposals, the federal brief also suggested other alternatives: remedial programs aimed at students early in their schooling so as to prevent educational disadvantages from the outset; intensive recruitment of qualified minorities coupled to special medical school-oriented tutorial programs; overcoming financial barriers to both undergraduate and graduate education by waiving fees or providing special scholarships and other forms of financial aid; and increasing the number of positions in the medical school "so that more minority members, in absolute numbers, will be entitled to admission."[61] This shift to an expanded set of policy alter-

natives was the product not only of a different set of authors
(the principal writer of the California brief had died before the
federal brief was written) but also the result of a change in
tactics.

"An amicus brief provides a different type of forum for expressing a client's position than a litigant's brief," Poltrock explained, defending the shift in emphasis in the federal brief:
"[The brief] gives the attorney leeway to express how he would
solve the policy if he were sitting on the court. The amicus brief
grants a far greater leeway to expound on wider questions than
is afforded by a brief written to defend a litigant's interests in a
particular case."[62] The freedom afforded to amici brief writers
enabled them to pursue a type of social commentary not available through a litigant's brief. It also allowed them to amelio-
rate conflicts within their sponsoring organizations.

The need to placate the growing internal opposition to the
AFT's position stimulated the expanded options posed by the
federal brief. A more thoughtful and carefully prepared proposal might deflect some of the criticisms directed at Shanker's
support of Bakke. Originally Shanker and his followers had so
thoroughly dominated the executive committee that there had
been little opportunity for his opponents to argue for a pro-
Davis brief. But with the announcement of the AFT stand in the
California court, opponents to the brief's position began to
organize within the union. The director of the California affiliate, Raul Teilhet, called for a retraction of the California brief
and urged the AFT to defend rather than attack Davis's special
admissions program. Assisted by representatives from the Chicago and District of Columbia chapters, Teilhet led a floor fight
at the August 1977 national AFT convention seeking to repudiate the "anti-quota" briefs.[63] Other organizations, such as the
United Professors of California, the largest AFT college affiliate
in California, publicized their opposition to the union's stand in
letters to the editors of all the major state newspapers and to the
New York Times and the *Washington Post*.[64]

The AFT is committed to "democracy in education and education in democracy"; it is pledged "to the support and promotion of the ideals of democracy."[65] Yet an intense minority saw
the union's *Bakke* policy as imposed from above and not ex-

pressive of members' attitudes. This minority was not insub-
stantial in number or power. Three of the four largest and most
powerful AFT chapters (the exception being Shanker's home
base, the New York City chapter) had gone on record as critics
of his decision to oppose affirmative action. And the dissent was
not without potential costs. One former Shanker aide who left
the union to join the rival National Education Association
(NEA) saw Shanker as "brilliant and right most of the time,"
but ready to force "his political will on the rest of the union. If
you do dissent, he remembers—and he frequently punishes."
Another former supporter explained Shanker's aversion to dissent as a product of Shanker's "major fear . . . a split in the
union."[66] In the opinion of these members, dissent was seen not
as a healthy manifestation of the organization's diversity, but as
a threat to its existence.

If a number of the union objected to what it saw as the illegit-
imately imposed will of its president, why did these members
not defect to the NEA, which supported Davis? Why, in the face
of substantial dissension within the most powerful and influential locals, was Shanker not rebuked by severely curtailing his
powers and prerogatives? The threat of revolt or defection was
not hypothetical; at least once before, the AFT had lost a number
of adherents when conservative members, upset by the militant
positions the union had taken, left to form the National Association of Professional Educators in 1975.[67]

Members dissatisfied with the policy stances taken by their
organization had three options. They could drop out of the organization and establish a rival organization, as had the members of the National Association of Professional Educators.
They could modify the organization by replacing the leadership
or by establishing new policy-making procedures. Or they could
modify their own relationship with the organization, leaving it
or retaining formal membership, but losing interest in its affairs.
In such a case, the decision to choose one option over another
depends on several factors, most of which relate to the structure
of incentives or motivations giving the organization its life. One
of these we have already seen in our analysis of the American
Civil Liberties Union.

One explanation for the absence of mass defections from the

AFT over *Bakke* is the separation between ownership and control in large modern organizations.[68] Like stockholders in a large corporation, the union member's share of the "collective good" provided by the organization was too minute to warrant challenging the leaders; the return on the invested effort would be insignificant in light of the energy expended.[69] Thus if the individual's motives to affiliate with the union were self-interested ones, and if he or she desired to maximize the return on the time, energy, and other resources contributed in remaining a union member, there was little incentive to attempt to change the policy process. What impact his efforts would make was offset by the costs accruing from action. Concurrently, the leader's calculation of the risk of alienating members' loyalties to the organization if he espoused an unpopular policy was influenced by similar considerations. Fears of participant rebellion tend to be discounted to the degree that the policy issue is tangential to the association's primary purposes. A member's threat to leave will influence a leader's action only if the member's value to the organization was great and if the member has meaningful alternatives to which to turn should he or she leave.

An alternative explanation depends on the special role played by the union in the member's life. Unlike European unions, American trade unions "tend to play a specific rather than diffuse role in the lives of their members."[70] Where European union members may look for philosophical and political guidance from their union in addition to improved wages and working conditions, American union members expect primarily discrete material benefits from their association. Tangible, not ideological, benefits are the primary incentives for their continued participation. Because these material benefits are measured in dollars and cents, they provide union members with "a relatively unambiguous means for judging the worth of the association." So long as leaders deliver "money benefits that substantially exceed the costs of membership,"[71] leaders have considerable leeway in pursuing peripheral organizational activities. Therefore members may not choose to disassociate themselves from organizations expressing personally objectionable policies. The association's ideological claims are so little valued in comparison with the benefits it delivers that sharp philosophical differences do not cause organizational rupture.

Utilitarian incentives seemed to have outweighed ideological differences in the AFT at that time. Improvements in the material status of union members attest to the strength of these incentives. For example, the salaries of the sixty-six thousand members of Shanker's New York City local doubled in real dollars between 1962 and 1976. Shanker has also won a lucrative pension plan that guarantees retirement at full pay after thirty years of service and free medical and dental care for his members.

The AFT, however, not only champions its members' financial interests before school boards during contract negotiations, it also devotes its resources to successful political activities. One study, after evaluating the responses of "key educational policymakers in the Education Department of HEW and on the staffs of congressional committees," ranked the AFT among the eighteen educational interest groups most effective in representing its members' interests "in the field of educational policy."[72] The union is not afraid to use its clout in national elections either. Shanker's efforts in behalf of Jimmy Carter's presidential candidacy in 1976 may have been crucial to Carter's victory.[73] The AFT also contributed more than a million dollars to candidates committed to "pro-teacher" legislation in the 1976 and 1980 elections.[74]

The primacy of utilitarian incentives should not obscure the importance of the associational and promotional values served by the AFT. The union's success can also be traced to its effectiveness in providing its members with a sense of self-worth, with the prestigious accolade of being "professionals." Fifteen years ago, teachers in the major urban centers of the East were crippled by the image of an "old school marm who slaved for the benefit of the children and was not expected to demand anything better."[75] Today, the AFT members share not only tremendous gains in working conditions and salaries but also the awareness that they are members of the eleventh largest union in the AFL-CIO. Shanker, their president, is the head of the labor organization's powerful Department for Professional Employees and at one time was considered a potential successor to George Meany as AFL-CIO President.

As would be expected in a complex organization composed of complex individuals, the reasons why individual members stayed in the AFT were many and varied. Probably most members agreed with Shanker and therefore suffered no conflict between the interests and promotional aspects of their membership. It is difficult to determine for certain how many disagreed and whether, in general, that disagreement was intense or mild. However, leaders of the opposition forces estimated that twenty-five to thirty percent of the members were intensely upset. This small but vocal group of dissidents retained its allegiance to the union because of the valued material benefits provided by the relationship and because of its usual agreement with the ideology of the AFT.[76] The AFT's traditional support of civil rights and its militant defense of teachers' interests helped maintain the loyalties of all but a few.

For the most part, then, the utilitarian benefits of participation in the organization outweighed individual members' unhappiness with either the specific policy stances taken by the national leadership or Shanker's efforts to dominate the policy formation process. The battery of checks at the disposal of the leader offset member disenchantment. And the resiliency of its utilitarian foundations allowed the AFT to resist considerable dissension over social policies without being seriously threatened by a mass exodus of angry members. In short, the American Federation of Teachers persisted because it delivered. But did the AFT deliver an "education" to its members?

Clearly, the rival elite within the AFT did have the opportunity to learn. The struggle between Shanker's "Unity" coalition and the West Coast chapter activated the contending blocs of leaders. However, Shanker's small efforts at accommodation were that—small. He did not modify his preferred policy stance —an explicit opposition to quotas in school admissions—, although he did make more explicit and detailed the alternatives he found acceptable to this kind of affirmative action. This would appear to be a minor concession.

Unlike Columbia's situation, and like Pennsylvania's, organization members were not exposed to the contending positions until after the brief was presented to the Court. However, here unlike Pennsylvania's experiences, dissenters did not acquiesce but sought to overrule their president's actions. The university and AFT were exposed to two different kinds of debates. The Pennsylvania brief was met with outrage less for what it said about affirmative action than about what it implied about the distribution of authority within a university. The rival claims about authority, not the brief's moderate defense of the university's discretionary powers over its admissions, were seen as important. The AFT brief was attacked for its position on the substantive issue of quotas; the question of who speaks for the organization was only part of the broader conflict. The battle was over principled outcomes, not procedures. In such a situation, where the content of the brief was the important issue in the intraorganizational contest, the brief's submission did not eviscerate discussion and education.

Vocal opponents to the brief were concentrated in three AFT chapters (San Francisco, Chicago, and the District of Columbia); there is little evidence that the great mass of the members were actively engaged in or aware of the dispute over *Bakke*. Except for the reports of the August convention, the issue was not raised in the union's newsletter. The debate was confined to the upper levels of the organization and did not penetrate down to most of the members. The AFT did not deliver an "education" on affirmative action to its members.

Organizational Myopia

The Legal Services Corporation (LSC) was a "managerial" organization which exhibited significant "oligarchic" features. The story of its involvement in *Bakke* provides some insight about the relationship between an organization's decision-making process and the anticipations and expectations of organizational allies and resource suppliers.[77]

The Legal Services Corporation was established as a private, nonprofit corporation by an act of Congress in 1974. Funded by the federal government, it provides legal assistance in civil cases for individuals unable to hire private representation.[78] The corporation assumed responsibility for the 258 preexisting legal service programs funded by the Community Services Administration's Office of Legal Services. The LSC was thus the inheritor of the national government's efforts to secure organized legal assistance for the poor that began in 1964 with the creation of the Neighborhood Legal Services program of the Office of Economic Opportunity.

The genesis of the LSC lay in the political vicissitudes experienced by its predecessors. The Neighborhood Legal Services agency, established during the first outpouring of Great Society legislation,[79] sought to supplement the privately funded legal aid societies that had provided the only legal assistance available to the American poor. Its ten-year existence was turbulent; efforts by Neighborhood Legal Services attorneys to protect clients' interests in veterans' benefits, welfare regulations, housing evictions, and unemployment compensation cases brought the agency into frequent conflict with other public organizations and led to accusations that the program spent its time harassing local and state governments.[80] For example, one affiliate in 1970, the California Rural Legal Assistance program (CRLA), was disbanded by then California governor Ronald Reagan. Exercising his statutory power to dismantle the program, Reagan sought to punish the CRLA for successfully obstructing his efforts to terminate two hundred million dollars in Medicaid benefits. Governor Reagan appealed to President Nixon and the Office of Economic Opportunity's director, Donald Rumsfeld, to uphold the veto, but a Nixon-appointed investigatory panel cleared the CRLA of all one hundred charges of malfeasance and impropriety leveled by Reagan, forcing the President to reinstate the program. In 1973, however, Nixon appointed as his new OEO chief Howard J. Phillips, an opponent of free legal services.[81]

Concerned by what they perceived as a systematic campaign to eliminate federally funded legal services for the poor, several members of the House and Senate, together with advocacy organizations like the American Civil Liberties Union and the American Bar Association, led a drive in 1971 to establish an independent, publicly financed legal service corporation. Encouraged by the support for the idea in the Ash Commission on Executive Reorganization report, Representative William Steiger of Wisconsin and Senator Walter Mondale of Minnesota introduced a bill in March proposing the formation of the LSC. Three months later, President Nixon responded by offering a restricted version of the Mondale-Steiger proposal, and the foundation was laid for an intense legislative struggle. The two proposals differed on the issue of appointment of the board of directors. The Mondale-Steiger bill would have created a nineteen-member board, nine of whom were to be appointed by the President while the others would be selected by organizations such as the American Bar Association.[82] Nixon insisted that all the directors be presidential appointees and sought to confine the board to eleven members.[83] After one presidential veto, a lingering death in a House-Senate conference, and a Senate filibuster, Nixon's positions won. He signed the law establishing the LSC on July 25, 1974.

The LSC's enabling act instructed it "to provide equal access to the system of justice in our Nation for individuals who seek redress of grievances." The organization's leaders interpreted this charge as a commitment to "the principle of equality under the law." Its president maintainted before Congress that, "Legal institutions and legal rules are the framework within which our social and economic systems operate; they establish basic arrangements by which public and private grievances of our citizens are resolved. If one segment of our population is denied the use of the legal system, that system becomes dangerously skewed and the fundamental principle of equality under the law is undermined."[84] In order to realize this ideal, the LSC distributes money to 315 locally administered legal programs offering free legal help to poor clients on civil matters. The corporation also provides these programs with support services, technical assistance, research, and staff recruitment and training.

An organizational ideology of facilitating democratic government by introducing the interests of the impoverished through the avenue of civil litigation animated the corporation's staff. It also led to the decision to write a brief in *Bakke*. As one member of the legal staff stated, the brief reflected the organization's commitment to increasing the number of minority attorneys in the American legal profession, a commitment which he saw as implied in the LSC's special mandate from Congress.[85] If the corporation was to be successful in acquiring the legal talent necessary to carry out its objectives, the supply of minority attorneys must be drastically increased. In 1977, fifteen percent of its full-time lawyers were from minority backgrounds; minorities at that time comprised only two percent of the legal profession, and more were needed as an essential source for manning the operations of the LSC.[86]

The brief itself was drafted by Alice Daniels, the corporation's general counsel, and her immediate subordinate. They were careful to see that the brief's legal arguments were solidly founded and legally defensible. It was only after the brief was filed in the Supreme Court, however, that members of the board had an opportunity to read and discuss the document. After a short but heated exchange, the directors ratified the brief by a bare majority vote. Many of the members, noting that the brief's submission was an accomplished fact, sought to present a united front to an expected backlash from Congress.[87] Their expectations were not to be disappointed.

The annual authorization of the LSC was debated on the House floor three weeks after the corporation filed its brief. Congressman John Ashbrook of Ohio, one of the LSC's original foes, charged it with the willful violation of its charter by "representing" the interests of the Davis "law school" [sic] in its *Bakke* amicus brief. The congressman characterized the LSC's actions as "irresponsible," countermanding the House's explicit decision "to get the government out of the business of requiring schools and employers to use race or sex quotas in admitting students" in Titles VI and VII of the 1964 Civil Rights Act and in the "anti-busing" provisions of the Education Amendments Act of 1974. Ashbrook introduced an amendment forbidding the LSC from filing any amicus brief or providing any legal assistance in race- or sex-related litigation.[88]

During the debate on Ashbrook's amendment, Representative Thomas Hagendorn of Minnesota offered an alternative which required "the Corporation shall not itself participate in litigation on behalf of clients other than the Corporation." Describing the logic of the LSC's justification for intervening in *Bakke* as "somewhat tortuous," Hagendorn pointed out that the LSC charter did not "authorize the growing number of amicus briefs . . . [in which] the Corporation might choose to involve itself on behalf of its own ideological crusades" in order to protect such "extremely indirect and highly dubious interests" as those advanced in its *Bakke* brief. With fewer than six percent of the House members on the floor, the Hagendorn amendment passed by a 26 to 5 vote.[89]

Four months later, a similar scene was acted out on the Senate floor. Senator S. I. Hayakawa of California challenged Senate Bill 1303, the companion to the House legislation debated in June. Repeating Hagendorn's "tortured logic" argument, Senator Hayakawa accused the LSC of attempting "to convert a civil rights issue into a poverty issue." Hayakawa then offered an amendment to the Senate bill restating in substance the language of the Hagendorn amendment to the House bill.

During a debate involving several key Senate supporters of the LSC (Orrin Hatch, Gaylord Nelson, and Edward Kennedy), Senator John Chafee of Rhode Island admitted to the LSC's critics that "there is no question that it was a mistake for the Corporation to get into the *Bakke* case." Pressed by other Senators about the meaning of his amendment, Hayakawa acknowledged that his proposal clarified rather than revised the prior law on the subject.[90] In part because of this admission, the Hayakawa amendment was passed by the Senate, reconciled with the Hagendorn proposal by the conference committee, and enacted into the LSC reauthorization law in December 1977.

In retrospect, it is puzzling that the LSC's legal staff did not foresee the turmoil its activities in *Bakke* would engender. While the LSC reauthorization and appropriations legislation emerged relatively unscathed from the intense congressional attacks against its "ideological crusade," the staff felt "harried" by the criticisms and was fearful about the political implications for the future.[91] Representatives of local legal services programs have noticed a growing conservatism in the headquarter's interpretation of organizational policies. And this conservative attitude has, in turn, had a chilling effect on the activities of some local programs.[92] Apparently, congressional displeasure was effectively communicated without the need for draconian measures.

The political myopia manifested by the LSC brief writers can be seen as an affliction common to many organizations—the confining effect of organizational self-image. To some extent, most organizations need to develop a set of beliefs, an "ideological system," upon which to develop a stable identity. While some organizations can afford to exist as lifeless structures made up of roles and administrative procedures and directed to limited ends in which there is little personal investment, many others acquire a distinctive identity which fosters the accomplishment of the more arduous objectives they are created to attain.[93] A strong sense of identity helps to maintain organizational stability in the face of the uncertain synthesis of past commitments, present demands, and future opportunities that is the life history of many organizations. Since utilitarian devices often fail to achieve the fervent adherence to organizational goals necessary to carry out an agency's purpose, a distinctive sense of mission is useful in activating participants' energies.

In the LSC's case, the two staff members responsible for writing and submitting the brief bearing the corporation's imprimatur believed that they were complying with the congressional mandate to advance the interests of the poor. More important, neither "really thought about the very politically sensitive nature of *Bakke*" and did not "think of the brief's filing as a political act" apart from the narrow legal merits of the case.[94] This failure to foresee the implications of intervening in so politically controversial a case as *Bakke* may be the product of the LSC's self-image as a "non-political" institution. Prominent in the statements made by the organization and by its supporters was the refrain that the LSC must be insulated "from partisan politics."[95] As a member of the House subcommittee that monitors LSC activities stated in his defense of the corporation's reauthorization, "with the exception of the *Bakke* case," the LSC is "not involved in politics"[96] This emphasis on the putative nonpolitical character of the organization was not new; the rationale was invoked by LSC supporters during the original battle to create the corporation. The Mondale-Steiger bill spoke of protecting legal services programs from "extraneous interference and control." President Nixon repeated the sentiment when he sent his version up to Capitol Hill. "If we are to preserve the strength of the program, we must make it immune to political pressures and make it a permanent part of our system of justice."[97] The need to "remove [federally funded legal services] from political influence"[98] was therefore one of the few topics on which both sides could agree. Independence would insure that legal services to the poor would not become a perennial chesspiece in a game of legislative politics.

Hopes for the establishment of a legal services program unaffected by political considerations appear naive. Although the act creating the corporation specified that it "shall not be considered a department, agency, or instrumentality, of the Federal Government, and that except for personnel compensation and benefits, officers and employees of the Corporation shall not be considered officers and employees of the Federal Government,"[99] the LSC is dependent on Congress for its funding and accountable to Congress for its operations. Direct congressional supervision forces the corporation to satisfy multiple sets of clients: the LSC must respond to the expectations not only of the impoverished who seek legal assistance and of the legal cadres funded to provide such assistance but also to its opponents and supporters in the national legislature. By submitting an amicus brief without consulting its board of directors, the Washington office's legal staff lost the opportunity to be alerted to the implications of overlooking one set of expectations in its efforts to satisfy another set. The wider perspective afforded the directors in their roles as representatives of the corporation before Congress might have alerted the staff to the challenges certain to come from Congress. The failure to notify the ostensible policy makers of the organization—the board of directors—reflected the narrowing of perspective attending the reliance on the organizational ideology of remaining nonpolitical. To see only the technical arguments presented by the case while being insensitive to the questions about public ordering of private relationships underlying it is a symptom of a most unhappy variant of the affliction called "legalism"—"the ethical attitude that holds moral conduct to be a matter of rule following, and moral relationships to consist of duties and rights determined by rules." [100]

A Tangled Web of Friends

The National Legal Aid and Defender Association (NLADA) represented fifteen hundred public defense and poverty law offices and six thousand member attorneys in 1977. It presented itself as the spokesperson for "the great majority of defender offices, coordinated assigned counsel systems, and legal aid societies in the United States." [101] In this capacity, it has filed amicus briefs in state and federal court cases affecting criminal justice defendants' rights and the delivery of legal services to the poor. It has lobbied before state and federal legislatures, both to present testimony on criminal justice topics and in support of funding the LSC and its local affiliates. It has also provided technical services to its members, from locating forensic experts and psychologists to cosponsoring the National College of Criminal Defense Attorneys and Public Defenders in Houston, Texas. The association has been instrumental in developing national standards for poverty law programs in civil and criminal litigation. [102]

Although the NLADA did not participate as an amicus in *De-Funis*, several of its constituent legal aid societies did join the NAACP brief supporting the University of Washington Law School special admissions program. They had argued that the traditional entry criteria to professional schools reflected "little or no demonstrable relationship to . . . [professional] school performance" and that a return to such criteria would involve "a return to a discriminatory system which does not satisfy the requirements of the equal protection clause, the rule of *Griggs* v. *Duke Power*, and Title VI of the Civil Rights Act of 1964." [103] The Constitution, judicial precedents, and congressional actions, they maintained, forbid the use of performance measures that unnecessarily restrict minority access to educational and employment opportunities.

Despite pressures from the participating legal aid societies, the NLADA's executive committee declined to become involved in *DeFunis* because there was insufficient time to canvass the organization's members. Being a membership association rather than a "managerial" organization like the Legal Services Corporation, the executive committee felt obliged to be sensitive to the members' claims to be consulted. However, qualms about acting without consultation were not so apparent in *Bakke*. The intervening years had underscored the importance of cases that challenged affirmative action, and, as one member of the Washington staff recounted, "We were convinced we had to state our support of affirmative action." The president and acting executive director, assisted by the national headquarters staff, decided to join one of the many coalition briefs. Like the LSC legal staff, the NLADA staff viewed *Bakke* as a threat to its organizational interest in maintaining the supply of minority attorneys necessary to staff poverty law programs. The imminence of the peril outweighed concerns about consulting the members.[104]

There had been some discussion among the executive leaders and staff about endorsing the LSC brief. But since the NLADA aggressively lobbied for the LSC's founding and funding, some feared the LSC would suffer from too public an identification with one of its primary support groups. Others were apprehensive about congressional response to LSC's involvement in *Bakke*. Unaffected by the "neutrality" myth to which the LSC's staff had succumbed, the NLADA staff foresaw the outrage that could result if a federally funded agency took a stand on so controversial an issue.[105]

The NLADA's leaders decided to join a brief cosponsored by such disparate organizations as the National Council of Churches of Christ in the United States of America; the American Coalition of Citizens with Disabilities; the Americans for Democratic Action; the International Union of Electrical, Radio, and Machine Workers (AFL-CIO); the National Education Association; and the Young Women's Christian Association. The NLADA chose to endorse this brief not because it expressed the association's interests particularly well, but because of other factors: time pressures foreclosed the writing of a distinctive NLADA-oriented brief; the principal backers of the National

Council of Churches' brief were well known to the NLADA and the latter had great confidence in their abilities; the brief had already been endorsed by key allies; and the NLADA expected to increase the impact of its actions in *Bakke* by joining a solidly written brief backed by several powerful and respected private organizations. The National Council of Churches' brief had one major shortcoming: it failed to stress the association's immediate concern about an adequate supply of minority attorneys. Despite this problem, the NLADA endorsed the brief.

The primary consideration for the NLADA was meeting the expectations of important allies. As a member of the Action for Legal Rights Coalition which had campaigned for the establishment of the Legal Services Corporation in 1971–1974, the NLADA developed close relationships with other advocacy organizations such as the National Lawyers Guild. These relationships were important because, as common concerns arose, each organization was able to support the efforts and supplement the energies of the other. Slowly, a community of interest developed, and continued relationships became valued for their own sake; they provided associational benefits that cemented alliances beyond the momentary dictates of transient issues. The "community" in the "civil rights community" was not illusionary; there was a commonality of interests and efforts that created enduring interorganizational and interpersonal ties.

The contacts were not only social but professional. One of the major avenues of communication among advocacy organizations was the crosscutting connection afforded by private attorneys who represented several civil rights-oriented organizations. Perhaps the best known of these lawyers was Joseph Rauh, a long time civil rights activist. A member of the NAACP board, Rauh was also a vice-president of the Americans for Democratic Action and was responsible for inducing the ADA to join the National Council of Churches' brief. A man who had cultivated contacts in almost every civil rights group active in Washington, Rauh alerted several organizations to *Bakke*'s significance and by doing so provided the opportunity for a large number of organizations to participate in *Bakke* who had not done so in *DeFunis*. Richard Sobol, the principal author of the

National Council of Churches' brief, was another attorney who used his professional contacts to forge a coalition brief. As the legal counsel for the International Union of Electrical, Radio, and Machine Workers, Sobol directed the union's attention to *Bakke* and won their support for the Davis special admissions program. Another source of informal contacts among advocacy organizations was afforded by overlapping memberships. Several members of the National Lawyers Guild served as attorneys in the legal aid programs represented by the NLADA, and the ACLU listed as dues-payers many NLADA and Guild members. These interweaving threads of participation acted as avenues for communicating the interests, concerns, and positions of one organization to another.

Interviews with members of "oligarchic" organizations emphasized the conditioning influence of allies' expectations. While it was true that the amicus process in *Bakke* served a variety of roles and needs—advancing specific interests, broadening debate to ensure clarification of the case's implications and complications, laying a basis for future arguments, publicizing the existence of new organizations, consoling members through symbolic participation in important issues—amici briefs also helped renew ties among like-minded organizations, ties vital in national policy making.

The nation's capital has been characterized as a community in which what you can do is dependent upon whom you know.[106] The web of governmental and private relationships is so complex, the system of checks and balances and institutional overlap so bewildering, that any organization seeking to attain its objectives through political actions is compelled to develop alliances with compatible associations both within and outside of the government. Coalition building is thus one common consequence of the uncertainties of political activity. It can also be prudent to ensure that certain internally divisive issues are farmed out to the coalition for resolution, thereby diminishing the chance that confrontation will occur within the organization. The AFL-CIO, for example, practices a policy of creating separate coalitions to pursue promotional objectives in order to "mitigate the internal strain" and to "provide an organizational distance from the union itself." [107] Membership dissension or public outrage is then directed at the coalition, not at its sponsors.

An organization's need to maintain harmonious relationships does not always prevent it from an occasional break with its friends over an especially important issue. As with the American Jewish Congress's experience in *Bakke*, some issues can be so crucial to an organization's sense of mission that it is willing to risk a breakdown in peaceful contacts with its routine workmates in order to defend its conception of the values at stake. The NLADA, on the other hand, was an example of an organization where the staff and leaders assessed the advantages of affirming its connections with its traditional allies to be greater than the possible disaffection of its own members.

Unlike the LSC, the National Legal Aid and Defender Association was careful to respond to the influential actors in its environment. Its endorsement of the National Council of Churches' brief was prompted by the fear that not to be counted in would indicate a falling-out among friends. Given the chance to assert its support of its friends by the activities of coalition-building attorneys such as Joseph Rauh and Richard Sobol, the association's national staff seized upon the opportunity to consolidate its relations with its fellow participants in the dance of advocacy-group politics. The cost exacted by the decision to placate allies and friends, however, was the failure to solicit membership views, a cost that might have been higher if dissidents in the organization had had the occasion to organize and express their unhappiness with the case or the brief before it was filed. As it turned out, members' responses to the NLADA's actions were "mixed." While a substantial number of letters— "two or three hundred" [108]—deplored the position taken in the brief, there was no concerted effort to overturn the executive leaders and staff's decision. According to one critic, "it was too late to do anything useful. We were faced with the accomplished fact." [109] More pertinent was the lack of a convenient forum for the opposition to coalesce and make their views known. The AFT had held a union convention less than a month after its brief was filed. The coalition brief bearing the NLADA's name was submitted in June 1977; its members did not meet in convention until the early part of 1978.

Bakke was more "educational" or instructive for the "managerial" Legal Services Corporation than it was for the membership-based NLADA. In both organizations there was little opportunity for learning—for the contest of views which prompted a strengthening or reappraisal of personal beliefs—during the brief-authorizing process. But the LSC's leaders and staffs did modify their behavior after the expression of congressional outrage about the LSC's involvement in *Bakke*. To the degree education changes behavior, the LSC was one of the few organizations for which its activities in *Bakke* resulted in a substantial modification of its organizational practices.

Oligarchic Behavior and the Costs of Efficiency

Explanations for oligarchic forms of organizational politics typically rely on rather simplistic notions about human nature and the gratifications of power. Michels, for one, stressed the status and monetary benefits accruing to leaders. But, whatever the inducements of the "lust for power," the pressures toward oligarchy in *Bakke* flowed from sources far more complex than is normally realized.

Time and resource limitations imposed constraints on the policy processes of several organizations. Oligarchic maneuverings in the National Legal Aid and Defender Association resulted from pressures to beat a deadline. The lost opportunities for swift action in support of organizational objectives and the costs of the resources necessary to educate the mass membership about the issues confronting the association virtually foreclosed the chance for participation or debate on a mass scale. Michels's counsel on the inevitable frustrations of democratic ideals in large bureaucratic organizations intimates that leaders must make a choice between attaining the objectives of the organization or imbuing it with the kind of procedures which allow "balanced representation" among internal group interests and of processes which provide means "for adjudicating conflicts."[110] Small wonder so many organizational leaders were convinced that such a choice must be made. And what might appear at first to be the evil machinations of self-selected groups on reflection turned out to be the sincere effort of hard-pressed individuals attempting to protect organizational interests on the front line of daily activity.

Situations like those at the University of Pennsylvania suggest that Michels's theory of organizational leadership requires a significant modification of emphasis. Michels emphasized how the status benefits of the office led leaders to pursue greater power for themselves; the thrusts toward an efficient organization were transformed into pressures for personal aggrandizement. But Michels may have misconstrued an important aspect of leadership in modern organizations, and by so doing misunderstood one of the nuances of authority in a democracy. As Theodore Lowi has suggested in a different context, leaders in a democratic society are curiously ambivalent about power: they pursue it while being deeply troubled about it.[111] Seeking power for one's office rather than one's person is a satisfying way of justifying the pursuit of power. And, whatever the personal satisfaction thus afforded to the occupier of the office, both the office-holders and their attentive publics see the legitimacy of their actions as flowing from the authority of the position and not the person. University of Pennsylvania president Meyerson adamantly refused to open the brief-authoring process to the faculty because he felt obliged to defend what he understood to be the legitimate prerogatives of his office. As a sympathetic critic of Meyerson's position explained, "Meyerson wasn't attempting to grab power; he was attempting to defend what he believed to be his authority as university president. He didn't give an inch in *Bakke* because he feared the faculty would use it as a pretext to take the proverbial mile"[112]—to demand an ever-increasing control over university affairs. Thus Meyerson's intransigence might be more accurately depicted as a defense of presidential powers than as a process of "empire" building.

The cases of the American Federation of Teachers and the American Civil Liberties Union illustrate the power of organizational membership incentives and how the attractions of continued participation in the association and general commitment to its purposes can overcome internal disagreements. The battery of checks and benefits at the leader's disposal can offset membership disenchantment by providing important and direct material incentives, as in the AFT, or the symbolic reassurance of participation in an organization dedicated to public values, as in the ACLU. Thus cohesion can be maintained through processes quite apart from a consensus of attitude.

The threat of "sanctions against recalcitrant individuals or factions" is another powerful force maintaining individual allegiances.[113] While most discussions on the usefulness of sanctions either underplay their role or overemphasize the personal loss suffered by being excluded from an organizational membership,[114] an often overlooked factor is the individual's calculation of the effects of being excluded on the continuing health of the organization itself. If one's compulsory or voluntary withdrawal from the organization will contribute to its destruction, and if one highly values the long-term nature of the enterprise, the threat of being excluded may be very powerful indeed. If there are no alternative associations to shoulder the burden if the original organization is allowed to die, some individuals may be strongly motivated to continue their membership even if it requires acquiescing to policies they would otherwise strenuously repudiate. Several members of the ACLU explained their continued association with the organization in these terms. For them, the worthiness of the ACLU's overall objectives outweighed what they perceived as the wrong-headedness of its *Bakke* policy. For them, to dissociate from the organization, and thereby contribute to the potential frustration of other important objectives, was to evade personal commitments. Thus loyalty to an organization may be derived not only from material returns or associational pleasures, but from promotional ends.

The organization of mass associations is complex and volatile, and the leaders of these associations are susceptible to many of the same shortcomings as their followers. Organizations are composed of active and passive leaders as well as active and passive followers. One manifestation of leadership passivity in *Bakke* was an excessive deference to staff judgments. In such organizations as the National Fund for Minority Engineering Students, the "lay leaders" were dependent on "professional leaders" to guide their deliberations. This kind of dependence may lead to the inducement of organizational myopia, the failure to discern the long-term consequences of a policy, and may place the association at the mercy of organizational and occupational ideologies, narrowing the horizons of discussion and producing that peculiar form of tunnel vision which impeded creative policy making in the Legal Services Corporation.

Despite these qualifications, Michels's efforts to define and explain leadership in large groups in terms of personal interests as well as organizational necessities can not be overlooked completely. Some leaders did exclude member participation or exercise the instruments of control at their disposal in order to pursue personal notions of what public policy ought to be. AFT president Shanker may have supported Bakke's challenge of the Davis program because the interests of some of his followers were at stake, but it was clear that a personal commitment to the traditional equal opportunity formula as equal treatment predisposed him to reject quota-oriented affirmative action programs as unwise. Other leaders may have been induced to take the stands they did because of the status benefits personally available to them. The heads of private associations are in daily contact with executives of other associations. They tend to cue their actions from the attitudes of these peers, not from the expectations of their followers. Thus the principal reference group is not the membership but the status group comprised of other associations' leaders, a reference group which is not always sensitive to organizational boundaries or loyalties. Perhaps this occurred in the National Legal Aid and Defender Association. The leaders of the "oligarchic" organizations involved in *Bakke* were aware of the distracting effects of time pressures, personal views, or peer group influences. Some readily admitted to sponsoring briefs that were highly unpopular with their members, having been persuaded to act to support values they believed more important than member participation. As the leader of an industrial union explained, "We are a union of working stiffs, the great number of whom are more worried about rising prices and job security than they are about advancing civil rights. We [the union leadership] did what we thought we should do, not what the members would want to be done." Others felt that, if given the opportunity, their members would willingly endorse the views expressed in the briefs. The executive director of a service organization defended her decision to join the National Council of Churches' brief in these terms: "I am only a conduit for my followers. . . . I've been chief of this organization long enough to know what they want even before they do. When I heard that the Children's Defense Fund was getting signatures to a brief, I called over and offered our services. I'm sure any member would agree with my action." [115] An observer might have been less sanguine about membership responses. As Luttberg and Zeigler discovered in their study of the Oregon Education Association, [116] leaders can overstate their intuitive powers when it comes to sensing their members' attitudes. The gap between what leaders imagine their members' feelings to be and what those feelings actually are can be quite large.

Organizations manifesting oligarchic behaviors in *Bakke* seemed more concerned with advancing specific policy preferences or meeting external pressures than they were with soliciting membership opinion. They were concerned about "efficiency" and "effectiveness" more than participation. But acting oligarchically could also have "costs."

Many oligarchic organizations were inefficient when evaluated by their own self-imposed criteria of efficiency. The considerations that motivated their behavior, the goals they set for themselves, were not accomplished. Two criteria of efficiency invoked by most oligarchic amici organizations to justify their actions in *Bakke* were achievement of a desired outcome—either influencing the Court's judgment or appeasing important clienteles—and disposal of the issue with a minimum use of organizational resources.

Few briefs were likely to meet the stringent demands of both criteria. The type of clear, articulate presentation liable to affect the Court's deliberations was the sort of statement that might antagonize significant portions of all but the most homogeneous organizations. Furthermore, the disagreements among organizations as to what ensures an influential brief—the varying contentions of amicus brief folklore, which jostle over the comparative merits of sponsorship by large numbers of normally nonlitigative groups (e.g., the National Council of Churches), authorship by a well-known name in legal scholarship (Columbia University et al.), or dependence on an established organizational expertise (like the ACLU)—substantiate the problematic character of imputing influence to any particular brief. One can count the number of times a brief was cited in a judicial opinion or search for arguments and language in the opinion which appeared to have been extracted from a brief, but it is difficult to know whether the use of a brief by a judge proves it to be a cause for decision or only an apt expression of a judicial opinion. Of course the latter function ought not to be disparaged; to the extent that a court's authority depends upon the persuasiveness of its pronouncement of a judgment, providing the vocabulary and style to make that pronouncement eloquent and appealing is an important service indeed.

Keeping these cautionary thoughts in mind, the brief submitted by Columbia, Harvard, Stanford, and Pennsylvania appears to have been the most explicitly effective, very possibly because it represented a constituency similar to that of the case itself. Justice Powell frequently cited the universities' brief; its defense of academic control over admissions played a pivotal role in his defense of affirmative action admissions programs.[117] Justice Blackmun was also reputed to have been influenced by the universities' premise that diversity was a reputable and necessary component of the admissions decision, at least as represented by McGeorge Bundy's vigorous defense of the notion in an article in the *Atlantic Monthly*.[118]

With the exception of the ACLU's brief, which several other participants in *Bakke* amici organizations viewed as an impressive performance, the briefs submitted by other oligarchic organizations appeared to have been relatively ineffectual. The arguments made in the briefs sponsored by the American Federation of Teachers, the National Legal Aid and Defender Association, and the Legal Services Corporation broke no new ground, and the potential contributions of the LSC's efforts were eviscerated by the turmoil attending its release and the congressional challenge of its legitimacy. Whatever impact these three organizations may have had on the Court was probably confined to alerting the Court to the case's importance and the individual and organizational interests at stake in its resolution, although it is unlikely that they needed the reminder.

Affecting the Court is only part of the notion of efficiency as influence; the other is affecting the attitudes and actions of the organization's clienteles and members. If effectiveness is understood also as the appeasement of important actors within and outside the organization, the performance of oligarchic organizations was debatable. Organizations characterized by the oligarchic process of domination, such as the AFT and the University of Pennsylvania, subordinated group harmony to expediency, rejecting the demands of dissenting leaders and members for involvement in the brief-writing and approval process. Domination, the clearcut victory of the views of one portion of an organization over another with little or no effort to establish a common ground for common action, gave rise to challenges of Shanker's policy on *Bakke* at the AFT convention and the public repudiation of the brief by several affiliates of the union. Faculty outrage at the process culminating in Pennsylvania's endorsement of a *Bakke* brief was further evidence of the conflict within organizations exhibiting dominating forms of oligarchic behavior.

Associations that exhibited the less aggressive form of oligarchic decision making, where there was an intentional effort to avoid confrontation, such as the NLADA and the LSC, reflected a mixed situation. The LSC suffered considerably at the hands of unfriendly Congressmen, and the results of the abuse led to a retreat from an energetic interpretation of its mandate for action. The NLADA, on the other hand, seemed to suffer little from its involvement in *Bakke*. Though some segments of the organization may have hoped either to see a different position taken or not to have intervened at all, most members appeared to accept the brief as a fact and turned their energies to other, more pressing matters.

The ACLU would seem to straddle the distinction between domination and avoidance of confrontation. While the pro-

Davis activists won over the pro-Bakke group, the policy process leading up to their victory was characterized more by avoidance than by a concerted effort to confront the problem on the part of the leadership at the national level. Although the Union may have suffered some loss of members because of dissatisfaction with its *Bakke* policy, any fallout was overshadowed by the far greater loss in members and funds as a result of ACLU policy in the Nazi-Skokie controversy. Member dissention was also ameliorated by the unique ties of symbolism that exist between the organization and its traditional membership.

The costs extracted by these lost opportunities for membership participation were not surprising. Oligarchic organizations characteristically manifest highly personalized patterns of conflict despite the absence of significant membership involvement. There are ways of acknowledging conflict which do not cause antagonism. Some organizations were able to have participation *and* efficient policy making.

Oligarchy did seem to minimize the demand on organizational resources. The ACLU, for example, enjoyed an expeditious resolution of a long-standing controversy in which the formal policy makers seemed unable to come to agreement on the issues. By deferring to its legal staff and the general counsel elected by the board, the board of directors freed itself of the burden of decision. However, if the *Bakke* position contributed to the decline in members and funds generally attributed to the Skokie case, the loss of financial resources may have been greater than the savings in time and energy.

The Legal Services Corporation, like the ACLU, may have given up some measure of long-term financial security in exchange for the short-term economies attendant upon swift production of a brief. The failure of the LSC's legal counsel to recognize the political repercussions of involving a publicly funded organization in so volatile a controversy as *Bakke* left the organization vulnerable to reprisals from critics in the Congress. By neglecting to alert potential allies in the organization and in the legislature before the filing of the brief, the LSC legal counsel and her staff subjected the organization to considerable fault finding when it came before Congress during the appropriations and reauthorization hearings and debates. Though the legislative consequences of congressional disapproval were relatively minor—the amendment forbidding LSC participation as an amicus in cases not directly affecting its interests was a restatement of prevailing policy rather than the imposition of new and more stringent guidelines—the LSC president and board of directors reacted to the criticisms by taking a more restrictive reading of the corporation's mandate than they had done before.

The other oligarchic organizations examined suffered very little loss in resources or members as a result of their participation in *Bakke*. Even the most dissident elements of the American Federation of Teachers did not leave the union because of its *Bakke* position. While the University of Pennsylvania might have lost some alumni contributions or other gifts, the development office saw no *Bakke*-related decline in contributions to the university.[119] The NLADA Washington headquarters reported no discernible increase or decrease in members or funding in the months after the submission of the coalition brief bearing its name. In these three cases, the expeditious writing and filing of the briefs did not engender uneconomic consequences when measured in members or finances. To the extent that the efficiency of a brief is judged in reference to its demands on organizational assets, the AFT's, NLADA's, and University of Pennsylvania's briefs were efficient.

Finally, did education of the members occur within oligarchic organizations? While the elites within organizations like the American Federation of Teachers may have learned, the education seemed confined to these elites, not diffused among the members. What had been an educational process in the American Civil Liberties Union up to that point—a continuing examination and discussion of what the organization's stance ought to be on affirmative action—was not pursued in *Bakke*. The decision by the legal staff and the general counsel to offer a strong pro-Davis brief without consulting the board or the membership of the affiliates destroyed an opportunity for intraorganizational exchanges on the issue.

Our theory of education has emphasized *how* policies were created rather than the *substance* of those policies. Participa-

TABLE 3　Education and Organizational Leadership Style

Leadership Style	Level of Educational Activity in Organization						
	(High 1)	(2)	(3)	(4)	(Low 5)	(Don't know)	Total
	Percentage (and number) of respondents						
Oligarchic organizations	2% (4)	5% (8)	8% (13)	42% (71)	37% (63)	6% (10)	100% (169)
Democratic organizations	36 (54)	52 (79)	7 (10)	5 (8)	0 (0)	0 (0)	100 (151)
Managerial organizations	12 (5)	5 (2)	46 (19)	17 (7)	15 (6)	5 (2)	100 (41)
Total	(63)	(89)	(42)	(86)	(69)	(12)	(361)

NOTE: Data on perception of level of educational activity were elicited by use of the following interview question: Do you agree with the statement: "Discussions about *Bakke* in my organization provided me with the kinds of facts, ideas, statements of principles, and interests which helped me confirm an existing opinion or form a new one on affirmative action." Respondents ranked their agreement with this statement as from 1 ("strongly agree") to 5 ("strongly disagree").

tion in policy making which helped members to develop new opinions or to deepen their understanding of existing opinions would be educational. Few oligarchic organizations had the breadth and type of discussion which facilitated this type of reflection. Litigation provided an opportunity to expound preexisting views in oligarchic organizations.

It is difficult to objectify education. As a social and psychological phenomenon, education exists in the mind of the beholder. However, one way to test for education is to analyze the perceptions of the participants. Did *they* think they learned in *Bakke*? Participants from oligarchic organizations tended not to interpret their organizations' activities as educational. (See table 3.) When asked what they wanted from their organization's discussion, many responded in terms similar to our theory of education. They wanted principles for action that recognized the realities of American life but did not counsel despair. They wanted facts to settle the factual disputes and ideas to clarify their confusion about the conflicting values implicated in the debate. They wanted to learn *what* they should do, and what were the advantages and limitations of alternative positions in *Bakke*. In brief, they wanted to be educated, and most felt they had not been by their organizations' actions in *Bakke*.

Conversely, participants in "democratic" organizations were more likely to be satisfied with their organizations' efforts. Eighty-eight percent (133 of 151) mildly or strongly agreed with the statement that they had been educated about affirmative action through their organizations' deliberations.

CHAPTER IV

THE ANAGRAMS OF DEMOCRACY

The traditional justification for the amicus curiae process is its contributions to a well-informed judiciary. Alerted to ideas, arguments, and facts unknown to the litigants or not in their best interests to present to the court, judges are aided in developing coherent policies by "friends-of-the-court." However, few briefs in *Bakke* did more than echo the arguments of the parties, and what original contributions were made may have been lost amidst the deluge of fifteen hundred pages of amici briefs. At least in *Bakke*, the amicus process served more directly "political" purposes. It offered organizations the chance to exert the leverage of prestige and numbers on judicial policy making.

This process of organizational advocacy raised a classic problem in democratic theory—the tension between leadership and representation, between being responsible to the long-term interests of an organization and being receptive to the preferences of the led. When so many organizational leaders and staffs felt they could not afford to be democratic, what induced other leaders and staffs to attempt to reconcile participation and effective organizational action? If education is one of the multiple roles leaders and staffs are called upon to perform, why did some organizations educate their members when others could not or would not?

The Multiplicities of Democracy

Organizational democracy requires leaders to take seriously their duty to involve members in policy making and members to acknowledge their responsibility to participate. These responsibilities arise not because the members' views are necessarily more "correct" than those of the leaders but because of the organization's obligation to give individuals the opportunity to learn. Disagreement and dissent are appreciated as signs of healthy organizational decision making as well as the necessary costs of democratic procedures. Informed discussion and debate encourage active participation and help ensure that members' agreement with policies is more than a simple acquiescence to decisions made in different arenas.

Democratic organizations are therefore more than aggregations of individual interests or instruments articulating or mobilizing the preexisting sentiments of an association. They seek also to "shape and alter and elevate the notions and values and goals" of their members.[1] Of course not all "democratic" organizations place the same emphasis on this goal nor are all equally successful in attaining it. Nevertheless, the leaders and members of democratic organizations in *Bakke* were implicated in a quest to learn—to improve preexisting judgments or to establish well-considered and supported opinions about affirmative action. Democratic organizations in *Bakke* did serve as "classrooms" for their members, a function best illustrated by the members' own words:

"I wavered on the question. Our arguments about *Bakke* caused me to discover it was the sort of issue one could not be certain about."

"At first I leaned towards Bakke's side. I *learned* [emphasis added] why Davis should be supported."

"We talked so much that I sometimes saw us as a college b.s. session."

"At the beginning, I thought Bakke was right. Now I know he's right, and I have facts to support it."

"I may not know any better what is the right thing to do, but I do know what things we should not be doing."[2]

What happened within democratic organizations to stimulate these positive assessments?

Democratic organizations in *Bakke* displayed several styles of decision-making behaviors. Each behavior brought with it a corresponding type of education or stimulating environment. Each behavior also provided a way to distinguish between more and less democratic organizations and between greater and fewer opportunities to learn.

The weakest or least demanding form of democratic behavior was *bargaining*[3]—the standard political practice of attack and defense where desires remain substantially unchanged. Bargaining occurred when members of an association failed to see the controversy as a non-zero-sum game. This practice emphasized threats and promises of deprivation or gratification among the organizations' participants and threatened to destroy the underlying trust any association needs in order to preserve cooperative arrangements within it. In *Bakke*, associations like the Carter Administration suffered a rupture of the commonality of principles and interests that give associations their cohesiveness. Democratic organizations that pursued bargaining strategies were the least conducive to nourishing—unpolarized—conflict.

A stronger form of democratic behavior was *compromise*. Compromising organizations in *Bakke* avoided polarized confrontations by translating conflicts over principles into conflicts over more easily negotiable interests. Organizations that adhered to a compromise approach exhibited a shaping of value premises that minimized the threat of a direct confrontation over differing goals. The staff leaders of the Equal Employment Advisory Council attempted to transform disagreement over fundamental values into differences of opinion over the personal interests at stake, so the debate involved the interest-oriented issue of "How am I to be injured or advantaged?" rather than the principle-oriented one of "What important values are being fostered or curtailed?" The narrowing of conflict facilitated negotiation, transforming a contest premised on indivisible goods into one resting on a calculation of divisible goods attained or denied.

Another ingredient aiding a compromise approach was the reservoir of trust found in an organization. The underlying sense of loyalty to the organization that permeated the relationships within it allowed conflict to be seen as nonthreatening, a "normal rather than pathological" condition.[4] Disagreements over policies were accepted as healthy differences of opinion over the best means to attain shared goals rather than acts of apostasy or defection. The liberating influence of this bedrock of homogeneous interest contributed to a narrowing of the scope of conflict. In the case of the Equal Employment Advisory Council, the limiting of the debate over what values ought to be endorsed in *Bakke* helped the association to develop a persuasive statement—one expressing its unique legal expertise, experience, and resources—which may have contributed substantially to the Court's awareness of the consequences and complications of the alternative resolutions to the issues posed by *Bakke*.

The organizations most conducive to the discovery of new ideas and information by their participants were those committed to *integration*. Unlike organizations that followed a compromise strategy that encouraged avoidance of conflict by side-stepping differences in principles, integrative organizations sought to confront directly the sources of division within the association. The internal policies of such organizations were marked by an appreciation of the positive elements of conflict, a willingness to use opposition and dissent as mechanisms to elicit discussion and to compel members to reexamine settled attitudes and to defend consciously the values by which they justified individual preferences. The hoped-for outcome was a new appreciation of old values shared by the participants or the discovery of new bases of agreement upon which organizational understanding could form. Democratic practices of this type clearly demanded more from an association than the presence of consultative mechanisms ensuring staff and leadership compliance with the sentiments and preferences of the members. The organization was not seen as a mechanical device for trans-

mitting preformed views but as an arena for enlightening understanding of the stakes at contest.

What accounts for these different patterns of democratic
organizational behaviors? Why were only eleven of the forty-
seven democratic organizations integrative, while over half
(twenty-seven) were compromising and nine bargaining? All the
organizations accepted the legitimacy of dissent; all encouraged
communication with and among members. They were all, by
comparison with oligarchic organizations, willing to pay the
costs of disagreement and opposition.

A further question is whether interest groups, minority-
defense organizations, or public-interest advocates were more
likely to express a specific type of democratic behavior. One
might surmise that interest groups, with their closely defined
interest structures, are more conducive to compromise, while
the homogeneous interests and broader purposes of minority-
defense organizations lend themselves to integration, and the
disparate coalitions that may characterize public-interest advocates led to bargaining. However, structure-of-interest did not
predict decision-making style within democratic organizations
(lambda = .06).[5]

Another possibility is that organizational complexity affected
the behavior of democratic organizations. The fact that complexity did not differentiate between oligarchic and democratic
organizations[6] does not preclude its significance within democratic organizations. The more complex an organization—the
greater the number of members, the more dispersed the members are geographically, the larger its bureaucracy, the more
federated its structure—the more difficult it is for leaders to
control the organization and therefore the more difficult it may
be to practice integration. However, like structure-of-interest,
organizational complexity was a poor predictor, with one exception. Membership size was moderately related to decision-
making form (see table 4). Ironically, despite fears about the inability of organizations with mass memberships to promote
democratic participation, such organizations were more likely
to manifest integrative behaviors than were smaller organizations in *Bakke*. Apparently, size alone need not preclude organizational education.

TABLE 4 Organizational Complexity and Democratic Forms of
Decision Making

Decision-Making Style	Geographical Dispersion			
	National	State[a]	City	Total
Bargaining	67% (6)	11% (1)	22% (2)	100% (9)
Compromise	52 (14)	19 (5)	30 (8)	101[b] (27)
Integrative	91 (10)	9 (1)	0 (0)	100 (11)
	(30)	(7)	(10)	(47)

$\theta = -.1972 = -.20$

	Membership Size				
	0–1,000	1,001–10,000	10,001–50,000	50,000+	Total
Bargaining	89% (8)	0% (0)	11% (1)	0% (0)	100% (9)
Compromise	74 (20)	11 (3)	7 (2)	7 (2)	99[b] (27)
Integrative	18 (2)	18 (2)	18 (2)	45 (5)	99[b] (11)
	(30)	(5)	(5)	(7)	(47)

$\theta = .4585 = .46$

	Size of Bureaucracy (ratio of staff to members)			
	1/100	1–2/100	3+/100	Total
Bargaining	44% (4)	33% (3)	22% (2)	99%[b] (9)
Compromise	56 (15)	22 (6)	22 (6)	100 (27)
Integrative	18 (2)	73 (8)	9 (1)	100 (11)
	(21)	(17)	(9)	(47)

$\theta = .0955 = .10$

	Organizational Structure		
	Centralized	Federated	Total
Bargaining	33% (3)	67% (6)	100% (9)
Compromise	78 (21)	22 (6)	100 (27)
Integrative	45 (5)	55 (6)	100 (11)
	(29)	(18)	(47)

$\lambda = .1053 = .11$

[a] State and substate organizations (4 and 3 respectively) were collapsed into single category "State."
[b] Does not equal 100% because of rounding.

Polarization, or the degree of personalized conflict within the organization, served to distinguish between bargaining and other forms of democratic decision behaviors. This was to be expected, of course, since bargaining lends itself to higher levels of polarization. Seventy-eight percent of bargaining organizations suffered high polarization, contrasted with only eleven percent of compromise, and none of integrative organizations.[7] However, since most compromise (sixty-three percent) and integrative (ninety-one percent) organizations clustered in the low polarization category, the predictive power of polarization was a low .26. While high levels of polarization were closely associated with bargaining behavior in *Bakke*, it did not differentiate well between compromise and integrative behaviors.

The best predictor of decision-making behavior was leadership style. Those organizations whose leaders and members were more likely to respond positively to the statement "My organization's leaders acted to insure the fullest discussion of *Bakke*, communicated the alternatives we could pursue, and responded positively to membership preferences" were also more likely to be integrative.[8] Leadership style seems to be the best explanation of organizational preferences for bargaining, compromise, and integration.

Compromise affected an organization's decision making in the earlier analysis of the Equal Employment Advisory Council (see Chapter 2). The staff and executive leadership's commitment to facilitating the organization's actions prompted them to find a common ground, based on the organization's purpose, upon which consensus could be formed. What had threatened to be a bargaining form of policy making—with its accompanying recriminations and threats to organizational stability—was transformed into a compromise form. By shifting debate from a confrontation over principles to an assessment of the specific organizational interests at stake, the EEAC was able to defuse a potentially explosive argument. This kind of shift might, however, decrease the education achieved by narrowing the focus from principle to self-interest. Other cases illustrate the origins of bargaining and integration approaches and the translation of these leadership styles into actual behavior.

The Organization as a Marketplace

The efforts of President Carter's Administration to develop an amicus brief in *Bakke* engendered an unprecedented degree of public fervor. Accounts of the infighting in the Administration over the brief ran daily in the pages of the *New York Times* and the *Washington Post*. The intense lobbying and debate in the government were hardly surprising; the values at stake in *Bakke* were not only highly philosophical but also highly political, and a newly elected government could ill afford to severely irritate its supporters. What was surprising was the public nature of the conflict and the apparent willingness of disparate camps in the government to appeal to the public through media "leaks" in order to elicit support for their positions.[9]

The President's problems with *Bakke* were also surprising given the Justice Department's long experience in using the amicus process. Although some private groups rely extensively on the process to further their preferences, the Justice Department was the first to use it in a concerted effort to lobby the courts. President Theodore Roosevelt's attorney general, Charles J. Bonaparte, is credited with initiating an aggressive amicus curiae strategy on behalf of civil rights for Negroes which came before the Supreme Court during the 1906 through 1909 Court terms.[10] Not until the late forties did the federal government begin its four-decade-long amicus campaign to vindicate the Fifth and Fourteenth Amendment rights of minorities.

At first, the Justice Department was not receptive to the idea of acting as an amicus in the case that ultimately stimulated its efforts on behalf of civil rights. Despite lobbying by advocacy organizations in the *Restrictive Covenant Cases*, the department reserved its decision whether to intervene until the beginning of the 1947 Supreme Court term. Then, at the prompting of the President's Committee on Civil Rights, an organization mandated by President Truman to hold hearings and make recommendations on how to implement the Bill of Rights, and under pressure from many "different religious, racial, welfare, and civil rights organizations, urging the Government to enter the litigation,"[11] Attorney General Tom Clark and Solicitor General Philip Perlman decided to file an amicus brief in the case. Although the advocacy-groups' pressures to intervene were not the sole factor in the Justice Department's decision—the general political orientation of the administration and the efforts of other concerned governmental agencies were at least as important—the apparent victory of their activities led the organizations involved to campaign aggressively in future civil rights cases for government participation. Their efforts culminated in the outgoing Truman Administration's decision to file perhaps the most important brief on behalf of the petitioner in *Brown* v. *Board of Education*.[12] Since then, the Justice Department has been a party to, formal intervenor in, or amicus filer in virtually every significant civil rights case that has reached the Supreme Court.

The major exception was *DeFunis*. Despite promptings from the Solicitor General's office and by at least two governmental agencies—the Civil Service Commission and the Equal Employment Opportunity Commission—the Nixon Administration vetoed efforts to file a government amicus brief in that case. Although accounts purporting to explain the government's reluctance to participate in conflict with one another, it is clear that Solicitor General Robert Bork campaigned for a brief supporting Marco DeFunis's attack on the special admissions program at the University of Washington Law School. The Civil Service Commission, a potential defendant in Title VII employment actions, joined Bork in lobbying the Administration for a brief repudiating quotas, fearing that a "pro-quota" decision by the Court would be applied to the Civil Service Commission's merit system of government employment. The Equal Employment Opportunity Commission, with some support from the Department of Health, Education, and Welfare, insisted that the government was obligated by the Civil Rights Act of 1964, and especially Title VII of that act, to promote the educational and employment opportunities of minorities. Members of President Nixon's White House staff who were responsible for civil rights matters were reluctant to press for any brief, fearing that if the Administration approved one, it would support DeFunis's position. It was better to have no brief, Leonard Garment and Bradley Patterson (Nixon's special assistants on race and urban policy) believed, than to have a brief submitted on the "wrong" side. Hence those individuals in the Administration most receptive to the concerns of minorities were the ones pressing most ardently against the filing of any brief. Partly as a consequence of objections from his staff and partly because his closest aides, John Ehrlichmann and H. R. Haldeman, argued that it would be politically unwise to take a position in the controversy, President Nixon decided that no government brief would be submitted.[13]

The Nixon Administration's failure to approve a brief in *DeFunis* portended the difficulties that President Carter would confront in *Bakke*. The same factors of political calculation, internal division, and external pressure operative in *DeFunis* made themselves felt in *Bakke*. But the factors took on an added significance when a Democratic president who had campaigned aggressively for the black and minority vote became involved.

Officials from the University of California met with members of the Administration in late February 1977, shortly after the Supreme Court granted *certiorari* in *Bakke*. President David S. Saxon discussed the question of whether an amicus brief should be filed by the government with HEW Secretary Joseph Califano, and later pursued the matter with Commissioner of Education Ernest Boyer. At the same time the two principal brief-writers for the university, Archibald Cox and Paul Mishkin, contacted Solicitor General Wade McCree and Drew Days, Assistant Attorney General in charge of the Civil Rights Division. The university also contacted other members of the Justice Department and the Carter Administration in hopes of inducing the government to enter the case on its behalf.[14]

Despite the unusual failure of the Supreme Court to invite the Justice Department's participation in a case so explicitly dealing with the national interest, Days instructed his staff to solicit the opinions of the various governmental agencies and offices on the questions of whether to intervene in *Bakke* and in support of which party. The response was unanimous; all supported intervention. Days and second Assistant Solicitor General Frank Easterbrook cited this response as the basis for their recommendation to offer an amicus brief on *Bakke* in separate memoranda addressed to the Solicitor General. After consulting with the interested agencies in mid-June and gaining approval of an outline for the proposed brief that endorsed affirmative action while rejecting rigid quotas, Days and two members of the Civil Rights Division legal staff wrote a first draft. McCree assigned the task of reviewing and revising it to his first and second assistants, Lawrence Wallace and Frank Easterbrook. Thus began the first of perhaps as many as seven separate drafts of the brief.

While the Justice Department was coordinating the views of other concerned governmental agencies and developing its intended brief, groups inside and outside the Administration began to lobby for a brief that would comply with their policy preferences. Califano explicitly endorsed Davis Medical School's special admissions program in March and stated that he would consult with the Attorney General about a government brief in support of that program.[15] Although he later withdrew his support of quota-based admissions programs, perhaps because of intense pressures from the Jewish community, according to one newspaper account, from American Federation of Teachers' president Albert Shanker, and from the Carter White House,[16] the secretary continued his campaign within the Administration for a pro-Davis brief. A task force was established in the HEW's Office of Education to produce data to be used in Califano's lobbying efforts,[17] and the acting general counsel for HEW, St. John Barrett, mailed a letter to Assistant Attorney General Days pressing for a brief defending the Davis program.[18]

Califano's campaign may have been counterproductive. Members of the Justice Department, especially the Solicitor General's Office, saw his action as an attempt to stampede the Administration into supporting the Davis Medical School. And despite frequent meetings in June with attorneys representing such private organizations as the National Conference of Black Lawyers, the Council on Legal Education Opportunity, the University of Washington, the National Lawyers Guild, and the Institute for the Study of Educational Policy; and press statements from the Congressional Black Caucus and Senator Edward Brooke of Massachusetts,[19] those drafting the brief continued to support affirmative action programs but not the use of quotas.

The prouniversity forces were not the only ones mobilized during the spring and summer of 1977. A delegation representing eight national Jewish organizations[20] met with Califano on June 7 in a fruitless attempt to persuade him that quotas were forbidden by statute, constitutional interpretation, and logic.[21] A month and a half later they again asked Califano to reevaluate his position in support of quotas.[22] Finally convinced that the secretary's opinion was beyond any hope of converting, the Jewish organizations sought to develop support for Bakke's challenge of Davis in the Justice Department, the Civil Service Commission, and the White House. Organizations representing white ethnic groups joined in the effort to solicit governmental endorsement of Bakke's positions.

By this time the original deadline for submission of amici briefs had passed. While President Carter had indicated in a July 28 press conference that Attorney General Griffin Bell and HEW Secretary Califano were working on a brief, and implied that a pro-Davis statement was the probable result, no definite decision had yet been made about which side should be endorsed.[23] When Bell announced in an August 8 press conference that a decision to file a brief supporting Davis had been made, members of the Justice Department were caught completely by surprise and a spokesperson for the department publicly denied Bell's announcement. A Justice Department representative reportedly stated, "Bell opened his mouth at a press conference and the wrong words came out."[24]

Pressure began to mount within the White House for circulating a copy of the proposed brief. Alerted to the political ramifications of a pro-Bakke brief by black and other civil rights organizations and fearing that the brief might not accurately reflect the Administration's position on affirmative action, Carter's chief advisor on domestic policy, Stuart Eizenstat; and the President's counsel, Robert Lipshutz; joined by chief of the White House staff Hamilton Jordan; asked Attorney General Bell to allow them to see the brief. Bell resisted these efforts until September 1. The attorney general had confidence in his subordinates' ability to write a satisfying brief—after all, McCree had been the first black man elected a city judge in Detroit and had been one of the most respected members of the United States Court of Appeals before his appointment to the office of Solicitor General, and Days had been a NAACP Legal Defense Fund staff attorney before being appointed as Assistant Attorney General. Bell also sought to defend the prerogatives of his own department and to protect the traditional independence of the Solicitor General's Office from direct presidential pressures.

However, the attorney general finally relented and personally delivered a copy of the proposed brief to the President in the Oval Office. Under Carter's instructions, Eizenstat reviewed the draft, concluding it was lacking in logic, style, organization, and political savvy. In a memorandum to the President, Eizenstat argued that the brief failed to represent the thinking of the United States government on affirmative action and that it could be used to challenge the federal government's affirmative action programs for minorities, women, the handicapped, and veterans. Moreover, the brief depended excessively on a trial and appellate record that was too weak to carry its evidentiary burden. The criticisms were relayed to Bell's special assistant, Terry Adamson, who in turn brought them to the attorney general. Those suggestions from Eizenstat that struck Adamson and Bell as pertinent were included in a memorandum to McCree. In an effort to insulate the solicitor general from the political turmoil in the Administration, Bell and Adamson did not tell McCree that the suggestions had come from the White House.

Copies of the eighty-eight-page draft Bell delivered to Carter were leaked to the press. From then on, the political struggles and infighting in the Administration over the *Bakke* brief were front-page news in the nation's major papers. Although accounts conflict, it is clear that someone on Carter's immediate staff was responsible for the original "leak"; some members of the Justice Department believed the draft was placed in the hands of a *New York Times* reporter so that private organizations could carry on the battle without the President's personal intervention. If that was the case, the strategy backfired. Not only did opposing forces in the Administration continue their struggle by the selective use of leaks to marshal outside support and pressure for their positions, but organizations outside the Administration began even more aggressive campaigns to coax endorsement of a brief more to their liking.

By the second week of September, McCree and Days were personally engaged in drafting and refining the government brief. A new, revised version of the September 1 draft was sent to Eizenstat on the ninth and circulated among the interested parties within the Administration. Eizenstat was mollified by the inclusion of several of his recommendations, but he still urged a softening of the "anti-quota" language. At the invitation of McCree, members of the Black Congressional Caucus received copies of the draft, and their remarks pointedly indicated that the brief's orientation was unacceptable to them and their constituents. During a hurried telephone call, McCree outlined to Adamson four points McCree felt the finished brief should contain: race may be taken into account to offset the effects of prior and continuing discrimination; an explicit finding of prior discrimination by an institution is not necessary to legitimate that institution's voluntary efforts to counteract the persistent effects of past discrimination; the language repudiating rigid quota programs as devices for relieving discrimination absent a legislative, judicial, or administrative finding of discriminatory behavior should be softened; and the Supreme Court should be advised to remand the case to the California courts to determine whether Davis Medical School actually practiced a quota-based special admissions program. Eizenstat was heartened by this shift in emphasis and told McCree that the brief was now acceptable to the Administration.[25]

The news that Carter had accepted McCree's suggested outline did not reduce the frenzied lobbying efforts of groups inside and outside the Administration. Representatives of fifteen black organizations demanded that Carter go on record in favor of affirmative action programs like Davis's.[26] Representatives from the Polish-American Congress vainly sought an appointment with Attorney General Bell in order to discuss supporting Bakke.[27] News accounts of a "spirited" cabinet meeting where Califano, Department of Housing and Urban Development Secretary Patricia Harris, Labor Secretary Ray Marshall, and Am-

bassador to the United Nations Andrew Young clashed with
Griffin Bell and Carter's aides over the brief were published on
September 13.[28] On that day Nathaniel Jones of the NAACP,
Jack Greenberg of the NAACP Legal Defense Fund, former Secretary of Transportation William Coleman, and three members
of the Congressional Black Caucus called upon the solicitor general, hoping to dissuade him from pressing for an antiquota
component to the brief.[29] The following day the Congressional
Black Caucus openly criticized the President for accepting the
September 9 draft,[30] and groups on both sides of the controversy
privately threatened the Administration with dire tales of fearful repercussions in the 1980 presidential election.

Despite newspaper accounts quoting Administration sources
as saying that "the more the President senses this would be a big
mistake in the black community, he will draw back from" an
explicit rejection of racial quotas,[31] the brief that was filed in the
Office of the Clerk of the Supreme Court on September 19 did
assert that should an admissions process fail to allow for the
"fair comparison of regular and special applicants by the regular admissions committee," it would indicate that "race had . . .
been used improperly." While not the ringing repudiation of
quotas that news accounts had prepared the public to expect,
the brief did argue for the permissibility of "minority-sensitive"
programs while rejecting "[a]ny system which requires that considerations of relative abilities and qualifications be subordinated to considerations of race" as possessing "the attributes of
a quota system which is deemed to be impermissible."[32]

But the brief did not assert that Bakke had demonstrated his
right to be admitted to Davis. It spoke of the need "to restore
victims of discrimination to the position they would have occupied but for the discrimination" and the need "to make a fair
assessment of their achievements and potential," but it had in
mind minority students, not Allan Bakke. It also questioned
whether there was sufficient evidence in the record to prove that
Davis used an impermissible form of quotas. Lacking that proof,
the brief advised the Supreme Court to remand the case to the
lower courts for further proceedings.[33]

By contrast, the earlier draft released on September 12 had

insisted that "[r]ace should be used in making admission decisions only to assist in promoting the fairness of an evaluation
that is otherwise racially neutral." It had argued that precise racial quotas were unconstitutional if they used "race as a tool of
exclusion" against whites. According to some reports, the draft
had concluded that there was sufficient evidence that Bakke had
been unconstitutionally discriminated against and should be admitted to Davis Medical School.[34] The brief presented to the Supreme Court now insisted that the trial record did not make
"clear . . . whether the Davis program operated in this manner."
Despite the uncontroverted statements of the admissions committee chairman that the special admissions subcommittee offered minority candidates to the full committee until the sixteen
slots were filled,[35] the Carter brief asserted that it was still uncertain if the process was competitive or exclusionary. During a
period of fewer than two weeks, something had caused the brief
to shift from the positive statement that the Davis program was
exclusionary to the waffling comment that it may or may not
have been so.

The Administration's brief seemed to be a calculated effort to
appease contending groups in the *Bakke* controversy. Such politics of calculation are not unusual in government amicus writing. Nixon's decision not to participate in *DeFunis* was in large
part the result of a prudent assessment of the political liabilities
and advantages of taking a position in a controversial case. Nor
was the degree of political fighting characterizing the Carter
brief unique; Daniel Berman's investigation of the politics leading to the government brief in *Brown* v. *Board of Education* reveals the same intensity of struggles and the same degree of acrimonious debate found in the politics of the *Bakke* brief.[36] But if
the story of the Administration's efforts to create a brief in
Bakke reflected a politics of "bargaining" rather than "integration" or "compromise," it also revealed the shortcomings of a
policy-making process in which "everyone in the nation was try-
ing to help us write the brief."[37]

The government's brief was the product of accommodational
politics; the need to satisfy an amalgam of varying and conflicting demands fostered accommodation, not integration, of ob-

jectives. And accommodation as a process of mediating differences does have particular attractions to the political being. Presidential politics is often more a process of offending the least number of individuals and groups than it is one of satisfying the most. Timid and circumscribed statements such as the *Bakke* brief may not win too many friends, but they are unlikely to create too many enemies. The politics of bargaining and accommodation may also be attractive to the Supreme Court because of its institutional needs. In any organization, the presence of "veto" groups can check or impede policy making. Accommodational tactics are necessary to appease them, especially when efforts at integration or compromise are unsuccessful. To the extent that the controversy in the Carter Administration was a microcosm of the pressures and divisions within the nation as a whole, the public account of its difficulties and its final stance may have provided valuable clues to a Court searching for a statesmanlike but pragmatic resolution to the quarrel. In some ways the final brief was the kind of legal-political compromise with a broad appeal to which the Court might be attracted.

Ironically, the appeal of a political bargain is also a reminder of the limits of accommodational processes. Despite reports that "the Administration was bound to stir strong opposition no matter what choice it made, so Carter and Bell decided to uphold the position they both favored,"[38] many members of the public viewed the outcome as a flagrant example of government by pressure group. Members of the Supreme Court were reportedly upset at the public spectacle of the heated debate in the Administration. There were reports that Chief Justice Burger and Associate Justice Blackmun informed the solicitor general "'in no uncertain terms'" that the Court "was offended and displeased by the numerous leaks of early drafts of the brief . . . and that the justices felt the resultant uproar had subjected them to improper public pressure."[39] The Justice Department's staff was concerned with what it perceived as the unwarranted and overzealous intrusion of the President's advisors in the brief-writing process. While respecting the fact that the President would be held politically responsible for the actions of his Justice Department, the department's attorneys felt that the White House should defer to their expertise on the law. Once again, the legal actors invoked a claim of authority premised on their special training and experience. (For similar reasons, the White House's efforts in 1978 to modify an amicus brief submitted by the Solicitor General's Office in a veteran's preference case was rebuked by personnel in the Justice Department.) [40]

The story of the Carter Administration's efforts in *Bakke* is one about the intransigency of men and women, rather than of their willingness to develop mutually acceptable and effective policies. There was a rupture in the commonality of principles and interests that defined the association. This breakdown of relationships could not be blamed on ignorance or on failure to provide communication ties among the participants. The contending sides were well aware of the values and interests at stake in *Bakke*. Nor was rupture the product of an imposition of one view on a dissenting minority, as it had been in many oligarchic organizations. Members of the Administration encouraged and facilitated discussion, even though they were unable to maintain civility within those discussions. Carter and his immediate lieutenants took seriously their reconstructive role, but they were unable to display the blend of abilities found in compromise and integrative organizations—principled convictions coupled to the knack for flexibility. By attempting to negotiate a policy representing the lowest common denominator among the conflicting views, they frustrated the expression of a well-considered and argued opinion.

The Carter Administration's attempt to construct consensus among so many divergent viewpoints weakened rather than strengthened its capacity to generate a provocative, well-considered policy statement. Unlike the Equal Employment Advisory Council, where internal divisions forced a narrowed but more focused brief, the government lost focus in its brief as it side-stepped the issue. The earlier draft had stated clearly what was and was not permissible in voluntary programs of racial preferences. It promised a highly integrative policy statement—the product of a robust debate which sought to identify a principled position on a difficult question. But as the Administration's leaders shifted their concerns from a proclamation of government policy to an accommodational, "least offensive" stance, the sharpness of the original statement was blunted. This shifting emphasis was accelerated by the national media's attentiveness and the weak norms of confidentiality in the Administration. The more exposed the policy process became to public scrutiny, the less room the Administration had to maneuver. Confidentiality may help compromise and integration; the lack of it may induce bargaining. The *Bakke* issue seemed to be lost in the clamor of a "marketplace." Haggling and bargaining displaced debate and discussion. Allen Sindler states the consequences of all of this: "The Justice Department's brief . . . bore the marks of the conflict that produced it. A draft brief developed for one legal/political position (affirmative action and Bakke, yes; quotas and the Davis program, no) had to be reworked on a crash basis to sustain a different legal/presidential position (affirmative action, yes; Bakke and the Davis program, remand). Not unexpectedly under such circumstances, the resulting brief exhibited an odd mixture of old and new positions that did not fully cohere, whether viewed as a legal argument for the Court or as a presidential policy statement for the public."[41] But the brief did succeed as an organizational device to maintain cohesion.

In contrast to the Nixon decision in *DeFunis*, Carter decided to intervene in a volatile case whose political impact might adversely affect his hopes for reelection. Given the conflicting allegiances of important Administration members such as Attorney General Bell; Health, Education and Welfare Secretary Califano; and United Nations Ambassador Young, the threat to the cohesion of the association was real. The shattering of the uneasy relationships that typify executive coalitions might exact costs that reached well beyond the specific issue of special admissions programs. In viewing these political costs, the judgment to authorize a brief in *Bakke* reflected a commitment to principles; the particular implementation of those principles was dictated by the unreconstructed preferences of the subgroups and the executive's needs to paper over internal divisions so as to present a united front to the public. The Carter brief suggested that some democratic organizations were willing to sacrifice policy preferences in order to preserve cohesion.

The Carter Administration was not unique. While the most dramatic of the bargaining organizations, it was only one of eleven such organizations. Other bargaining organizations, like the Asian-American Bar Association of the Greater Bay Area, the American Federation of State, County, and Municipal Employees, and the Council of Supervisors and Administrators of New York City, were obliged to placate internal groups by a negotiated brief. They encouraged discussion but allowed it to get out of control. Rather than an exchange of views, organizational debates became highly polarized confrontations between opposed groups. Thus bargaining organizations, while democratic in their approach to participation and discussion, were much like oligarchic organizations where conflict frustrated rather than facilitated learning among participants.

Teachers and Students

Conflict need not become as polarized as it did in bargaining organizations such as the Carter Administration, nor must it be evaded, as it was in compromise organizations like the Equal Employment Advisory Council. In organizations like the American Jewish Congress and the National Association for the Advancement of Colored People, conflict was used to create informed members and effective policy statements. Their decision making was integrative.

The American Jewish Congress (AJC) and the NAACP demonstrate how organizations can be similar with respect to the ways in which they make decisions while radically different in the substance of those decisions. Both represent self-conscious and well-organized cultural groups and both have successfully effected major social changes in America, often jointly. The NAACP's campaign to overturn restrictive covenants in *Shelley* v. *Kraemer* was abetted by the effective amicus brief written by Arthur Goldberg for the American Jewish Congress.[42] The AJC also submitted a thoughtful and persuasive amicus brief supporting the NAACP's arguments in *Brown* v. *Board of Educa-*

tion.[43] Both associations are dedicated to membership participation and to consensus building. Despite these similarities, however, the AJC and the NAACP offered briefs that highlighted the major divisions in principles and interests between the contending camps in *Bakke* and the persisting differences between the two major ethnic blocs in the civil rights community—Jews and blacks.

Although founded in 1918 by Jewish immigrants to the United States to combat the rising tide of anti-Semitism, the American Jewish Congress did not devote its energies to litigation as a catalyst for social change until the establishment of its Commission on Law and Social Action.[44] In contrast to the approaches of the two other major Jewish defense organizations, the Anti-Defamation League and the American Jewish Committee, the Congress's Commission on Law and Social Action rejects the strategy of educating the public away from its anti-Semitic prejudices through campaigns of persuasion and "good will" propaganda, preferring to attack discrimination through direct legal and legislative action. Utilizing the tools of sociological research to uncover subtle patterns of discrimination, the Commission exercises its legal expertise and the American Jewish Congress's resources to ferret out and destroy systemic forms of discrimination against Jews.

DeFunis v. *Odegaard* brought to a head the issue of affirmative action for the AJC.[45] In the late sixties and early seventies the association searched for a middle ground between the complete repudiation of quota-based affirmative action programs and a grudging acceptance of the need for results-oriented preference programs. In 1972 the national biennial convention adopted a resolution which sought to "find a balanced position, one that recognizes the imperative need to increase the educational and employment opportunities of minority group members while, at the same time, recognizing the evils inherent in a quota system." The convention promulgated four principles by which the American Jewish Congress was to determine whether a goal was an acceptable but limited device to secure meaningful equal opportunity or an unacceptable imposition of "mechanical quotas."[46]

Two of the principles called for policies of nondiscrimination; two accepted limited use of goals and numerical targets. While opposing "the use of quotas in employment and university admissions," the convention did endorse "goals, with appropriate safeguards, for increased minority representation in employment." Aggressive recruitment campaigns, the use of culturally bias-free, job-related examinations, and manpower training programs were offered as permissible means to increase minority employment opportunities. Provided they were implemented in a fair and consistent manner, explicit goals for employment were also acceptable. In this context, fairness and consistency meant that no one would be discharged to make places available for minorities, that "minimum and reasonable qualifications" must be met by all applicants, that the goals should be based on the proportion of qualified minority applicants "within the relevant job market," and finally, that goals should be "reviewed annually and discontinued when the past imbalance has been corrected." But the AJC was not willing to endorse parallel measures in minority admissions. Although it accepted open admissions programs, "remedial programs" like the Council on Legal Education Opportunity's, "vigorous recruitment efforts," and "flexible admission criteria," the American Jewish Congress specifically rejected "quotas or percentage goals." It was willing to be lenient in employment but not in university admissions.[46]

Equanimity characterized the debate over the principles at the convention. Although supporters and opponents of quotas put their views forward in a forceful manner, their attacks and challenges were directed at the ideas spoken, not at the speakers. The balance of the debate was mirrored by the balance in the resolution. But even this limited acceptance of goals did not go unchallenged. Some members argued that any endorsement of goals logically implied an endorsement of quotas. Theodore Mann, one of the principal instigators of an antiquota position, stated on the convention floor that since goals must be operationally specified in order to provide evidence of their successful achievement, they lead to the de facto imposition of quotas and thus negate the antidiscriminatory principles articulated by the resolution. Mann's fears did not go unanswered. A council member from Washington, D.C., warned that too strident a rejection of goals could leave the American Jewish Congress vulnerable to charges of "selling out" the civil rights movement. He wanted to maintain the ambiguity of a position rejecting the concept of quotas while affirming the careful use of goals, in order to find a common ground of agreement with blacks and other minorities.

Disagreements over the organization's policy on affirmative action were not confined to the convention. While not all the local chapters were affected by the controversy, at least three of the largest and most important found themselves struggling with it. Conflict was intense in the New York and D.C. chapters, and only slightly less in one of the West Coast chapters. For example, as new programs and challenges to established programs of preferences arose, the Brooklyn chapter continually returned to the question whether any type of quota was justifiable. In late summer 1973, with the first preferential university admissions case on the Supreme Court's docket, Jack Elkin and Lillian Steinberg organized a series of debates. Representatives from the NAACP and the dean of a major New York City law school argued the pros and cons of *DeFunis* and answered questions from the floor. As a member of the audience remembered, "Those debates did more to explain what was happening than did the preceding two years of discussion."[47] For some, the valuable aspect of the talks was who did the speaking. "Somehow it made a difference that a black man was defending quotas. Here was one victim of the old type of quotas justifying a new type."[48] The dialectic of the debate between committed individuals helped to attach the significance of human lives to the abstract arguments attacking or defending preferences.

One constant refrain in interviews with leaders and members of the AJC was that discussion helped to crystallize individual thinking on the implications and consequences of alternative affirmative action programs. As in Tocqueville's image, the organization served as a "schoolhouse"; the supportive atmosphere provided the access to knowledge and the willingness to test ideas which promoted teaching and learning among its members.

Richard Cohen, the AJC's associate executive director, explained in 1977 how the debates in 1972 and 1973 helped him to understand affirmative action: "We [the Jewish community] have learned the hard way about the abuse of quotas. But cases like these [*DeFunis* and *Bakke*] dealt with the good-intentioned use of quotas to solve a problem. Personally, I abhor quotas, but I loathe racism as well. Somehow, we had to take a stand; there were no easy answers." The discussion within the organization helped him make a choice: "Reverse discrimination isn't an intellectual problem. It is a human one. No matter how much I read, I needed to see others struggling with the problem. Their questions, their fears helped me. A close friend confided to me that she wished quotas would go away. She feared their use because of their history of abuse. But how can we answer blacks' arguments? Here it was [1973], almost twenty years after the school desegregation case, and there still was no greater percentage of black lawyers than there were in 1954."[49]

A decision on quotas required a judgment—"a balance between the promise of present benefit and future danger." Cohen became convinced that a decision against quotas need not foreclose the chance for real improvements in opportunities for blacks. "I don't want to sound paternalistic," he said, "but I feel that quotas hurt everyone, especially blacks. We must break with the assumption that race should determine who gets where. We all suffer if we don't. We [the AJC] are committed to affirmative action. We have worked hard for remedial training, nonracial evaluations of credentials, intensive recruiting of minority candidates. These things do work without the price demanded by quotas." Cohen confessed that he had not changed his position. "From the beginning, I didn't want quotas." Nevertheless, he felt that the organization's discussions had taught him something important. The AJC "is not a monolithic group. We differ, sometimes violently, among ourselves. And I really think we learn from those differences."[50]

Cohen, like many others, was torn between his attachment to two social values—an opposition to the governmental contribution to the subjugation or stigmatization of racial or ethnic minorities, and a commitment to the ethic of individualism, the belief that society and individual freedom are best served by judging a person solely on his or her personal merit and not on membership in a favored or disfavored group. Unlike organizations such as the Equal Employment Advisory Council, the American Jewish Congress's difficulties with this problem did not cause its members to shift their concerns from principled to interest advocacy. The organization's members maintained their adherence to principle. Nor did the decision to take a firm and clear-cut stand on a difficult issue result in large-scale dissent or emigration among the members.

One of the original members of the bloc arguing for a pro-quota brief conceded that the debate within the AJC was occasionally bitter but "a general sense of good will persisted between both sides. We had so long struggled shoulder-to-shoulder against the injustices of our society that it was difficult to see our differences as one [*sic*] between enemies. The other side was wrong, not racist." The absence of intense animosity, the reluctance of individuals on either side to see the argument as one between angels and devils, allowed an "agreement to disagree" to serve as the basis for welding together agreement on the substance. Integration as a decision-making process seemed to depend upon mutual trust and respect among the organization's participants.

Not all Jewish organizations were as fortunate as the AJC in this respect. In *DeFunis*, two were riven by their staffs' failure to consult the members. The Commission on Social Action of the Union of American Hebrew Congregations participated in a brief supporting the minority preference program at the University of Washington Law School. The commission is the union's staff arm, mandated to monitor legislative action affecting the interests of Reform Judaism and to assist congregations in developing social action programs which "apply locally the ethical principles of Judaism to the problems of the world we live in."[51] The decision to join a coalition brief was made by five members of the commission without consulting either the general board or the membership, most of whom did not discover the commission's involvement until newspaper accounts brought it to general attention. Considerable internal disagreement over the commission's stance caused a reorganization of its structure, an expansion of the governing board to include representatives from a broader spectrum of confederated groups in the union than had been the case before the *DeFunis* controversy. A sharply divided (15–14) commission declined to offer an amicus brief in *Bakke*, stating that "because of irreconcilable differences among our constituency over this case, and in view of the degree in which attitudes have frozen since the *DeFunis* case, it would be improper to identify this organization with the position [the university's] which is so clearly a minority within the Union. We have chosen, therefore, not to enter the *Bakke* case as a 'friend of the court.'"[52] The general assembly of the union ratified the commission's decision at their November 1977 meeting, re-affirming their support for affirmative action while specifically rejecting quotas as an acceptable means for attaining equal opportunity.[53]

Another Jewish organization, the National Council of Jewish Women, was also criticized by its members for supporting the University of Washington in *DeFunis*. The council's director of national affairs, its Washington, D.C. representative, and its president decided to side with supporters of affirmative action without clearing the decision with other leaders or members. After calls for their impeachment and angry denunciations of their stance, the director resigned and the two elected officers sought to make amends by declaring their opposition to quotas. The National Council of Jewish Women did not participate in *Bakke*.[54]

Unlike these oligarchic organizations, the American Jewish Congress could depend on strong agreement for its policy statements in *DeFunis*. At the suggestion of its co-chairman, the AJC's governing council ordered the Commission on Law and Social Action to offer a brief which supported the notion of affirmative action but explicitly denounced "the concept that race is a job-related qualification for lawyers or any other profession or occupation" and deplored "the legitimation of racial quotas or balancing."[55] The governing council reviewed the brief after it had been submitted to the Court and passed a resolution affirming AJC endorsement of the brief.

The 1974 resolution was a carefully reworded and elaborated version of the 1972 statement, expanding the grounds for the Congress's opposition to quotas while reaffirming more traditional modes of affirmative action such as vigorous recruitment efforts and remedial training programs. The language accepting goals from the 1972 document was now revised to express a clear-cut repudiation of them in all cases except those where a court or administrative agency ordered their use after a finding of past discrimination. Goals were to be used only to assess good-faith efforts, not as devices to secure fixed representation of racial or ethnic groups. "Applicants for employment and university admission should be considered in a 'racially neutral way,'" read the Philadelphia resolution, paraphrasing Justice Douglas's words in *DeFunis*.[56]

The question of affirmative action was "the most difficult issue the American Jewish Congress has faced in the last thirty years," the emeritus director of the Commission on Law and Social Action stated.[57] A great deal of thought, discussion, and both personal and collective soul-searching underlay the decision to confront that special "dilemma for liberals"—recognizing the need for "realistic paths" to the achievement of "equality in fact as well as theory" while rejecting "mathematical formulas" as a basis for action.[58] The difficulty was made even greater by the fear that a pro-DeFunis or Bakke stance would be interpreted as the opening round in a struggle between the narrow self-interests of Jews and blacks, groups historically allied in the American civil rights movement. It was partly to allay the "Jew versus black" aspect of the controversy that the American Jewish Congress actively recruited white ethnic organizations as cosponsors to its *Bakke* brief.[59]

The Congress's concern with the possible repercussions of opposing quotas was not unrealistic; charges that the organization had surrendered principle to self-interest were frequent in statements to the media made by members of the black, Latino, and feminist communities. Kenneth Clark, psychology professor at the City University of New York and a respected spokesperson for blacks, explained his disappointment with the posture of Jewish organizations: "It is as if some of our old friends completely wiped out their knowledge of everything they knew and fought against through the Sixties. They seem to want to believe that there is no racism in America any more and they have to know better." [60]

Harold Fleming, writing in the pages of *City* magazine two years before *DeFunis*, dismissed Jewish aversion to the newer, more demanding forms of affirmative action as "easily understood" since in cities like New York, "Jews are heavily concentrated in the teaching profession" and feel threatened by "black pressures for . . . a larger share of teaching and administrative positions at a time of shrinking rather than expanding job opportunities." [61] He concluded that Jewish rejection of quota programs was intended to protect their own newly won positions in American society, not to oppose on principle all uses of voluntary, numbers-based preferential programs.

Sociological facts help to explain such suspicions of selfish motives behind the Jewish community's claim of a principled, "clear and uninhibited consensus." [62] Although Jews constitute less than three percent of the population, they are disproportionately represented in the teaching, medical, and other professional sectors of society, in part because of past limitations on economic opportunities open to them and in part because of cultural predilections and accidents of geographical distribution. Having overcome the disabling effects of past anti-Semitic prejudices, [63] Jews are now overrepresented in the very areas that blacks and other minorities see as demanding the greatest degree of redistribution among racial and ethnic groups.

Questions of motivation are always difficult to answer. Any association's stated list of principles is a complex code requiring careful deciphering. Some statements of principle are made because an influential minority in the organization feels strongly about them despite any likelihood that the principles are attainable in the foreseeable future. Others represent a concession to the expectations of an important ally who demands the principle's inclusion. Yet others are trial balloons, sent aloft to test the crosswinds of political pressures, while others are intended as ballast to be sacrificed should they impede more central purposes. Some principled positions are the products not of purposive design but of forces emerging from past commitments and interactions, representing "a compromise of the interests of several groups of potential participants."[64] The fact that a principled position happens also to serve self-interest does not prove it is hypocritically held.

In the light of the myriad possibilities, the Congress's decision to become involved in *Bakke* was probably the product of a mixture of motives, some rooted in a concern for the well-being of its constituents' interests, some founded in the association's mission to preserve Jewish cultural values, and some tied to a defense of more overarching values it thought necessary to the well-being of American society. Although primarily a Jewish-defense organization, the AJC has long acted on the premise that efforts advancing the "general interest" serve to protect the particular interests of the Jewish community. For example, its amicus defense of public school children whose religious beliefs forbade them to salute the American flag was instrumental in persuading the Supreme Court to overturn compulsory flag salutes in *West Virginia Board of Education* v. *Barnette.*[65] It intervened in the case not because of any direct economic or associational interest of its own but rather to champion the general principles of religious freedom and the value of free speech. The same public-interest concerns animated the 1974 Philadelphia resolution on affirmative action:

We believe this racial quota is bad for blacks, bad for Jews, bad for all minorities and bad for the total American community. If we are to live in a healthy democratic society, we must alleviate the grave intergroup tensions that threaten upheavals in our urban areas. In the words of Jeremiah, *we must strive for the welfare of the community in which we live, for in its welfare shall we find our own welfare.*[66]

The general welfare theme surfaced in its brief in *Bakke*: "[I]t has always been the conviction of this organization that the security and the constitutional rights of American Jews can best be protected by helping to preserve the security and constitutional rights of all Americans, irrespective of race, creed or national origin, including specifically the right to equal educational opportunity for all individuals."[67]

The synthesis of self-interest and idealistic principles helps explain traditional Jewish disenchantment with quota-oriented affirmative action. The AJC and other like-minded organizations feared that the drive for equal rights had become a drive for the rights of some people at the expense of others. As one sympathetic commentator on the "War Inside the Jews" has noted, "It is absolutely critical to an understanding of the Jewish position on these matters to know that Jews, however reluctantly they have come to their present position, perceive themselves as defenders of justice and not as its betrayers in the name of narrow self-interest. For it has yet to be made clear . . . how the move toward quotas accomplishes anything more than transferring disadvantage from one undeserving victim to another."[68]

This uneasiness with the spectre of an egalitarian movement directed at the conscious redistribution of social benefits and burdens on a racial or ethnic basis is not a recent phenomenon. As early as 1964, Joseph Robison of the Congress's Commission on Law and Social Action invoked the analogy of two runners, one of whom suffers the disability of historic discrimination, competing in a race, in order to warn that the "relatively simple" and therefore attractive solution of disabling the other runner "runs counter to the basic concept that guilt is personal and that punishment may not be imposed without fault." The principle of equality is a "powerful weapon against bias," not an instrument to favor the black by injuring the white.[69] This rejection of those affirmative action programs which injure innocent white third parties was at the heart of the Jewish opposition to "benign quotas."

The NAACP took a different view of the situation.[70] The nation's oldest and largest minority-defense organization, the NAACP saw Davis's special admissions process and other result-oriented preferential programs as "constitutionally permitted and statutorily authorized devices for ameliorating the racial exclusion that would otherwise exist."[71] Preferences for blacks and other minorities were not infringements of the general principle of equal opportunity, but rather the only reasonably effective mechanism of securing meaningful access to the opportunities the Constitution guarantees.

The NAACP had some difficulties coming to this conclusion.

In the 1950s and early 1960s, the organization had insisted on a strict color-blind reading of the constitutional objective of equal protection. The NAACP's brief in *Brown* v. *Board of Education* had insisted that the "evidence makes clear that it was the intent of the proponents of the Fourteenth Amendment, and the substantial understanding of its opponents, that it would, of its own force, prohibit all state action predicated upon race or color. . . . [A]s a matter of law, race is not an allowable basis of differentiation in procedural action." [72] In the companion case attacking racial segregation in the District of Columbia public schools, the NAACP pled, "Do not deny any child the right to go to the school of his or her choice on the grounds of race or color within the normal limits of your districting system. . . . Do not assign them on the basis of race, and we have no complaint." [73]

In the 1963 hearings on the Civil Rights Act, Roy Wilkins, the NAACP's executive director from 1955 to 1977, condemned the use of employment quotas as "evil" and feared they would be used to diminish, not enlarge, black opportunities. [74] However, by the mid-sixties, the improving status of blacks still lagged behind their rising expectations. The traditional equal opportunity-antidiscrimination formula did not seem capable of bringing about the desired changes in economic and social status with sufficient speed. The so-called Young Turk revolt in the conventions of 1967 and 1968, which pressed for greater militancy on the part of the NAACP, also contributed to the pressures for moving beyond "color-blind" politics.

"Our problem," explained Roy Wilkins, discussing the turmoil in the NAACP during the late sixties "was how to come to grips with what seemed to be a failing faith in the 'equal opportunity' ideal." Just as the organization had flourished with the triumph of the old formula, it now threatened to fall along with the formula. "Our declining membership, and my problems with the board, were largely the result of having nothing spectacular to offer." Wilkins recognized the necessity of doing something, but he could not endorse quotas. "How could we argue we were against racism and then demand racial rights?" [75]

Not all of the New York office personnel or the members of

the national board shared Wilkins's misgivings. There is evidence from internal memoranda circulated in the NAACP's New York headquarters that some national leaders and staff members, such as Nathaniel Jones, the organization's general counsel; and Herbert Hill, the NAACP's labor director; were convinced at the outset that preferences were necessary to realize the promise of equal opportunity.[76] But many other leaders and members shared Wilkins's fear that quotas would stimulate latent race consciousness or destroy the symbolic power of the "color-blind" principle of antidiscrimination.[77]

The division within the NAACP reflected differences of opinion within the black community itself. Blacks were not then or now unanimous in their support of quotas. Some conservative black intellectuals argue, like Thomas Sowell, that "what all the arguments and campaigns for quotas are really saying, loud and clear, is that *black people just don't have it*, and that they will have to be *given* something in order to have something. The devastating impact of this message on black people—particularly black young people—will outweigh the few extra jobs that may result from this strategy."[78] A black lawyer, J. A. McPherson, writing on his experience in law school, seems to support Sowell's prediction. "Traditionally, first year law students are supposed to be afraid, or at least awed; but our fear was compounded by the uncommunicated realization that perhaps we were not authentic law students, and the uneasy suspicion that our classmates knew we were not."[79] These concerns were not confined to black professionals or intellectuals. A Gallup Poll released in March, 1977, found that a majority of nonwhites— and therefore presumably a substantial number of blacks— opposed preferential treatment of minorities in college admissions and employment (sixty-four percent opposed, twenty-seven percent supported).[80] A poll conducted by the *New York Times* and CBS News during the month oral arguments in *Bakke* were made before the Supreme Court indicated that forty-two percent of black respondents disapproved of "quota"-based preferential college admissions programs for qualified black applicants.[81] More recently, a *Washington Post* and ABC News poll asked blacks and whites to respond to the statement, "Because of past discrimination, blacks who need it should get some help from the government that white people in similar economic circumstances don't get." Forty-six percent of the blacks opposed such help.[82]

Opposition to quota programs within the NAACP was not solely concerned with the color-conscious nature of such programs. Some objected to the investment of organizational time and effort in pushing for such programs in areas other than employment. In the words of one former member who had expressed concern over the direction NAACP litigation and lobbying had taken during the late sixties and early seventies, "I left not so much because of any differences over our policy on quotas as over my apprehension that the NAACP was frittering away its energies over policies that promised much but probably resulted in very little."[83]

The debate over affirmative action and quotas occurred within the national board and among local chapters during the years 1967 through 1972. The first preference programs affected minority employment opportunities in the construction industry. The board had little difficulty in supporting such programs as the Philadelphia Plan, which required employment of minorities in levels approximating their numbers in the general population. In the robust economy of the sixties, improvements for blacks did not menace whites. The economy was expanding at an unprecedented rate and seemed capable of employing all who wished to work. "Quotas" appeared in this light more like flexible goals than mandatory or exclusionary preferences. When the Philadelphia Plan was offered to the members at the 1970 national convention, it was ratified by an overwhelming majority vote. A year earlier, the 1969 convention listened as its national chairman rejected the more radical demand for monetary "reparations" or partial compensation from white organizations—specifically, churches—for the injuries inflicted upon blacks. The NAACP did not demand retribution for the "blood guilt" of white racism, declared Bishop Stephen Gill Spottswood in his keynote address, but the movement toward some measurable equity among the races.[84]

Preferences in professional school admissions were not so

easily dealt with. Where the economy seemed able to make room for almost all job seekers, professional schools had to turn away many qualified applicants. Preferences in this context threatened to be exclusionary. If places were to be opened for blacks, some whites would have to be denied admission.

There were at least seven board meetings between 1967 and 1972 during which quotas in professional education were discussed. Some agreed with Wilkins that quotas, as distinguished from flexible "goals or targets," threatened blacks' best interests.[85] Supporters of preferences, such as general counsel Nathaniel Jones, argued that these dangers had to be weighed against the benefits and insisted that the issue of "restrictive quotas" was a "phony" one. As Jones was later to say, "black people are not advocating 'quotas' for the simple reason that 'quotas' have served to exclude them from jobs and schools to a far greater extent than any other group. The use of 'quotas' against blacks is what has made affirmative action now necessary."[86]

Away from the association's New York headquarters, regional chapters were struggling with the issue on their own. One chapter in Montgomery County, Maryland, voted to oppose all numerically based preferences in higher education. Other chapters such as the Chicago affiliate were unable to settle on a common position. As one Chicago member remarked, "We knew we couldn't agree, so we decided not to talk." In Atlanta supporters of racial preferences and "quotas" won over opponents, and Atlanta joined D.C., New York, and California as vigorous proponents of preferences.

The intensity of feeling on the issue is difficult to assess. Few informants were willing to characterize either the board's or the chapters' deliberations on racial preferences in the years before *DeFunis* as highly polarized—Chicago seemed to be the lone exception. Like the American Jewish Congress, the NAACP seemed dedicated to robust but nonpersonalized debates. However, the national board, the majority of whose members are elected by the chapters, became the final forum for the controversy. In 1972, as *DeFunis* drew nearer, opponents of preferences found themselves part of a dwindling minority within the

NAACP. "I wouldn't say a consensus was forming," explained Wilkins, "but at least an amicable accord was being reached."[87] The board members were persuaded that something more immediate than the promise of equal opportunity was needed—results were needed. The interchange of ideas and arguments and the pressures for action from the local chapters overcame doubts about quotas. Thus, fired by anger and frustration over the slow progress being made in remedying past injustices, the board members approved stricter and stricter forms of quota programs. Quotas were first supported in blue-collar employment, then in professional and managerial occupations, and eventually in college admissions programs.

The organization's gradual acceptance of more exacting forms of racial preferences can be seen in the convention debates and resolutions between 1964 and 1977. Resolutions passed by the national conventions in the mid-sixties emphasized the need for "equal opportunity" and basic civil rights. By 1972, "parity" had replaced "equal opportunity" as the keynote of convention resolutions.[88] After a heated debate, the 1974 convention in New Orleans adopted a resolution rebuking "the phony emotion-charged issue that the means to end two hundred years of oppression is 'reverse discrimination'" and declaring the NAACP's support of the University of Washington and its battle against Marco DeFunis. The convention was not yet willing, however, to accept quotas as the official policy of the NAACP. Instead, the resolution emphasized the "unfair," racially biased nature of professional school admissions tests as the basis for its defense of the University of Washington.[89] But the leadership's position was clear. As Chairman Spottswood pointed out in his opening address, "We advocate affirmative action with established goals, timetables and minimums" because, "without this, how can progress be measured?"[90] A year later at the sixty-sixth Annual Convention in Washington, D.C., one of the most vocal defenders of racial preferences in the NAACP, Herbert Hill, restated the "hard-line" position on quotas. "It should be evident that what is really involved in the debate over affirmative action is not that blacks will be given preferences over whites but that a substantial body of law now requires that discriminatory systems which operate to favor whites at the expense of blacks must be eliminated."[91] Finally, in 1977, the NAACP convention passed a resolution announcing its support of the University of California, Davis admissions program specifically and of the use of "race as a selection factor" generally.[92]

This shift from the *Brown*-era color-blind stance to the *Bakke*-era color-conscious approach resulted from the concern about "another lost generation." An attorney active in NAACP litigation in California recalls, "The decision to support [quota forms of] affirmative action expressed a commitment by us to attain the promise of equality now, not twenty or thirty years from now."[93] Invoking the same sentiment, several individuals prominent in local NAACP affiliates feared that the promise of *Brown* would be lost to another generation of blacks. "Most of our children born since 1954 have been condemned to segregated schools. How many more years will it be before we see *Brown*'s mandate fulfilled?" Responding to the suggestion that "benign quotas" might produce newer, more sophisticated forms of segregation, the assistant general counsel of the NAACP answered, "That is a risk we're willing to take. There's no other game in town."[94] No other alternative reasonably promised to be as effective.

What had seemed to work for other ethnic groups was not working for blacks; the removal of artificial barriers had not resulted in the integration of blacks into American economic and political life. As one civil rights tactician pointed out in 1965, "facile analogies with the experience of various ethnic immigrant groups . . . do not hold." Unlike some other ethnic groups such as the Jews and Asians, blacks, commonly punished in slavery for reading, lacked the history of literacy which helps stimulate intellectual and economic advancement. Their families having often been dispersed by slavery and its aftermath, blacks also lack the sort of history of family stability that characterizes Jews, Italians, and other immigrant groups. The slave codes forbidding to many the right to marry and rear children also frustrated cultural transmission among black generations. Institutions of prejudice and oppression against blacks persisted after emancipation into the twentieth century. More important, "Jews are white and have the option of relinquishing their cultural-religious identity"; most blacks are denied such an option. Finally, the changing economic structure of America makes analogies with immigrant experiences in the early twentieth century inappropriate. Turn-of-the-century America was characterized by expansion—territorially and economically. The last decade has been one of stagnation in economics "in the midst of a technological revolution which is . . . destroying unskilled and semiskilled jobs—jobs in which Negroes are disproportionately concentrated." [95]

Since the natural processes of mobility and advancement did not work for the majority of blacks, many NAACP members thought, people must act to remedy the continuing effects of past injustices. This was not a repudiation of the principle of individual merit or accomplishment. As Vernon Jordan, then executive director of the National Urban League, explained in a speech before the American Jewish Committee (a speech which was quoted approvingly in the NAACP's magazine, *The Crisis*), "We have no quarrel with the merit system nor with the concept that rigid numerical quotas that overlook individual differences and attributes are wrong. But we reject the suggestion that a merit system is actually in operation today. Nor do we accept that merit can be accurately measured by tests." [96]

The NAACP's leaders' campaign for an endorsement of racial preferences and the frustration many members felt at the slowness with which existing antidiscrimination programs were effecting changes in the status of blacks were not the only forces at work in molding members' views. Like the American Civil Liberties Union, the NAACP suffered a decline in membership during the seventies. [97] Many saw the seventies as a period during which economic, not traditional civil rights, issues headed the public agenda—*Bakke* being the exception. As some of the urgency of the cause the NAACP was committed to champion appeared to wane, marginal members left and switched their support to concerns more pressing to them, such as the environment. Those remaining in the NAACP were more receptive to the emphasis on quotas than were those who had departed. [98] This blend of positive efforts by leaders, the frustrations of some individuals, and greater receptivity on the part of core members facilitated the construction of a consensus.

Educating a Democracy

Organizational action in *Bakke* posed one perennial problem of political action: how to reconcile responsive with responsible government. The demand that a brief purporting to represent an organization should approximate the actual sentiments of the members is a demand for something more than the authenticity of an organizational statement. The demand reflects a faith in the power of participation as a mechanism to strengthen the quality of a belief and to insure that leaders and members act responsibly. It is a demand for a *governing* rather than a *dominating* majority.

James Madison argued that governing majorities are animated by a sense of restraint imbued through constitutional checks and social forces. Though comprised of "factions," groups of citizens whose interests are adverse either "to the rights of all citizens" or to the collective "interests of the community," a governing majority is capable of ascending beyond "the great variety of interests, parties, and sects which it embraces" to champion the principles "of justice and the general good."[99] The governing majority rests its fate on its representatives' ability to consolidate "local prejudices and mistaken rivalships" into "one harmonious interest."[100] The "cool and deliberate sense of the community" is forged through the educative process of debate and compromise. The "communion of interests and sympathy of sentiments" which, while not lifting men up to the level of angels,[101] nevertheless makes them something higher than the beasts, is clarified though never fully realized through the process of discussion and pragmatic adjustment. It is restraint and diversity that legitimate the majority's claim to rule, not the force of mere numbers.[102]

Dominating majorities, by contrast, lack the liberating effects of debate, which prompt the truest possible expression of the common interest. Falling prey to the fallacy of pure democracy, the assumption that an equality of political rights ensures an identity of interests and sentiments, dominating majorities are susceptible to the debilitating arrogance attending the sovereignty of numbers. Lacking the discipline and heterogeneity which transform tyranny into legitimate rule, they are condemned to a condition of "consensual authoritarianism"[103] in which individual liberty is throttled by social norms.[104]

Madison's treatment of governing majorities concentrates on their sensitivity to multiple viewpoints, their openness to being persuaded, and their obligation to provide the opportunity for minority views to be voiced and for new majorities to form. He hoped that in such majorities, leadership would be the crucial ingredient translating many interests into a consensus that approximates the true common interest. The dialectic of debate, discussion, and compromise enables the leader to meld the raw materials of diverse individual interests into a coherent whole. These emphases on responsiveness to individual wants and responsibility to shared interests and principles are familiar by now, for they are the elements defining the democratic leadership style. The same sense of sensitivity, openness, and alertness to the riches of diversity exemplified the most successful democratic organizations in *Bakke*.

In much the same manner, Madison's description of the deficiencies of dominating majorities calls to mind several key features of the oligarchic style. Both fail to draw upon the full intellectual and political resources of the organization: the dominating majority recklessly disregards the views, wants, or abilities of the minority; the oligarchic leader in *Bakke* relied on his or her own expertise or on the limited resources of the staff. Most important, both are characterized by an excessive deference to one aspect of the whole. The dominating majority depends on the momentary aggregation of interests to supply the motive power to its action; the oligarchic organization placed its trust in the personal commitments of a few elite members or in the professional competence of the staff. By comparison, although they relied on staff expertise, the leaders and members of democratic organizations were not captured by them.

Why did democratic organizations pursue a governing rather than a dominating strategy? The self-perceptions of leaders and members seemed to be the key, but the evidence suggesting why some sets of leaders and members sought a democratic style is limited.

Organizations manifesting an integrative strategy, like the

NAACP and the American Jewish Congress, tended to possess three elements. Their leaders and members had internalized a set of values that emphasized the desirability and healthiness of discussion; the give-and-take characteristic of informed debate had long been a routine fixture of organizational procedures. Moreover, the ideological nature of the purposes that these organizations were established to attain or defend was conducive to engendering opposition and discussion. Many of the associations displaying an integrative effort were formed as means to express principled views of society and human relationships. Although in both the organizations cited above the discrete interests of the members were affected by the choices to be made, these organizations had long represented themselves to the public and to their own participants as committed to values that transcended momentary self-interests. Finally the nature of the membership body itself was an important determinant. In many cases, the members of "integrative" organizations were highly homogeneous in their personal backgrounds and life histories. There existed a fortunate congruence of individual interests and principles that produced commonality beyond the specific values the association was established to promote or defend.

It is significant that many (seven of eleven) of the organizations successful in pursuing integrative approaches were ones that straddled the distinction between interest-based and outward-regarding associations.[105] Just as many democratic interest groups involved in *Bakke* followed a compromise strategy, a strategy attractive to them because of the prominent role played by interests or incentives to active organizational membership, so the bifocal nature of minority-defense organizations such as the American Jewish Congress and the NAACP made an integrative strategy attractive. The melding of individual interests and other-regarding principles that define the organizational motives of such associations provided the assurance of personal fidelity to shared values and the sensitivity to the importance of principles that are the prerequisites to the successful use of integration. However, too strong a dependency on principles—shorn of discrete personal investment in the stakes of organizational existence—hindered integration and forced some organizations, like the Carter Administration, to turn to bargaining modes of agreement.

Consensus or majority support was not an inevitable product of a "democratic" approach. An organization's efforts to establish a common, principled position on a significant problem may uncover hitherto unrecognized divisions within the membership over values too critical to be compromised or integrated. The shared community of principles once thought to define the association can prove to be illusory. Unless the organization can find a new basis for common action or is able to avoid situations forcing a confrontation over the newly discovered differences, it may suffer mass protests or defections. The Carter Administration suffered such a fate. Its efforts to encourage discussion led to polarized confrontations that shook its confidence in its common quest. Here, structure did seem to exacerbate an already unsettled situation. The Administration lacked the homogeneity of background that characterized so many integrative organizations and the homogeneity of specific interests that characterized many compromise organizations. The diffuse structure of the federal government and the special symbolic importance of its stand in cases like *Bakke* accounted for much of the intensity of the conflict within the Administration. Since most participants were unwilling to exit from the organization, they exercised their voice more intensely.

That so few organizations exhibited even limited opportunities for education as we have defined it may be a cause for concern. Extra- and intraorganizational pressures accounted for much of the resistance in *Bakke* amici organizations. But they did not account for it all.

CHAPTER V

THE LAWYER
AS AN ORGANIZATIONAL
LEADER

Recurrent in these accounts of the organizational use of the amicus process in *Bakke* was the special roles played by the legally trained participants—organizational and private attorneys. In organizations like the Equal Employment Advisory Council, lawyers were able to forestall a battle within the membership over the acceptability of quota programs by shifting discussion to the narrower question of the inconsistent affirmative action regulations imposed on private industry. In the American Civil Liberties Union and other organizations where bitter confrontations among the members prevented consensus, lawyers were active participants in all the struggling groups. The decision to file and the final form of the brief were the result of the united efforts of the legal staff and the board's elected general counsel to impose a solution on a divided membership. Lawyers helped to coordinate organizational coalitions by convincing organizations such as the National Medical and Dental Association to join with like-minded groups in *Bakke*.[1] Attorneys thus served as instigators, decision makers, and coordinators in the litigational battle over affirmative action.

These roles suggest several questions: Did the prominence of lawyers in amicus policy making affect the nature of organizational education? Did the nature of the legal craft and the dependence on lawyers characteristic of any organization pursuing influence through the amicus process narrow the opportunities for vigorous debate in many organizations? Did lawyer-leaders stifle learning in *Bakke*?

Most explanations of organizational action in the legal process overlook the role of the lawyer as an organizational leader. No longer—if they ever were—simple facilitators of organizational ends, law-trained participants have become creators of group interests and principles. As the activities of courts have become more important to organizations, his possession of expertise has strengthened the lawyer's claim to an independent voice in the organization's council.

Lawyers have always played an influential role in organizations that employed them or sought their donated counsel. In the sixties and seventies lawyers came into their own as leaders. What was prophesied in several studies of lawyers in the late sixties and early seventies has become the reality: some lawyers have transformed their role as legal experts into a source of power in the organization.[2] Changing perspectives of lawyers' legitimate functions on the part of both lawyers themselves and other organization members have encouraged legal professionals to challenge laypeople for policy-making positions in the organization. The presence and powers of lawyers help explain the willingness of so many organizations to become involved in as controversial an issue as *Bakke* and may explain the diminishing importance of nonlegal perspectives in organizational decision making. Organizational advocacy in *Bakke* cannot be understood adequately without understanding the roles played by organizational lawyers. This issue of role can be broken down into three questions: What does it mean to say that lawyers are "organizational leaders"? Why have they gained this role? What were the organizational consequences of lawyer leadership in *Bakke*?

Organizations and the Amicus Process

Conventional explanations of organizational litigation emphasize four considerations: alternative political avenues, the resources available for investment, a calculus of comparative risks
and benefits, and environmental pressures.

Alternatives—the more promising the chances for success in
the courtroom are compared with other political institutions,
the more likely an organization will pursue a litigation strategy.[3]
Resources—the lower the costs of participation and the more
important the interest or principle at stake are, the higher the
probability the organization will use the legal process.[4] *Risks*—
organizations will assess the *risks* of a disastrous court decision
harming organizational values relative to the benefits of a judicial victory; the greater the potential risks compared to the possible benefits, the less the likelihood of organizational involvement.[5] *Pressures*—lacking an important stake in the outcome of
the case, the organization will intervene only if important allies,
contributors, or supporters pressure it to participate.[6]

Organizational advocacy in *Bakke* largely confirmed these
hypotheses. Because the case was already well along in the judicial process, concerns about initiating litigation and the accompanying perils of an adverse court decision were not pertinent.
The amicus process itself helps minimize costs and risks while
emphasizing the potential rewards and benefits of participation.
Most organizations perceived the value of involvement as high.

For most organizations, the manpower costs of participation
were marginal. "In-house" legal staffs or private attorneys contributing their services wrote the briefs. The efforts of coalition-
building attorneys gave rise to "coalition-briefs"—briefs written by one or a few organizations and offered to others for their
endorsement—that made the cost of participation negligible for
those lacking the resources or interest to write their own briefs.

The costs of participation were not reducible to tangible resources alone. Involvement in a controversy with the emotional
and intellectual content of *Bakke* was likely to heighten existing
divisions in all but the most homogeneous organizations and
to strain relations among allies. Traditional collaborators such

as the American Civil Liberties Union and the American Jewish Congress found themselves on opposite sides of the issue, while organizations like the Equal Employment Advisory Council spent months working out agreements among their divided memberships on the position to be taken in the case. The costs of participation can be high if organizational involvement threatens to erode the foundations of trust and goodwill that are vital to most associations.

Organizations varied considerably in the degree of conflict characterizing their involvement in *Bakke*. In some cases, the decision to offer a brief was made without recognizing the dangers of participation. The Legal Service Corporation's troubles during its 1977 congressional reauthorization hearings were due in part to the staff's independent decision to submit a brief. Other organizations, like the National Legal Aid and Defender Association, did assess the risks of internal disruption, but intervened in *Bakke* because the rewards promised to be greater. The strong personal convictions of leaders like American Federation of Teachers president Albert Shanker often ensured that a brief would be submitted despite resistance from powerful chapters in the national organization. The confrontation over the position of the brief endorsed by the University of Pennsylvania was an episode in the continuing struggle between the university president and the faculty over the policy-making powers of the administration. In organizations like the NAACP, the brief was the result not of evasion, ignorance, or leadership domination, but of the victory of a majority over a dissenting minority.

The Lawyer as Leader

The role of the lawyer in the decision to participate is subjected to cursory treatment in most discussions of litigation politics. Typically, the lawyer is seen as facilitating a predetermined organizational purpose,[7] or as contributing to the actual decision solely in the role of a legal expert outlining a strategy for legal action.[8] Studies that emphasize lawyers as players in the organizational decision-making process tend to focus on them as legal experts with some secondary organizational roles rather than as

organizational leaders who also provide legal services.[9] Stuart
Scheingold describes the lawyer's ability to use litigation to
stimulate the "political mobilization" of unorganized or qui-
escent groups by enhancing their "sense of efficacy."[10] Robert
Borosage argues that litigation "can serve as a catalyst for political consciousness and organizing." Both caution that the
pursuit of social reform through changes in the law can undermine as well as strengthen organizational advocacy. It can unduly emphasize the importance of lawyers, relegating the clients
they represent to a position as secondary and passive "players"
in the "game" of litigation.[11] It can also drive "a wedge between
political allies" since victory in the courtroom often "depends
on establishing a personal entitlement and . . . [therefore] distinguishing one's cause from others with similar claims."[12] Despite these warnings, Scheingold and Borosage still largely deal
with the lawyer's nonlitigation activities as if they were ancillary to his or her function as a legal advisor.

Concentration on the instrumental tasks of the lawyer overlooks the variety of roles played by lawyers for amici organizations in *Bakke*. Many organizations found that the case presented questions that were not settled by existing policies. The
issue of affirmative action posed difficult choices among different
mixes of acceptable equalities and inequalities. Philip Selznick
suggests that, in situations where organizations are called upon
to adapt to new problems or demands, they will rely on "institutional" leaders. Unlike the managerial leader who concentrates on routine matters of organizational life, the institutional
leader is obligated "to define the ends of group existence, to design an enterprise distinctively adapted to these ends, and to see
that the design becomes a living reality." This creative type of
leadership emphasizes the need to develop policies for and consent within the organization.[13] Not unexpectedly, then, lawyers
were called upon to act not only as legal experts but as leaders
in the Selznick usage. They acted in an institutional rather than
managerial capacity, creating and enforcing policies.

Selznick's distinction between routine and creative forms of
leadership is difficult to assess in the concrete. More conventional measures of leadership such as the extent to which one

sets agendas or serves to aggregate support are more useful. If leadership is the power to initiate or set the agenda for organizational action, then lawyers were preponderantly the leaders of the amici organizations active in *Bakke*. Almost four-fifths of the respondents attributed the decision to intervene to the persuasive efforts of lawyers who were employed by, or were important allies of, the organization.[14] This statistic may be misleading since almost half (fifty-one of one hundred fifteen) of the organizations were either composed of lawyers as members (such as the American Bar Association) or pursued litigational objectives (such as the legal defense funds). However, in the sixty-four organizations not "legalistic" in membership or purposes, seventy-two percent of the respondents described the lawyers as the agenda setters.[15] Although the significance of the lawyer's role was diminished in nonlegal organizations, it was still seen as crucial in more than two-thirds of the responses.

Still, to define organizational leadership as the power to initiate action overlooks the quality of leadership which carries through action. Certainly the distinction between successful and unsuccessful leaders is their ability to aggregate sufficient support to defeat opposing views and to turn a proposal into a policy.

Table 5 presents data on those who played such "entrepreneurial" roles in *Bakke* amici organizations. Relatively few cared to characterize their organization as encouraging membership participation through formal mechanisms like convention debates and votes or by canvassing member sentiments. A larger group (thirty percent) preferred to label their organizations' policy making as a struggle among elites. The general membership played a more passive role in this situation as observers of the activities of rival leaders or staff groups. The "struggle" respondents generally represented bargaining organizations such as the Carter Administration, but a few were from oligarchic organizations like the American Federation of Teachers. (Ten of the one hundred nine "struggle" repondents were from such organizations: one from the ACLU, four from the American Federation of Teachers, three from the American Subcontractors Association, and two from the American Bar Association.) The

TABLE 5 Policy Making in Civilian- vs. Lawyer-Led Organizations

Characteristics of Policy Making in Organization	Members of Civilian-led Organizations[d]		Members of Lawyer-led Organizations[e]		Total Members	
Broad membership participation[a]	37%	(43)	3%	(7)	14%	(50)
Elite domination[b]	19	(22)	73	(180)	56	(202)
Struggle among elites[c]	44	(51)	24	(58)	30	(100)
Total	100	(116)	100	(245)	100	(361)

NOTE: Data on policy-making procedure were elicited by use of the following question: "How would you describe the type of process your organization used in authorizing its brief for *Bakke*?" (Probe: "Who (name, title, address) was responsible for getting the brief approved? Who (name, title, address) led the opposition to the brief?")

[a] Convention discussion or vote, formal or informal canvassing of membership sentiments, application of prior organizational policy clearly supporting brief's position.

[b] Decision made by executive officers and staff members.

[c] Conflict among different groups in the organization's leadership.

[d] Respondents describing the leader as non-law trained.

[e] Respondents describing the leader as law-trained.

largest number of respondents chose the "elite domination" label for their organizations. Such leadership domination was identified with organizations such as the Antioch School of Law, the National Council of Churches, and the United Farm Workers.

Sixty-eight percent of the respondents said that attorneys had acted as the leaders of the major groups within the organization struggling to win endorsement of a specific policy in *Bakke*. The lawyer-leader was especially prominent in organizations perceived as being dominated by elites. In other words, there was some association between the likelihood that an organization would display an oligarchic style and the presence of an attorney acting in a nonlegal capacity. This role as an aggregator of support for one position or another was not confined to lawyers in organizations with law-related purposes.[16]

The role played by lawyers in the decision to endorse a brief in *Bakke* contradicted the professional premise that the lawyer should serve in the capacity of a neutral expert. The American Bar Association's Code of Professional Responsibility demands that the client, not the lawyer, choose the legal action to be pursued. The lawyer may educate his or her client on the alternatives and their probable outcomes, but the decision to choose is reserved to the civilian, not to the legally trained advisor.[17] This standard of conduct is less rigorous in practice when lawyers serve an organizational rather than an individual client. As

full-time employees of an organization, lawyers have an opportunity to demonstrate their commitment to its goals and
their loyalty to its values. The resulting greater confidence in the
lawyer can allow him or her to play other roles for the organization: as a public relations expert; as an organizational representative before a court, a legislative committee, or an administrative agency hearing board; and as an "idea man" and policy
researcher. As the organization begins to rely on litigation to promote its interests, the nature of lawyers' tasks is transformed.
The lawyer becomes less an "individual counselor" and more
the "legal arm of the . . . organization."[18] Nevertheless, the lawyer is still seen as assisting rather than leading the organization's
members, providing them with "a fuller and richer participation in the legal process."[19] The lawyer is still the promoter of
another's goals. Even theorists sensitive to the opportunities for
persuasion inherent in an attorney's educative role see him or
her less as an independent leader than as a representative of a
set of values. Talcott Parsons argues that lawyers should not be
handmaidens to their client's whims, but should serve as a
"buffer between the illegitimate desires of [their] clients and the
social interest," charged with the duty of representing the "law"
as well as the client.[20]

Despite a persistent belief in the lawyer as a vehicle for professional values, the lawyer did act in an organizational capacity in
many *Bakke* amici groups. Did it matter that lawyers dominated the decision-making process in *Bakke*?

Data describing the attitudes of organizational leaders offering amici briefs in *Bakke* are not available. However, a comparison of the lawyer and civilian respondents to this study's
survey might provide some clues as to the similarities and differences between lawyer and civilian leaders. Respondents were
identified by other members of organizations as knowledgeable
about their organizations' activities in *Bakke*; many respondents served in elected or staff positions in those organizations.
One plausible way to assess the "fit" between civilian and lawyer leaders' views may then be to examine the responses of civilian (non–legally trained) and lawyer respondents.

In many respects, lawyer and civilian respondents were indistinguishable. They shared common socioeconomic backgrounds, claimed similar religious and political preferences, and exhibited comparable levels of education. The only pronounced difference was that of age (see table 6): civilian respondents tended to be older. However, when asked questions designed to elicit attitudes on the role of law and lawyers in the organization specifically and in society generally, the differences between lawyers and civilians were marked. Civilian respondents tended to be less sanguine about the relevance of litigation to organizational purposes and less confident in the ability of the legal process to change significant aspects of American life.

Responses to questions about the efficacy of the legal process and of legal training as enhancing problem-solving capacities tended to treat the law and the lawyer as contributors—but not the sole contributors— (see table 7, questions 1 and 2). Civilians, whether affiliated with law-related or with other organizations, stressed the relative unimportance of legal strategies and talents. Lawyers were more diversified in their responses, with those from organizations pursuing legal strategies somewhat more skeptical about the law's general effectiveness than lawyers working with non-law-oriented organizations. This paradox may be explained by the job-related frustrations of working for legal defense funds or service organizations. Daily contact with the ponderousness of the judicial process coupled to an awareness of the problems of compliance may prompt a clearer appreciation of the strengths and limitations of the legal process. In fact, the realization that changes in the law seldom produce changes in behavior has persuaded many lawyers to organize advocacy groups in order to create a supportive political base for change. The term "education" in the titles of the NAACP, Mexican-American, Puerto Rican, and American Indian legal defense and education funds suggest that they recognize the need to create coalitions of interest groups in support of the funds' activities. The Puerto Rican Legal Defense and Education Fund's legal director explained the fund's close ties with Aspira of America, the largest and oldest community agency serving Puerto Ricans, in terms of mobilizing political muscle: "We will be influential only if our clients are seen as being politi-

TABLE 6 Comparison of Backgrounds of Lawyer and Civilian Participants

	Civilian		Lawyer	
Religion				
None	15%	(31)	17%	(26)
Catholic	34	(70)	29	(45)
Protestant	31	(64)	30	(47)
Jewish	17	(34)	22	(34)
Other/ Declined to state	3	(7)	2	(3)
Total	100%	(206)	100%	(155)
Race				
White	65%	(133)	69%	(107)
Black	19	(39)	17	(27)
Spanish-surname	11	(23)	8	(12)
Other	5	(10)	6	(9)
Total	100%	(205)[a]	100%	(155)
Age				
Less than 30	10%	(21)	10%	(15)
30–45	29	(59)	43	(67)
46–60	53	(110)	44	(68)
Over 60	8	(16)	3	(5)
Total	100%	(206)	100%	(155)
Sex				
Male	62%	(128)	53%	(82)
Female	38	(78)	47	(73)
Total	100%	(206)	100%	(155)
Party affiliation				
Democratic	58%	(119)	62%	(96)
Republican	22	(46)	14	(21)
Independent	18	(37)	23	(36)
Other	2	(4)	1	(2)
Total	100%	(206)	100%	(155)
Ideology				
Liberal	31%	(64)	36%	(56)
Moderate	40	(82)	37	(57)
Conservative	28	(58)	26	(40)
Don't know/ Declined to state	1	(2)	1	(2)
Total	100%	(206)	100%	(155)
Income				
Less than $15,000	18%	(37)	9%	(14)
$15,000–24,999	26	(54)	31	(48)
$25,000–34,999	36	(73)	33	(51)
$35,000–44,999	13	(27)	10	(16)
More than $45,000	6	(12)	15	(23)
Declined to state	1	(2)	2	(3)
Total	100%	(205)[a]	100%	(155)
Years with organization				
Less than 5	22%	(45)	29%	(45)
5–10	37	(76)	40	(62)
11–15	27	(56)	25	(39)
More than 15	14	(29)	6	(9)
Total	100%	(206)	100%	(155)
Type of organizational affiliation				
Elected officer	38%	(78)	26%	(40)
Staff member	42	(87)	51	(79)
Regular member	15	(31)	11	(17)
"Ally"	5	(10)	12	(18)
Total	100%	(206)	100%	(154)[a]

[a] Missing datum

TABLE 7 Attitudes on Law and Lawyers by Legal Training and Orientation

Do you agree with the statement:	Agree[a]	Uncertain[b]	Disagree[c]	Don't know	Total
1. "The legal process can produce important social changes."					
Civilians					
legal organizations	23% (21)	37% (34)	39% (36)	1% (1)	100% (92)
nonlegal organizations	15 (17)	35 (40)	49 (56)	1 (1)	100 (114)
Total	18% (38)	36% (74)	45% (92)	1% (2)	100% (206)
Lawyers					
legal organizations	26% (25)	44% (43)	30% (29)	0% (0)	100% (97)
nonlegal organizations	35 (20)	40 (23)	24 (14)	2 (1)	101[d] (58)
Total	29% (45)	43% (66)	28% (43)	1% (1)	101% (155)
2. "Legal training equips the lawyer with the ability to solve many important social problems."					
Civilians					
legal organizations	30% (28)	41% (38)	27% (25)	2% (2)	100% (92)
nonlegal organizations	22 (25)	37 (42)	41 (47)	0 (0)	100 (114)
Total	26% (53)	39% (80)	35% (72)	1% (2)	101%[d] (206)
Lawyers					
legal organizations	34% (33)	46% (45)	20% (19)	0% (0)	100% (97)
nonlegal organizations	52 (30)	35 (20)	14 (8)	0 (0)	101[d] (58)
Total	41% (63)	42% (65)	17% (27)	0% (0)	100% (155)

[a] Respondents answering "strongly agree" or "mildly agree." [c] Respondents answering "strongly disagree" or "mildly disagree."
[b] Respondents answering "neither agree nor disagree." [d] Does not equal 100% because of rounding.

cally powerful. Litigation is our lever, but we need the base that Aspira provides to stand on."[21] Similar sentiments were voiced by several other lawyers active in the *Bakke* litigation.

When asked about the relevance of the law and the lawyer to their organizations' objectives (see table 8, questions 1 and 2), the civilian participants' answers tended to differ depending on the nature of the organizations' missions. Civilians from legal-oriented groups saw the relevance of legal training and processes as being more direct than did those from organizations pursuing goals not identified as legal. These differences proved more apparent than real, however, when the civilians were pressed to be specific in their definitions of an organization's objectives. Civilians in both law- and non-law-oriented associations agreed that lawyers performed the technical tasks of law well. The greater willingness of litigation-oriented organizations to perceive the law-trained as an important organizational resource is explained by the pertinence of legal skills to the organization's goals.

But was the *Bakke* controversy a legal issue in the narrow sense—involving a controversy over established rules recognized or made effective by a court of law? Or was it more broadly political or philosophical in nature, dealing with who we are as a community and with defining the responsibilities of a healthy society? (See table 9.) All interviewees recognized the political and philosophical ramifications of the case, but there was a tendency among respondents from law-related organizations to accept a "rule" distinction to the solution to *Bakke*. Both civilians and lawyers in these organizations were more likely to accept the idea that *Bakke* concerned the proper rules for deciding the acceptability of race-centered public programs than were the civilians from non-law-oriented associations. The lawyer respondents from the latter organizations also tended to identify the controversy over affirmative action as a contest between color-blind and remedial interpretations of the constitutional "rule" of equal protection. Why were lawyers and civilians from law-related organizations disposed to see *Bakke* as primarily a contest over differing judicial rules? Why were they willing to ignore the fact that the case operated at both levels of rules and politics?

Several sociologists have stressed the "limiting function of the end-in-view."[22] An organization's commitment to its goals will affect its perception of the world. The need to concentrate organizational energies limits the ability of organizational members to monitor non-goal-related aspects of their environment. This tunnel vision helps the members to focus their attention on the specific objectives of the organization, but at a cost. Commitments create a form of blindness, forcing an organization to proceed along a line of action with unforeseen consequences.[23] The particular blindness often afflicting legal institutions and actors is a concern with procedure over substance. The "end-in-view" of the law is not the attainment of some substantive outcome alone, but a commitment to acting within boundaries—to realizing goal X (e.g., justice) so as to minimize injury to values Y (e.g., due process) and Z (e.g., individual rights). The paradoxical conjunction among the lawyer and civilian respondents from law-oriented organizations of an alertness to the political

TABLE 8 Legal Training and Organizational Needs

Do you agree with the statement:	Agree[a]	Uncertain[b]	Disagree[c]	Don't know	Total
1. "My organization can depend heavily on the legal process to accomplish organizational goals."					
Civilians					
legal organizations	70% (64)	19% (17)	12% (11)	0% (0)	101%[d] (92)
nonlegal organizations	7 (8)	31 (35)	61 (69)	2 (2)	101%[d] (114)
Total	35% (72)	25% (52)	39% (80)	1% (2)	100% (206)
Lawyers					
legal organizations	52% (50)	27% (26)	18% (17)	4% (4)	101%[d] (97)
nonlegal organizations	48 (28)	26 (15)	17 (10)	9 (5)	100 (58)
Total	50% (78)	27% (41)	17% (27)	6% (9)	100% (155)
2. "Legal training is very important in helping solve my organization's problems."					
Civilians					
legal organizations	59% (54)	27% (25)	11% (10)	3% (3)	100% (92)
nonlegal organizations	27 (31)	21 (24)	52 (59)	0 (0)	100 (114)
Total	41% (85)	24% (49)	34% (69)	2% (3)	101%[d] (206)
Lawyers					
legal organizations	69% (67)	25% (24)	6% (6)	0% (0)	100% (97)
nonlegal organizations	40 (23)	39 (22)	19 (11)	2 (1)	100 (57)[e]
Total	58% (90)	30% (46)	11% (17)	1% (1)	100% (154)[e]

[a] Respondents answering "strongly agree" or "mildly agree."
[b] Respondents answering "neither agree nor disagree."
[c] Respondents answering "strongly disagree" or "mildly disagree."
[d] Does not equal 100% because of rounding.
[e] Missing datum.

TABLE 9 Perception of *Bakke* As a Legal Question

Do you agree with the statement:	Agree[a]	Uncertain[b]	Disagree[c]	Don't know	Total	
"*Bakke* is primarily a question of law, not of politics or philosophy." Civilians						
legal organizations	46% (42)	37% (34)	17% (16)	0% (0)	100%	(92)
nonlegal organizations	18 (20)	29 (33)	52 (59)	2 (2)	101[d]	(114)
Total	30% (62)	33% (67)	36% (75)	1% (2)	100%	(206)
Lawyers						
legal organizations	50% (48)	26% (25)	25% (24)	0% (0)	101%[d]	(97)
nonlegal organizations	45 (26)	43 (25)	12 (7)	0 (0)	100	(58)
Total	48% (74)	32% (50)	20% (31)	0% (0)	100%	(155)

[a] Respondents answering "strongly agree" or "mildly agree."   [c] Respondents answering "strongly disagree" or "mildly disagree."
[b] Respondents answering "neither agree nor disagree."   [d] Does not equal 100% because of rounding.

dimensions of litigation with the tendency to see *Bakke* as a debate over rules can then be seen as an expression of the "legalistic approach": "the structuring of . . . human relations into the form of claims and counterclaims under established rules, and the belief that the rules are 'there'."[24] And the propensity to view so important an issue as affirmative action as a question of duties and rights is thus not confined to the law-trained member alone.

I am choosing my words here with care. I realize I am invoking the much used and much abused concept of "legalism." The belief that *Bakke* posed a question of law—a search for the proper applicable rule or principle of constitutional interpretation—need not be legalistic. Legalism involves a particular attitude toward rules, a tendency toward the literal application of rules without consideration of the human or political consequences. It is legalistic to believe that *all* relations should be structured by established rules, but not to believe that *some* should. Nevertheless, in the context of *Bakke*, it was legalistic to rely on *legal* rules—judge- and lawyer-made rules—as solutions to the problems.

Bakke did not deal with matters of norm enforcement. Rather it challenged the two key political principles of our time: the principle of *non*discrimination (individual advancement according to individual merit) and the principle of *anti*discrimination (the humanitarian concern for victims of racial injustices).

To invoke legal rules to solve the social, political, and philosophical questions posed by *Bakke* does create an unwarranted dependence on a narrow set of concepts and ideas. And this dependence suggests another, more general explanation why laypeople affiliated with law-oriented organizations were susceptible to the claim that the case was a contest over legal rules.

Lawyers in the *Bakke* amicus process were inclined to see themselves as generalists while civilians tended to view lawyers as specialists. Although in general civilian participants were receptive to the lawyers' claim of expertise rooted in their technical competence, those civilians not affiliated with litigation-oriented associations tended to be more skeptical of this claim. More important was the willingness among civilian participants in litigation-oriented organizations to share their lawyers' perception of *Bakke* as a contest over rules. Given these civilians' distrust of lawyers' claims to be generalists, why did they subscribe to the myth of the expert generalist in *Bakke*? The answers lie in the special status accorded lawyers by respondents who saw the case as an issue in law, not as a broader question of politics and philosophy (see table 9).

The Myth of the Expert Generalist

Persistent in our legal and popular cultures is a belief in the lawyer as an expert generalist. The "expert" part of this belief follows from the perception that the lawyer possesses a unique skill and commands a special knowledge derived from his or her legal studies and professional experiences. The "generalist" portion flows from the notion that lawyers serve as the interpreters, the middlemen, in our society. One well-known critic of the legal process nevertheless praises the "generalist character of judges" and warns against deprecating the "generalist role" played by lawyers and judges "in a complex, highly differentiated society. The interpreter, the person who stands at the synapses and makes connections between subsystems and subcultures, is a vital part of any policy-making process."[25] This metaphor of lawyers as intermediaries in a communication network is a common characterization of their function. It promotes the image of the lawyer as an expert but disinterested broker of others' needs and interests. It emphasizes the skills in negotiation, conflict-resolution, and the analysis of questions from both sides of a dispute that lawyers develop through their studies and professional practice.

But lawyers are not generalists; most do not receive specialized training in disciplines apart from the law. While the curriculum of the modern law school often emphasizes the overlap between legal questions and problems in economics, philosophy, and public policy, lawyers seldom receive the type of intensive training in these disciplines that could provide them with independent expertise as economists, philosophers, or policy analysts. The lawyer-in-training is instructed in the practice of legal analysis with its propensity to emphasize hypothetical cases, the drive to cover the most extreme situation, and its focus on problems as questions or rights and duties. Moreover, "generalist" has two meanings, and the confusion implicit in the idea of an expert generalist is a product of confounding these meanings.

"Generalist" could mean the lawyer has the trained capacity to deal with many kinds of problems. This "strong" claim would imply that the lawyer is conversant in many disciplines' "languages" or perspectives and can use them to produce coherent policies on practical matters. Alternately, "generalist" could mean that the lawyer is subject to many different demands, and therefore he or she is obliged to respond to many different constituencies. This "weak" claim simply recognizes that the lawyer's function in American society is poorly defined. Unlike the "jack of all trades" premise of the stronger meaning of generalist, the weaker meaning suggests that the clear set of expectations and norms that delineate the roles of other professionals, such as the physician or the cleric, are absent for the lawyer. It does not support the assumption of a generalized talent or skill to deal with problems of broad social significance. If legal analysis is only one of many ways to deal with facts and to reason to conclusions, then the lawyer can not lay a unique claim to being a generalist under that word's stronger meaning.

There is another, perhaps more defensible, way of characterizing the expert generalist claim. Lawyers suggest that most of their important training comes after law school; as the lawyer moves from client to client, he or she acquires experience which transcends the client's concern about a particular interest. Lawyers also see themselves as operating at a low value-level which allows them to work with the fudged compromises implicit in the law and in most public discourse. Lawyers are experts in the art of the possible, developing skills in compromise and dispute settlement. And they know one strategy for coercion when all else fails—sue the opponent. They can claim to be generalists in the sense of being well-educated critics of what is laid before them; they are adept at translating abstract value claims into "common sense." But the essence of my criticism of the expert generalist claim is that lawyers are adept at thinking about means rather than ends. They may be induced to transform an organization's goals to fit the means they understand. The types of skills and experiences a lawyer develops tend to be procedural ones—skills in compromise and human relations. The experienced lawyer is more like the street-wise police officer or the talented politician than he or she is like other types of professionals. Lawyers tend to claim more than that they are expert negotiators. They claim a special status as the guardians of the Constitution, invoking the nature of law as a specialized language and the character of law as a repository of social values.

Several observers of the law and the legal profession have noted the capacity of legal language to provide a "secret" skill which distinguishes the trained practitioner from the uninstructed layperson. Philosophers of jurisprudence have argued that the ordinary language of the individual in the street and the specialized language of the law should be different in kind, not simply in degree.[26] Historians writing on the reformation of the American law school and of professional ethics and roles in the early twentieth century have commented on the apparent victory of the image of the lawyer as a social engineer and of law as a science conveying "mastery over the complex and disintegrating forces of social change."[27] Both radical critics of American law in the early seventies and less partisan specialists in linguistics have likened the law to a mystical process, complete with "arcane Latin phrases, elaborate rituals, and obscure pieces of paper" which "help to perpetuate the mystery of the Court and the priest-like status of the lawyer."[28] Others have suggested that the private and privileged character of the language has its own economy, serving as a medium to communicate technical knowledge efficiently among members of the profession while defining the boundaries of the profession.[29] Only well-trained professionals, or laypeople who go to considerable effort to master the language on their own, can make their way through the maze of the legal process.

But law is not only the special domain of the legal expert. It is also a repository of social values, a public resource providing an access to the history of a culture and a means to mold that culture's future. It constitutes a "resource of cultural value and creative power . . . whose use is unavoidably public in impact."[30] As a system of norms, the law is the product of the mediating forces of ideals and reality and thus can be neither an embodiment of pure principle nor a simple reflection of social structures, customs, or processes. All legal systems are required not only to offer intellectual elegance but to support a coherent set of interests and values. Due process, individual freedoms, and property rights are some of the values and interests protected by American law. Lawyers, as the professional guardians of the law, are accorded a special status as guardians of these values and interests. This status played an important role in *Bakke* (see table 10). An expert understanding of the law and the values it protects legitimated the lawyers' claim to decide the issues presented by *Bakke*.

Seen in this light, the amici briefs in *Bakke* could be interpreted as attempts to bridge the gap between the views and interests of the authoring group—lawyers employing the grammar and lexicon of their discipline—and the authorizing group—the organizations endorsing the briefs' positions. The briefs were attempts to express the perspective of the layperson through the specialized language of the legal expert. Inevitably, the success of these attempts was affected by the strengths and shortcomings of the professional guardians of the law.

Lawyers in many amici organizations capitalized on their spe-

TABLE 10 Lawyers As Expert Generalists in Amici Organizations

Role Played by Lawyers	Civilian Respondents	Lawyer Respondents	Total	
Guardians of the Constitution[a]	63% (47)	42% (35)	52%	(82)
Expert interpreters of the law[b]	33 (25)	57 (48)	46	(73)
Mechanics[c]	4 (3)	1 (1)	3	(4)
Total	100% (75)	100% (84)	101%[d]	(159)[e]

NOTE: Data elicited by use of the following question: "What special values or interests, if any, did the lawyers in your organization bring to the discussion of *Bakke* and the issue of affirmative action?" (Asked of those responding "Strongly agree" or "Agree" to question in Table 9.)
  [a] Respondents characterizing lawyers as protectors of constitutional values.
  [b] Respondents emphasizing the authority of lawyers as practitioners of the law.
  [c] Respondents describing lawyers in terms of their narrow, technical expertise or replying "none".
  [d] Total does not equal 100% because of rounding.
  [e] Total is 159 because of multiple responses.

cial status as "guardians" by taking the initiative in deciding whether a brief would be submitted and on whose side—Bakke's or the regents'. One example of this was the willingness of the lawyer-leaders in the American Association of University Professors (AAUP) to exploit their status as legal experts.

Peter Steiner, a Michigan law and economics professor, and at the time the AAUP's president, created an ad hoc committee of lawyers drawn from the organization's general council—William Van Alstyne of Duke Law School, Abraham Sofaer of Columbia, Kenneth Tollett of Howard, Terrance Sandalow of Michigan, and Matthew Finkin of Southern Methodist. The AAUP's general and associate counsels were also involved.[31]

The AAUP committee had no existing policy on which to draw in its deliberations. An April 5, 1977, memorandum to the committee's members listed sixteen "Association Policy Documents, Reports, and Resolutions which may pertain to issues raised by the *Bakke* case."[32] However, none of these statements dealt explicitly with affirmative action and the few that dealt with racially restricted admissions seemed to reject them.

The committee met frequently, sometimes in person, sometimes by telephone, during the first half of 1977. Van Alstyne urged that the AAUP should refuse to support quotas. But others, like Tollett, asserted that the matter was one best left to the discretion of individual university faculties. According to Tollett, *Bakke* posed a jurisdictional, not an equal protection, question. "I really wanted the Association to support California unequivocally. But I argued that the case affected the rights of faculties to determine their own admission standards. So long as no one was stigmatized by these standards, the Constitution was not involved. Moreover, we were making policy for university professors. The Association speaks for professors and their rights, not for students."[33] Sandalow, Finkin, and Sofaer supported Tollett, over Van Alstyne's vigorous dissent.

In a telephone conversation in late April, Van Alstyne warned Steiner that the upcoming Executive Committee meeting would be "raucous."[34] Van Alstyne was wrong. Steiner was able to persuade the Executive Committee in its May meeting to defer to the lawyers' expert judgment in this affair. One individual present at the meeting recounted Steiner's arguments. "He told the Executive [Committee] that the AAUP needed to make a statement and to do it swiftly. He urged acceptance of the *Bakke* committee's proposed brief. Faculty power over admissions, not racial quotas, was at stake here. He implied that the *Bakke* committee had done all the investigation that was necessary; the Executive should stand by that decision." Apparently, Steiner relied on a broader justification than *Bakke*'s threat to faculty autonomy. He also said that the question was a constitutional one, one best left to constitutional experts. At that point, Bill [Van Alstyne] objected—he said that the case was too important to be left to lawyers like him." Some members of the Executive Committee came to Van Alstyne's defense: "They feared *Bakke*, that quotas were a threat to the AAUP's principles of academic freedom and merit. They joined Bill and argued against any endorsement of the California program."[35]

The Van Alstyne position lost. Two AAUP respondents who voted to approve the brief saw *Bakke* as essentially a question of legal interpretation best left in the capable hands of the legal experts. The AAUP's brief was not released to the governing council until October 1977, four months after the brief had been filed with the Supreme Court.

The special role played by lawyers in the AAUP was not confined to that organization. Attorneys actively molded the stands taken by the national Fund for Minority Engineering Students and the ACLU. In each of these organizations, staff and private attorneys acted less as facilitators or coordinators than as commanders of organizational behavior.

The contrasts between lawyers as coordinators and as commanders are most striking in comparisons of the Equal Employment Advisory Council with the National Fund for Minority Engineering Students, and of the American Jewish Congress with the American Civil Liberties Union. The attorneys in the EEAC and the AJC were not afraid to become involved in their organizations' decision making, but their activities did not lead them to invoke their positions as lawyers to assert a right to settle the issue. The attorneys in the NFMES and the ACLU did so.

The EEAC legal staff sought to facilitate the expression of membership sentiment. They energetically produced the facts and ideas upon which the members of the executive and case selection committees drew in their discussion of *Bakke*'s ramifications. The members perceived their attorneys as facilitating and coordinating debate, not as dominating it. The paid counsel serving the NFMES, on the other hand, not only instigated that organization's participation in *Bakke*, but intentionally pushed the brief's statement beyond the fund's specific concern with the needs of minority engineering students. Shay and Marks admitted that they had used their position as legal advisors in order to strengthen Davis's case by enlarging the number and type of organizations endorsing its admissions program.

In the ACLU, lawyers served as the prime movers for the pro-Davis brief. Despite an intense and continuing disagreement among the elected leaders and members over affirmative action, the general counsel and the staff filed a brief without the general board's explicit approval of the brief's contents. Rather than facilitating organizational debate, they imposed a policy on the organization. The legitimacy of the attorneys' actions was not challenged, however, since the board acquiesced after the fact. The board had customarily delegated control over cases to the legal staff, and probably did so in this instance in order to foreclose the renewal of an intraorganizational conflict that threatened to rend the ACLU.

Like the ACLU, the lawyer-leaders in the AJC were the instigators of a brief, but unlike the ACLU and like the EEAC, the attorneys acted in a facilitative fashion. Both civilian- and lawyer-leaders valued the expression of contrary viewpoints, and, in the debate leading up to *DeFunis*, the members were routinely consulted and advised about the problems, choices, and consequences attending affirmative action. Broad agreement for backing Defunis's and Bakke's claims was carefully nurtured. Theodore Mann and the Commission on Social Action held strong personal and professional opinions about the cases, but they were committed to campaigning for the adoption of these opinions, not to the imposition of their views upon the American Jewish Congress.

Interviews with leaders and members of *Bakke* amici organizations suggest that the experiences of the AAUP, the NFMES, and the ACLU were representative of more organizations than were the experiences of organizations like the EEAC or the American Jewish Congress. Respondents from "oligarchic" organizations were more likely to entertain the notion that *Bakke* was a contest over legal rules rather than a broader dispute over general social values.[36] They were also more inclined to perceive the lawyer's role in larger terms.[37] This lends credence to the earlier speculation that a willingness to rely on the legally trained actor to make important decisions contributed to "oligarchic" behavior. Conversely, the same properties of restraint, dedication to member participation, and openness to different ideas and arguments that were identified as ingredients of the "democratic" style affected the activities of both civilian- and lawyer-leaders in those organizations.

The Costs of Lawyer-Leaders

The fact that the controversy over affirmative action first arose through the legal process, not through some other political process, undoubtedly accentuated the influence of the legally trained organizational leader. Nevertheless, the importance of the role he or she played in *Bakke* may be explained by factors other than context.

Bakke challenged many of the preconceptions of elite organization members. It is suggested that choices had to be made between values cherished by many Americans, the freedom to be judged on personal merit or need as against the right to be compensated for past or continuing unjust discriminations. By persuading civilians that *Bakke* should be viewed as primarily a "legal" issue—a controversy over what rule ought to be applied—lawyers appealed to their own status as legal experts and therefore to their claim to being expert generalists. Given the difficulties of deciding the *Bakke* question, the appeal of the idea of an expert generalist was intense. It promised that lawyers could construct a proposed rule that would settle the problem and enable one value to prevail over the other.

The persuasiveness of the expert generalist argument rests on the accuracy of characterizing *Bakke* as a conflict over rules. *Bakke* was not a conflict between preexisting rules, but a situation where new rules had to be created. The controversy over affirmative action was not the type of rule-bounded question susceptible to traditional jurisprudential understandings. Whether the Fourteenth Amendment's equal protection clause condones extraordinary exceptions to its individualistic, antiracist theme implicated a number of conflicting constitutional values. Since the grand principles of individual merit and of the humanitarian concern for the victims of racial prejudice were themselves challenged, a solution to *Bakke* could not be deduced from these major premises. *Bakke* presented a situation where the nation must develop new principles or radically recast old ones if the public's expectation of justice and fairness were to be satisfied. Citing the relevant rule was inapposite; the rule must be created, not simply interpreted.

If *Bakke* was a question of rule creation as opposed to rule application, then the appeal to the expert generalist and to the legalistic approach may have been fraudulent. Just as a court is least court-like when it legislates, so too the lawyer is least lawyer-like when he or she must apply the techniques of legal analysis to a non-rule-defined situation. The legal analyst cannot

claim a unique competence when creating new rules. The attorney is trained as an expert advocate, a training that does not
instill the capacity to be an objective assessor of contending values in concrete cases. The disciplines of economics, philosophy,
and policy analysis have at least an equal claim, and occasionally a superior claim, to decide in these circumstances. If *Bakke*
demanded redefinition of several major premises of American
life, then it required many types of expertise, not just one set of
experts, and therefore many types of leaders, not one type.

The prominence of lawyers in the *Bakke* controversy may also
explain an anomaly—the absence of the radical "group rights"
claim, the right of a corporate whole to exercise a power or
privilege independent of the rights of its individual members.

Despite the real differences in their views, both Bakke's and
the university's supporters focused on the importance of the individual. No participant or amicus organization endorsed or
gave serious attention to the concept of proportional representation of racial groups in the medical profession. The university
explicitly rejected that approach: "[P]roportional representation'—the notion of insuring representation of each group in
the student body in strict proportion to the percentage it com-
prises of the general population . . . is inapplicable. . . . The
Davis Task Force program makes no effort to achieve proportional representation."[38] In his defense of Davis's program in the
oral arguments before the Supreme Court, Archibald Cox went
even further. If the program were to "give rise to some notion of
group entitlement to numbers, regardless either of the ability of
the individual or of . . . their [*sic*] potential contribution to society . . . , I would first, as a faculty member, criticize and oppose it; as a constitutional lawyer, the further it went the more
doubts I would have."[39] Even the representatives of groups
likely to be most injured if Bakke's challenge were upheld
declined to argue a group-right position. The Black Students
Union of Yale Law School charged that Bakke, and not the supporters of the university, was asserting a "group right"; Bakke
was the party insisting that "by using [a racially oriented] classification, the school is denying a group [the white applicants] its
rights."[40]

Of course, relying on the literal meaning of statements such as these is dangerous. Some university supporters may have underplayed their preference for a group-rights position. The notion of group rights is radically redistributive; it demands a major restructuring of the ways in which resources and opportunities are apportioned in society. It promises both a group of new winners and losers and a new set of rules for the competition. The individualistic argument is distributive. Although new winners and losers may emerge, the competition continues on the basis of the traditional values of individual merit and accomplishment. If courts are perceived as susceptible to distributive arguments but resistant to redistributive ones, it is tactically sensible not to champion group rights. Other university supporters may have failed to recognize the group entitlement basis of their arguments for affirmative action. A claim for group rights may be implicit in any argument for minority representation. Of the 450 participants in the writing or approval of amici briefs interviewed, only one was willing to support proportional representation on a radical group-right basis.[41] All the others supporting the university saw racial membership as a convenient proxy for the individual's constitutional right to be free of racial discrimination. The group "stands" for the individual's right to be treated as an individual.

Organizations as forthright in their endorsement of statistical parity among the races as the National Conference of Black Lawyers did so not on the premise that such groups have a distinct right to a fair share of the medical profession but rather that in a race-blind society individual choices would naturally distribute physicians among racial groups in a random manner. The current unequal distribution of benefits and burdens among the races served in their view as evidence of invidious discrimination against individuals. For them, minority representation meant equalizing opportunities among groups as a short-term expedient for ensuring fair treatment of all individuals. Minority representation also seemed to promise a broadening of intellectual resources to the advantage of the whole society.

The litigants' and amici resistance to the radical group-right interpretation of equality was shared by all the courts involved in *Bakke.* The trial court judge quoted with approval a federal district court's judgment enjoining an affirmative employment program:

No one race or ethnic group should ever be accorded preferential treatment over another. No race or ethnic group should ever be granted privileges or immunities not given to every other race. There is no place for race or ethnic groupings in America. Only in individual accomplishment can equality be achieved.[42]

The California Supreme Court majority opinion adopted the language in *Shelley* v. *Kraemer* insisting that "the rights created by . . . the Fourteenth Amendment are . . . guaranteed to the individual. The rights established are personal rights." The guarantee of equal protection was meant to require members of all races to be "subject to equivalent burdens" and to benefit from equivalent opportunities.[43] Even the lone dissenter to the California decision reaffirmed the individualistic nature of the equal protection clause.

[T]he special admissions program did not contemplate, nor sanction, the admission of *unqualified* applicants simply because they were minorities. . . . [It] was implemented to serve the larger national interest of promoting an integrated society in which *persons* of all races are represented in all walks of life and at all income levels.[44]

The state, this opinion maintained, has a compelling interest in breaking down the artificial barriers to personal achievement by redressing the injustices of the past with preferences for the present. The majority and dissenting opinions thus endorsed the goals of individual achievement.

The federal court seemed as ignorant of the radical group-rights claim as the lower courts had been. Four justices declined to address the constitutional arguments at all. The five who did reach the constitutional issue split over whether the Fourteenth Amendment countenanced racially exclusionary processes. Although divided over the issue of means, they were united on the vision of the goal to be achieved: fairness to the individual. According to Justice Brennan, Davis's special admissions program "is consistent with the goal of putting minority applicants in the position they would have been in if not for the evil of racial discrimination."[45] Justice Marshall invoked the vision of "a fully integrated society, one in which the color of a person's skin will not determine the opportunities available to him or her."[46] While recognizing the need for "transitional" programs, Justice Blackmun wrote of his

earnest hope that the time will come when an "affirmative action" program is unnecessary. . . . Then persons will be regarded as persons, and discrimination of the type we address today will be an ugly feature of history that is instructive but that is behind us.[47]

Finally, Justice Powell expressed his commitment to "fairness in individual competition for opportunities":

The guarantee of equal protection cannot mean one thing when applied to one individual and something else when applied to a person of another color. If both are not accorded the same protection, then it is not equal.[48]

All five justices thus relied on the notion of equal opportunity.

Despite the absence of the "group-right" claim in the *Bakke* litigation, the idea of a group-oriented approach to attaining equality is not alien to America. The attractions of equal opportunity as the route to equality were diminished by the narrowed economic opportunities commencing in the late sixties. Moreover, American history is not void of occasions where group rights were treated as legitimate. The passage of the Wagner Act during the New Deal created special rights for a special group— "wage earners in industry"—and sought to equalize resources among competing groups.[49] Finally, and most important, arguments over group rights appeared in the pages of the *New Republic, Commentary, Change,* and in letters to the editors of newspapers like the *New York Times* and *Washington Post* at the same time that *Bakke* was being decided by the Supreme Court.

Why is American law blind to the appeals of group rights? The usual response in American legal thinking to the radical group-rights claim is to dismiss it as absurd. Laurence Tribe, a leading constitutional authority, finds it a "puzzling . . . proposition that a ban on denying 'to any person . . . the equal protection of the laws' . . . must be more concerned with justice to groups as collective wholes than with justice to individual human beings."[50] Even those who consider group rights plausible only give serious attention to the weak claim for group rights. Owen Fiss, for example, has proposed a "group-disadvantaging principle" to support preference programs. If a group forms a "natural class," possessing a unique identity in the public eye not reducible to the characteristics of any one member, and if its members are treated on the basis of the group identity and not on individual attributes, then the group may be the legitimate recipient of preferences. But Fiss makes it clear that the "natural class" is only a short-term expedient for identifying individuals who are deserving of "special solicitude." One of the justifications for the preferences is to "permit the fullest development of the individual members of the subordinate group." The new principle is thus more concerned with the group as a collectivity of disadvantaged members than with the rights of a group as a group. It is the aggregate claim of unjustly injured individuals that is vital in defining the group's claim to special treatment.[51]

The resistance of American law to group-rights arguments is limited to the area of racial or ethnic discrimination. In other areas of constitutional law, the courts have been willing to extend due process and equal protection guarantees to business firms, labor organizations, corporations, and trusteeships.[52] The acceptance of the independent status of economic association as an artificial "person" is not unique to American law; every society regards certain associations as legal entities.

American law accepts a group as a convenient device for protecting the individual against past and continuing discrimination, but it flounders when pushed to require statistical parity for groups as a right. It finds plausible a group's claim to affect the political process but rejects as absurd the claim to a share of any benefit as a right. According to much of American political teaching, politics is a process of group action and accommodation. Groups affected by a public program have a right to play a role in shaping and administering that program. But membership in such groups is seen as voluntary, overlapping, and changing. When the claim to rights and privileges as an identifiable group is voiced, American law lacks the capacity to accept the argument. Even as fervent a defender of affirmative action as the jurist Ronald Dworkin finds himself bound by the metaphor and forced to conclude "prejudice in official decisions is wrong, not because some group is worse off as a whole, but because it treats an individual with contempt."[53]

I have argued elsewhere that the inability of the law to entertain the group-rights claim is the product of neither ideology nor chance.[54] Instead, the answer is rooted in the types of metaphors American lawyers have developed to understand collective action. Specifically, the guarantee of equal protection to "persons" could not be extended to racial groups except as proxies for the individual rights of their members.

The limitations of the "person" metaphor bounded all the amici participants. No organization was willing to raise the group-rights argument in its brief. The expectation that the Court would find such an argument senseless made the claim irrelevant to constitutional litigation. This was true for organizations where lawyers served in coordinative and facilitative as well as command capacities. To an important extent, amici organizations were dominated by "law language." Organizations committed to robust debate were as susceptible to the power of this language as were organizations more oligarchic in their behaviors.

The explanation for this susceptibility is obvious but not satisfying. It is obvious that organizations seeking to exercise influence through the legal process are obliged to conform to the concepts and precepts of that process. In order to speak to lawyers and judges, one must "speak" the law. This explanation is not satisfying because it undervalues the special nature of *constitutional* as distinguished from other forms of litigation. Cases like *Bakke* are not civil suits in the normal sense of that term. They are exercises in preserving or remaking social, economic, and political arrangements. Courts do not legislate at the interstices of the law in cases like *Bakke*; they are molding the fundamental principles of a society. In a profound sense, constitutional litigation involves the continuing re-creation of a political regime. It deals with the fundamental make-up or essence of a political order, not with a dispute between aggrieved parties.

The value of constitutional discourse and decision in political dialogue is often justified by the moral influence exerted by the law on American life. But the Constitution "is not a mere lawyer's document, it is a vehicle of life, and its spirit is always the spirit of the age."[55] Debates among lawyers are not the same as those among philosophers or economists or congressmen. Law language narrows the debate and helps to simplify the complexities, but it may also impoverish public understanding of serious controversies. The contrasts between the richness, depth, and variety of ideas and arguments found in the public debate with the narrowness of the legal debate demonstrate the costs exacted by too heavy a reliance on the law to settle broad social issues.

This is not an indictment of the law. Legal reasoning promises plausibility, not certainty, for its conclusions. Nor is this a simple affirmation of the no longer novel insight that judicial decisions are poor mechanisms for resolving difficult problems. Its intent is far more modest: to remind ourselves that analyses of theories of equality are in large part evaluations and explanations of the power of political words. To look to the courts for guidance on affirmative action means to rely on the power of legal words to console or activate. Reliance on legal words forces a reliance on the conventions and contexts that the law uses to define what is sensible. But sensibleness has many meanings. What is legally sensible need not be synonymous with what is politically sensible. To rely excessively on the law's capacity to teach us about the difficult choices of public policy on affirmative action may foreclose the type of learning necessary to develop satisfactory—that is, politically prudent and responsible—answers on the issue. The dominance of lawyers as leaders and the limited conceptual capacities of law language made this broader form of education difficult to attain in *Bakke*.

Intellectual impoverishment was not the only cost of a reliance on the lawyer-leader. Losses in organizational vitality may also have resulted. Organizations that number their lay membership in the hundreds of thousands confront the problem of maintaining leadership accountability. The problem of accountability is especially acute for those organizations, such as the American Civil Liberties Union, where the members see themselves in supportive rather than participatory roles. In such organizations, the tendency for involvement in cases like *Bakke* to become lawyer-defined and controlled may make vigorous member participation in the organization's decision making even more difficult.

Litigation of any type, but especially through the amicus process, seldom motivates an organization's leadership to solicit membership views. Ideas, not votes, are seen to count in courtrooms. The leadership mobilizes an organization's intellectual resources, not its membership numbers. This general antiparticipatory bias of the legal process strengthens lawyers' predisposition to see themselves as the real actors in the judicial drama while relegating their clients to the role of paying spectators.[56] The bias fosters a distinction not only between the association's leadership and membership but also between the two sets of organizational leaders. The civilian leader is confined to the passive function of monitoring the actions of the expert legal practitioner. In fact, some civilian leaders expressed uneasiness with their organization's participation in litigation and suggested that lawyers were encroaching on the elected officers' prerogatives. Forty-three percent (eighty-nine of two hundred six) of the civilian respondents expressed apprehension about the growing influence of lawyers in the nonlegal decisions made by the organization. Interestingly, thirty-one percent (forty-eight of one hundred fifty-five) of the lawyer respondents voiced similar concerns. Perhaps this explains why the use of litigational devices like the amicus brief is still extraordinary for most organizations. Except for those organizations, such as the legal defense funds, already committed to litigation as a strategy, political participation through the legal process may unsettle many leaders. The reliance on the special expertise of an in-house legal staff or of attorneys providing *pro bono* aid may challenge civilian leaders' view of their own competence and hence their authority to lead.

There is no reason to subscribe to any sinister theory of conspiring lawyers attempting to usurp the authority of civilian leaders. The attorneys active in *Bakke* were, like their civilian colleagues, well intentioned and hard-working. Nor was *Bakke* unique in terms of the special prominence of lawyers as leaders. A century and a half ago, Tocqueville identified the bar as America's "aristocracy" and hoped that lawyers would serve as democracy's tutors.[57] Legal historians tell us that there has never been a golden age when lawyers were not involved in nonlegal roles either within organizations or in politics generally.[58] However, with the enormous changes in the practice of the law, the movement from an apprenticeship craft to a profession, and the growing assertiveness about rights and reliance on the courts to vindicate those rights, lawyers' opportunities to take advantage of nonlegal roles have increased. *Bakke* was one such opportunity.

Other studies suggest that *Bakke* was not an exceptional situation. Despite earlier research dismissing the importance of the role played by politicians with legal training, Engstrom and O'Connor discovered significant differences between the voting behavior of lawyer- and nonlawyer-legislators in the Louisiana House of Representatives.[59] Defending the pertinence of the "lawyer-dominance proposition," Albert Melone found that ninety percent of the delegates to the 1972 North Dakota Constitutional Convention saw lawyers as the dominant actors in the convention's proceedings.[60] It seems obvious that lawyers are acting in other situations as they did in *Bakke*. They are offering their special ways of enriching, and impoverishing, organizational decision making.

To some extent, this chapter's argument is an *ad hominem* one. It worries about an excessive reliance on lawyers and the law to settle the painful aspects of affirmative action. It argues for an extension of the debate over affirmative action to areas in addition to the legal, and it appeals to the commonsensical idea that problems like affirmative action are political and moral, not mere technocratic ones susceptible to legal skills alone. The 4–1–4 *Bakke* split in the Supreme Court, the specter of the Carter Administration's intensive infighting, and the widening division within the civil rights community all point to the conclusion that affirmative action cannot be resolved by ignoring the toughness of the issues involved or determined by the uncompromising victory of one side over the other. The unusually acrimonious language in the opinions of the Court in *Bakke*— the castigation of one another where more civilized modes of debate and expression of differences have traditionally prevailed[61]—suggests not only the limited ability of the courts to produce a persuasive and workable solution to this issue, but the attending necessity of involving the full competences of the political actors in erecting a structure of principle and interest capable of making defensible and desirable affirmative action policies.

CHAPTER VI

BEYOND *BAKKE*

B*akke* was neither the first nor the last affirmative action case to come before the Supreme Court. In its aftermath, the Court dealt with voluntary quotas in private employment and congressional "set-asides" for minority contractors. Although neither case attracted the public attention accorded *Bakke*, both were important in their own right. Given the magnitude of the economic and educational hurdles they must overcome, more minority members today could aspire to expanding job opportunities in blue-collar and skilled positions than to careers in the medical or legal professions.

United Steelworkers v. *Weber* was the next major affirmative action case. Brian Weber alleged that his rights to be treated without regard to race under Title VII of the 1964 Civil Rights Act had been violated by a craft training program administered by Kaiser Aluminum and Chemical Corporation and the United Steelworkers Union. The program reserved "for black employees 50% of the openings in an in-plant craft training program until the percentage of black craft workers in the plant is commensurate with the percentage of blacks in the local labor force." Justice Brennan, speaking for Justices Stewart, White, Blackmun, and Marshall, found the program permissible.[1]

Since the government was not involved, the case posed no "state action" question and therefore did not implicate the Fourteenth Amendment's equal protection clause. Instead, Weber's claims relied on the premise that Congress had outlawed all forms of racial discrimination in private employment when it wrote into Title VII the clause:

It shall be an unlawful employment practice for any employer, labor organization, or joint-management committee controlling apprenticeship or other training or retraining, including on-the-job training programs, to discriminate against any individual because of his race, color, religion, sex, or national origin in admission to, or employment in, any program established to provide apprenticeship or other training.[2]

According to Weber, the clear language of this act forbade even benign racial distinctions in employment training unless an authorized governmental body discovered a prior violation of the equal employment law.

Justice Brennan was unpersuaded. Relying on the "language and legislative history" of Title VII, he concluded it had not been Congress's intent to restrict private, voluntary experiments to "abolish traditional patterns of racial segregation and hierarchy" in employment. Since Congress had not specifically prohibited such experiments and since the Fourteenth Amendment did not apply, the actions of Kaiser and the union were unhindered by statutory or constitutional restrictions. Brennan acknowledged the possible abuses of such "benign" programs but found adequate safeguards in the challenged program. It did "not unnecessarily trammel the interests of white employees." No whites were fired to make places for blacks. Weber lost nothing he already possessed, only the opportunity for something more. Nor did the program impose "an absolute bar to the advancement" of whites; half the trainees were white, and Weber retained a chance for advancement. The program was a "temporary measure"; once the "manifest racial imbalance" in the labor pool was eliminated, the program would cease.[3]

The status of *Weber* is troublesome. The decision was five to two; two justices did not participate. Justice Powell was ill and unable to attend oral arguments, and Justice Stevens excused himself, reportedly because his former Chicago law firm did legal work for Kaiser. Based on their positions in *Bakke*, and later in *Fullilove* v. *Klutznick*, one might argue that their participation in *Weber* could well have reversed the Court's decision. As it was, Justices Rehnquist and Burger dissented, finding that the language, intent, and meaning of Title VII indicated "*no* racial discrimination in employment is permissible."[4] While voting with the Brennan majority, Justice Blackmun stated he shared some of the dissenters' "misgivings."[5] Since Stevens had written one of the plurality opinions in *Bakke* and was to offer a trenchant indictment of the majority holding in *Fullilove*, his participation might have changed Blackmun's vote and transformed a five to two victory for affirmative action into a four to four split, letting stand Weber's victory in the Fifth Circuit Court of Appeals.

Fullilove v. *Klutznick* was the next challenge to an affirmative action program. As part of the 1977 Public Works Employment Act, Congress set aside ten percent of the appropriations for minority contractors and subcontractors in public works projects. As in *Bakke*, the Court splintered into two plurality opinions, upholding the congressional set-aside by a six to three vote. Chief Justice Burger wrote one of the plurality opinions, holding that the set-aside constituted a "reasonably necessary means of furthering the compelling governmental interest in redressing the discrimination that affects minority contractors."[6] Speaking for himself and Justices Powell and White, Burger emphasized the breadth of congressional power to act against past and present discrimination. The special status and power conferred upon Congress by the spending and commerce clauses of Article I and the enabling clause of the Fourteenth Amendment allow Congress to act without the type of evidentiary record which a court or administrative agency would need to justify its action. Moreover, the scope of remedial powers granted Congress was greater than those given to the courts. Courts are authorized to act only when there is a constitutional or statutory violation; Congress is empowered to ferret out social evils. Burger stressed the programmatic justifications for the program: First, it was completely voluntary; no one was forced to apply to it. Second, the set-aside requirements were not inflexible; 1,261 waivers had been granted where the program's objectives could not reasonably be met.[7] The burden of the preferences fell "relatively lightly" on "innocent parties"; only .25 percent of all funds expended on construction in the United States was affected. And this policy did not seek to elevate any racial group to a superior position; it sought only to rectify an obvious inequality. For these reasons, Burger insisted that Congress was not compelled to "act in a wholly 'color-blind' fashion" and that its program passed muster under the strictest standard of equal protection.[8]

The plurality opinion offered by Justice Marshall and joined by Justices Brennan and Blackmun, applied the less demanding standard Brennan had adopted in *Bakke*. According to Marshall, "the racial classifications employed in the set-aside provision are substantially related to the achievement of the important and congressionally articulated goal of remedying the present effects of past discrimination."[9] Congress's actions were therefore constitutional.

Burger and Marshall were willing to defer to Congress's expertise and powers in this area of social policy, but the dissenting justices were not. Justice Stewart, joined by Justice Rehnquist, argued that *Fullilove* had reestablished the discredited *Plessy* v. *Ferguson* rule of preferences "based on lineage"—of a "government of privileges based on birth." No matter how immense the breadth of spending, commerce, and Fourteenth Amendment enforcement power granted to Congress, it was still bound by the restrictions of the Constitution. The same "color-blind" principle imposed on the states by the Fourteenth Amendment was imposed on Congress by the Fifth Amendment.[10] Stewart insisted, therefore, that if "a law is unconstitutional, it is no less unconstitutional just because it is a product of the Congress of the United States."[11]

Justice Stevens's dissent in *Fullilove* was even stronger than Stewart's. He could find no basis for the preferences in the Constitution or in the pragmatics of politics. "Because racial characteristics so seldom provide a relevant basis for disparate treatment, and because classifications based on race are potentially so harmful to the entire body politic," extraordinary purposes must be offered to support racially-based preferences. If the set-aside was intended as a reparation to racially injured groups, then the precepts of justice require that it be distributed among the "members of the injured class in an even handed way." But not all minority groups have an equal claim to preferences; Spanish-speaking individuals and Indians, for instance, lacked the history of injuries that would warrant similar treatment with blacks in the program. Moreover, it is the *least* disadvantaged of the minority group which stands to reap the largest benefit from this "perverse form of reparations." It is the successful, middle-class members who have the resources to take advantage of the set-asides, while "those most disadvantaged" and suffering the greatest "consequences of past laws" receive nothing. Not only had the dictates of justice been ignored, Stevens wrote, but the set-aside threatened to establish "a permanent source of justi-fication for grants of special privileges."[12] Stevens seemed an-gered by the absence of a "merit" basis to this program. At least the Davis program contested in *Bakke* sought minority students who were qualified to pursue professional studies and who promised to enrich education and society.

Fullilove differed in important respects from its predecessors. It touched upon the enormous discretionary powers of Con-gress, not the parochial decisions of an isolated school faculty or the private negotiations between a corporation and a union. The built-in checks afforded the national legislature (committee structures, the norms of accommodation and compromise, the bicameral division, the concurrence of the executive) would seem to assure that whatever policy survived the hurdles of law making would be sensitive to the multiplicity of interests and principles at stake. Perhaps this explains why the Chief Justice endorsed this form of affirmative action after rejecting all the others.

Bakke, Weber, and *Fullilove* suggest that members of the Court are cautiously feeling their way through the affirmative action thicket. Employing a trial-and-error learning strategy, the members seem to be receptive to new learning opportuni-ties. Nor did the amici organizations reject these new oppor-tunities to voice their convictions and concerns.

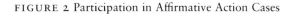

FIGURE 2 Participation in Affirmative Action Cases

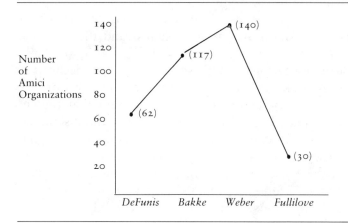

Weber attracted even more amici participation than *Bakke* had. The number of organizations offering amici briefs rose from one hundred seventeen in *Bakke* to one hundred forty in *Weber* (see figure 2). Much of this increase can be attributed to the many unions or union-affiliated organizations that rushed to support the United Steelworkers. Organizations like the Coalition of Black Trade Unionists and the National Union of Hospital and Health Care Employees which were not present in *Bakke* were in *Weber*. The AFL-CIO mobilized its constituent unions to defend the Steelworkers' claim to an unfettered collective-bargaining right.

Not only was the number of participants greater, so was the sophistication of their organizing efforts. The National Conference of Black Lawyers, the National Lawyers Guild, and the Center for Constitutional Rights established an Affirmative Action Coordinating Center to serve as a clearing house for arguments and facts supporting affirmative action.[13] Conservative legal defense funds such as the Southeastern Legal Foundation, the Washington Legal Foundation, and the United States Justice

Foundation intervened to assist the Pacific Legal Foundation's arguments in support of Brian Weber.

Noteworthy for their absence in *Weber* were Jewish organizations like the American Jewish Congress and the American Jewish Committee. Although no less opposed to quota-based affirmative action programs, these organizations declined to participate. A spokesperson for the American Jewish Congress explained why. "There was a strong possibility that the employer, Kaiser Steel, has indeed been guilty of racial discrimination against blacks. Before the training program was put into effect, there were only five black craftsmen out of 290 in craft positions at the Kaiser plant." While fearing that a court "decision upholding the quota . . . would permit virtually unlimited resort to race-conscious employment practices," the AJC's concern about Kaiser's past employment practices persuaded it that "supporting Brian Weber and condemning the Kaiser quota system would mean opposing race-conscious remedial action in a situation where it could be necessary and appropriate—that is, at the plant of a national corporation that may have engaged in illegal discrimination." [14]

While the struggle over affirmative action continued in the courts, the differing sides were searching for some common ground outside the legal process. Between *Bakke* and *Weber*, there were at least two major conferences where representatives from opposing organizations sought to establish a new consensus. In November 1978 the seventy-seven member-organizations of the Leadership Conference on Civil Rights recommitted themselves to the establishment "as a matter of right" of "education to the limit of each person's ability." [15] In the preceding month, the Anti-Defamation League joined with several of its antagonists in *Bakke*—the NAACP Legal Defense Fund, the Mexican-American Legal Defense Fund, and the University of California—in renewing its dedication to the proposition that education is one of the most important forces breaking down "barriers to equal opportunity" and that remedial programs coupled to "individualized admissions procedures" were the wisest means to overcoming racial disadvantage in higher education. Along with the American Council on Education, these four organizations formed the Committee for Equal Educational Opportunity to work toward expanded access to higher education, stating "We are determined to press toward our goal, because we are convinced that the future course of American society is inextricably linked to the equal opportunity of its members—because it is right."[16] Even before the Supreme Court handed down its decision in *Bakke*, representatives from the Anti-Defamation League, the United States Justice Department, the Association of American Law Schools, and Harvard University met under the auspices of the Education Commission of the States and the Justice Program of the Aspen Institute to discuss common concerns and to reestablish a dialogue among their organizations. As one participant said, "Whatever the court decided, we need the best ideas that can be generated by all of the interested parties."[17] The agreement formed in these meetings emphasized programs like that of the Council on Legal Education Opportunity. Individualized help offered in a non–racially exclusive manner was one of the few ideals shared by participants on both sides of the *Bakke* controversy.

Considering that many of the organizations active in these meetings were democratic ones in *Bakke*—and many of these were integrative as well—*Bakke* may have been one episode in a continuing process of education. The same factors prompting an openness to internal debate and discussion may have helped facilitate debate and perhaps learning among organizations.

Litigation and Education

Education involves talking and thinking. It depends upon the exchange of ideas, facts, and perspectives. But not just any kind of exchange suffices; as the experienced teacher knows, education must be challenging but not intimidating. The ideas, facts, and perspectives which are the materials of education must be presented in the right manner—sufficiently clear to be understood, sufficiently contingent to encourage reflection.

Amicus litigation would seem a promising forum for education. Amici briefs help the courts to overcome some cognitive limitations of the legal process. Although the courts have assumed the role of the principal moral forum for the nation, the institution where the great social issues of the day are ventilated, their ability to meet this role is frustrated by the adversary nature of normal litigation. Issues implicating vast networks of social and political relations are framed in the context of *A* vs. *B*, forced into the mode of two-party disputes wherein important third- and fourth- and fifth-party interests may be overlooked. The very strength of the legal process—its ability to simplify complex abstractions through the analysis of concrete cases—constitutes its most fundamental weakness. Some issues resist this simplifying and clarifying process; their resolution demands sensitivity to a multiplicity of facts, values, and prospectives posed by the problem. Affirmative action was such an issue.

Through the use of the amici process, organizations and individuals can learn about the facts and arguments which reflect the broader social significance of issues otherwise narrowed by the contest between two specific interests. The amicus process therefore promises to facilitate the legal process's role as a major forum for national education. But did it do so in *Bakke*? The answer is, not often.

Analysis of the literature dealing with political education suggests that conflict that nourishes discussion and participation that fosters responsibility encourage the mutuality, sensitivity to consequences, and principled action which is political education. Few organizations seemed capable of meeting this burden. Often conflict was so highly polarized that debate was diminished and opportunities for education were denied. In many organizations, members were treated as contributors and not as participants. In the American Civil Liberties Union, for example, members seemed more devoted to a symbolic affirmation of certain values than they were committed to participating in specific policy processes. Members in other organizations appeared more concerned with the material goods the organization delivered than with the promotional causes the organization pursued.

The opportunities for the right kinds of debate and exchange were frequently frustrated by organizational needs such as survival and identity. The realities of organizational existence may outweigh the instrumental roles played by an organization when policy must be formed. At times, a broad social issue may become entrapped in a more pressing organizational consideration, as in the debate in the University of Pennsylvania over who governs the university. Frequently, litigation in *Bakke* provided the opportunity for leaders to expound preexisting views rather than to reflect upon them; litigation served as a forum for the declaration of positions, not for dialogue. It would seem that oligarchy is a more likely behavior than democracy in elite organizations. There were, however, some positive findings. Fears that highly bureaucratized organizations will prevent democratic behaviors were unfounded in *Bakke*. Bureaucratization need not be accompanied by oligarchy. Nor need large size preclude education. Large organizations were no less able to encourage democratic policy making than were small organizations. Leadership style, not structural properties, best explained organizational behavior in *Bakke*.

If *Bakke* was a case of litigation as education, does it teach lessons of a broader application?

Can Courts Teach?

The most striking feature of American politics is our reliance on judges to decide great social issues. We invest faith in the courts, attributing to them qualities that are majestic. No doubt our willingness to turn to the courts as the first step in a strategy to change our world, rather than as a last resort,[18] reflects a belief that somehow courts can provide a quality lacking in other political institutions: the commitment to principle above interest. The frequent allusions in the United States to courts as teachers or as moral forums are expressions of this faith.

Bakke teaches that the court's abilities to instruct may be more limited than we suppose. If the participants in litigation rarely learn, rarely reflect on the alternatives, then the more passive audience of the public may never learn. We may expect too much of courts and the legal process, and, in turn and paradoxically, too little of the political process.

Richard Kluger has argued that "law in a democracy must contend with reality. It has to persuade. It has to induce compliance by its appeal to shared human values and social goals." No doubt he is right, but Kluger goes on to identify the Supreme Court with the "law." "The Justices stood at the very interface of man's susceptibility to destructive private impulse and his longing for reasoned social order."[19] This equation of the activities of courts and lawyers with the "law" is mistaken and misleading. If "law" has something to do with the exercise of power in a context of agreed upon rules and procedures and directed at the achievement of values which affect us all, then the "law" implicates all the formal parts of the political process—executive and legislative as well as judicial. In fact, the issue of the "lawful" status of affirmative action did engage the attention of such members of Congress as the Black Caucus. More important, the issue was subjected to a rich and robust debate in the national media and stimulated demonstrations in the streets, and discussions in university classrooms, industrial workplaces, and social clubs. Education was more likely to occur in these less formal surroundings than in the ritualized confines of the judicial process.

Affirmative action was an important issue before the *Bakke* case, but it had not previously attracted the volume of national attention that it did when this case came before the Supreme Court. The power of the judicial process to place items on the public agenda, to force attention to difficult or worrisome problems, is one reason why we value our courts in a special manner. But if *Bakke* stimulated discussion, it may also have impoverished it. As Chapter 5 showed, a reliance on judicial concepts and logic can be costly. That so large a number of individuals and organizations were mobilized by *Bakke* was a positive contribution of the judicial process; that they were mobilized in so restrictive a debate was one cost of litigation.

What Did *Bakke* Teach?

According to the paradigm underlying contemporary policy analysis, "values" expressed as principles or interests are translated, in part or in whole, into "policies" which correspondingly produce "results," some expected, many unexpected. The measure of a policy's effectiveness is the degree to which the results realize the values that justify the policy. Unfortunately, when we attempt to create a workable set of public policies dealing with questions like equality, we have insufficient data to determine the effectiveness of those policies by analyzing their results. We are either forced to guess where we are likely to end up if we pursue those policies or we must attempt to assess the quality of those policies by means other than product analysis.

One way to criticize public policies on equality is to examine the process by which those policies were developed. Problems met in developing defensible policies on the issue may help to uncover and explain the ambiguities, contradictions, and planned and unplanned consequences inherent in those policies. In other words, the problems that confronted attempts to formulate workable policies on the question of equality, the story of the disagreements and hammered-out compromises within the advocacy organizations involved in *Bakke*, may help us assess the merits of specific notions of what equality ought to require in contemporary American politics. Although this may be no more than a case study in American elite group thinking on equality, it may nonetheless serve to instruct us on the larger values at stake in the debate over equality.

Every regime is a testing ground for theories about men and their relationships with one another. *Bakke* was one such test. One way to analyze the ideas at contest there is in the light of the imperatives of politics itself.

Political action is a product of the interplay between at least two sets of values or beliefs. *First-order beliefs* are those primary values which tend to activate political behavior; they form the conceptual framework within which individuals think about things political. By contrast, *second-order beliefs* are those values and ideas which guide political action. Beliefs on the character of equality, democracy, and human freedom are second-order beliefs; they provide guidelines for action in specific cases, although they may themselves be ambiguous in their meanings.

Perhaps the most crucial first-order beliefs implicated in the controversy over affirmative action are those reflecting individual perceptions of human nature. Is man primarily a "good" creature, needing the proper nurture to realize his capacities, or is he essentially an "evil" being, one who requires discipline or is otherwise condemned to a life that is "solitary, poor, nasty, brutish, and short"? These "first-order" notions of human nature carry with them concomitant visions of what constitutes the proper ordering of human relationships and hence of the "good society" and government. Visions of what man's nature *is* affect visions of what men's relationships with one another can and will be.

Although one can trace the roots of these two perspectives at least as far back as Plato's discussion of the multiple natures of men in Book VII of *The Republic*, contemporary studies of American politics provide a more immediate lexical source. Commentators on American politics and political thought such as both Louis Hartz and Robert Dahl emphasize accommodational consensus as the hallmark of American politics. Conflict among men is ameliorated by the informal pressures of social norms and conformity.[20] By contrast, those who see the natural state of human relationships in terms of conflict among individual interests, and harmony as imposed by an external sovereign power, look to institutional forms of constraint as means to discipline the warfare that is human society.[21] In actual fact, of course, the American political system is based on both perspectives. For every assertion that man is by nature "ambitious, vindictive, and rapacious,"[22] in that most basic theoretic document on the American system, *The Federalist Papers*, there is a counterassertion that "there are other qualities in human nature which justify a certain portion of esteem and confidence."[23] The tension between the consensual- and the imposed-order orientations to the problem of human politics accounts in part for the bewilderment of those who attempt to explain American democracy through the categories of "liberal versus conservative" or "egalitarian versus libertarian"—beliefs that are second-order reflections of first-order orientations.

Clearly, the second-order beliefs take on their particular complexions from the character of the first-order orientations prompting them. For example, two orientations to the second-order belief in democracy can be differentiated. One reflects the "absolutist" tradition that views democracy as an end-in-itself, arguing that "each and every adult has the right to participate in political life because such participation is held to be a necessary element in his self-development."[24] Then there is the tradition, cited above, that sees democracy as an instrumental device to check each man's avarice and selfishness by the countervailing power of other men, since no one can ever be trusted to act other than upon his narrow self-interest.

Correspondingly, those who adhere to specific public policies may choose to do so because of a consensual- or imposed-order orientation to the world. The person prompted by a consensual outlook might champion welfare reform out of the conviction that a guarantee to subsistence income will free the individual to deal with loftier concerns than hunger or cold. The believer in imposed order, on the other hand, might pursue welfare reform as a device to purchase social peace from the poor by redistributing a portion of the economic pie. Superficially similar policy stances mask strikingly different perspectives on politics. Moreover, notions about the comparative virtues of the principles of equality and liberty in actual policy decisions reflect higher-order beliefs than simple differences between egalitarians and libertarians. To reduce *Bakke* to the antithesis "equality versus liberty," is to run the risk of parodying the real sources of division among the parties.

The most interesting and instructive differences among the *amici* organizations were not found in the expected disjunction between the pro- and anti-Bakke camps. The anticipated differences between the defenders of the University of California, Davis Medical School and the supporters of Allan Bakke's attack on the special admissions program were not as significant as the contrasting views *within* each bloc. What on the surface appeared to be a common adherence to the same activating principles on inspection became different perspectives producing only superficially similar public statements. In many respects, the position taken by the American Civil Liberties Union, which submitted a brief in support of the University of California, was closer in philosophic temper to that espoused in the American Jewish Congress's brief supporting Allan Bakke than to the NAACP's brief defending preference programs. On reflection, perhaps it should not be surprising to discover that ostensible allies often disagree more fundamentally than do official opponents. And these fundamental disagreements are often due to the influence of two very different perspectives on, or first-order beliefs about, the nature of human community.

All the amici briefs defended the value of individualism. However, they differed as to the status of that value: was individualism an end in itself or a means to an even more important value? A consensual orientation emphasizes the former. Organizations like the American Jewish Congress and the American Civil Liberties Union saw society as a product of individual talents and actions. Absent the distorting influences of factors such as racial identification, a healthy society would consist of consensual exchanges among free individuals. Both endorse "the ideal that all individuals are equally to count in society." [25] The consensual orientation is thus an expression of classic liberalism.

Organizations like the NAACP and the Italian-American Foundation, while differing on the specifics of Davis, nevertheless endorsed an instrumental notion of individualism. While not rejecting individual liberty, these organizations were sensitive to what they perceived to be the real nature of society. Individual merit is often a cover for entrenched interests. Those who are successful define what constitutes merit. Emphasizing individual merit means emphasizing the biases in current distributions of economic and social power and status. Therefore, power is necessary to check power, and the government is obligated to step in to rectify gross and enduring disparities in the powers of different groups. Thus the NAACP quoted from the Minority Report on Title VI of the Civil Rights Act:

". . .when legislation is enacted designed to benefit one segment or class of society, the usual result is the destruction of coexisting rights of the remainder of that society. One freedom is destroyed by governmental action to enforce another freedom." [26]

While a society of consensual individualism may be an attractive ideal, it is an unattainable one given the nature of human avarice.

The actual differences between these two perspectives on affirmative action are subtle ones. They are not as clear as the usual caricature of the conflict over affirmative action as a collision between "equal opportunity" and "equal results." If the controversy was in fact the reflection of a more fundamental struggle between world-views, then the debate at the level of principles is probably unresolvable. And if the past predicts the future, the uneasy coexistence of these two perspectives in American thinking suggests that neither perspective will ever be wholly victorious. The more probable resolution to the issue of affirmative action may be one founded in compromise, in some sort of pragmatic adjustment between the contending views. Perhaps Justice Powell's opinion in *Bakke* was a better prediction of what will happen than what ought to happen.

Powell's efforts to reconcile the value of nondiscrimination with the necessities of effective minority access to educational and employment opportunities were criticized by both sides as legitimizing subterfuges for racial preferences. Powell's acceptance of "the competitive consideration of race and ethnic origin"[27] will only drive "the Davis type of program underground," charged Nathan Glazer. "The fact is that in any system that goes beyond test scores and grades it is impossible for racial and ethnic considerations not to play a role in admissions." But Glazer, unlike other Powell critics, went on to urge that "despite these and other powerful substantive arguments against 'any consideration' of race and ethnicity, I believe we must accept Justice Powell's position. In a multi-ethnic society, while we would not want government to prescribe the degree of such considerations by imposing quotas and goals, we would want individuals and institutions to take these factors into account voluntarily and by their own lights. In a typical example, we would not want government to require a balanced ticket, but we would want the good sense of political leaders to operate so that all groups get political representation."[28]

Glazer is appealing to the peculiarly American brand of hardheaded practice we call pragmatism. Implicitly he urges us to reject publicly affirming the legitimacy of quotas absent a judicial, administrative, or legislative finding of a specific racial wrong. Such an affirmation would legitimize a principle which many would not want to universalize. But we should not attempt to confine social needs in too rigid a set of principles. Sensitive considerations of minority status coupled to informal quotas are realistic measures to accomplish change. What we refuse to do explicitly perhaps we should do implicitly.

Here may be the basis for a new, albeit unstated, consensus. It is the type of compromise many may find attractive. It promises some meaningful access for minorities while not threatening the nondiscrimination principle that so many value. Nor need such a pragmatic policy endanger the status of the law as an embodiment of higher ideals. That we occasionally must do things under the table which we would not recommend as an explicit public policy indicates the high regard in which we hold those ideals. Ideals provide guidance; they can not and should not be seen as blueprints for action. They provide goals to be enacted, but they cannot specify how those goals are to be achieved. This is the power of ideals in political action—what Hanna Pitkin has called the salutary and "continuing tension between ideal and achievement." [29] They prompt us to act, but they leave us the freedom to choose how and when to act.

This was the lesson taught by *Bakke*. None of the choices was fully satisfactory; each exacted costs as well as offered benefits. But choices must be made in politics, even if those choices are limited to unpalatable alternatives. That democratic organizations did struggle to make those choices in an informed manner, despite the stresses of controversy, suggests we are willing to learn—and that litigation, despite its limitations, can sometimes teach.

APPENDIX:
A NOTE ON METHODOLOGY

The classifications I have used in this study were obtained in the following ways:

Interest Orientation (Structure of Interest)

Interest groups are organizations that intervened in *Bakke* to protect the specific material interests or opportunities of their members. Interest group indicators used were: (1) organization members expected to benefit or suffer materially by the validation of racial preferences (American Subcontractors Association, the National Association of Minority Contractors, the Fraternal Order of Police); (2) organization members wholly employed in implementing, supervising, or coordinating affirmative action programs (Equal Employment Advisory Council, National Association of Affirmative Action Officers); (3) organizations that operated voluntary affirmative action programs and intervened specifically to protect those programs (University of Washington, Harvard, Stanford, Council on Legal Education Opportunity); (4) organizations that participated in order to defend their members' professional rights to make decisions, including granting racial preferences in admissions (American Association of University Professors, Association of American Law Schools, Association of American Medical Schools).

Minority defense organizations are organizations that participated in order to defend the values and interests of large groups of individuals sharing cultural or other intangible social ties. Indicators of minority-defense status were: (1) organizations perceived themselves (and were popularly viewed) primarily as spokespersons for, or legal defenders of, a specific cultural or racial group (National Association for the Advancement of Colored People, Mexican-American Legal Defense and

Educational Fund, American Jewish Congress); (2) social organizations were composed of homogeneous racial or ethnic memberships (Order Sons of Italy in America, Polish-American Congress); (3) organizations were not usually identified with a racial or ethnic constituency but leaders justified their intervention in *Bakke* on the grounds that minorities deserved special assistance (American Medical Students Association, American Coalition of Citizens with Disabilities).

Public-interest advocates are associations that promote causes or values and that are made up of members or contributors who neither suffered nor benefited directly from the court decision. Organizations were assigned to the public-interest advocate category if: (1) they were established to defend broadly based, principled visions of American society rather than any racial, ethnic, or economic group (American Civil Liberties Union, Young Americans for Freedom); (2) their leaders and members perceived the basis of their involvement not in terms of defending a racial or ethnic group's opportunities but of a dedication to an understanding of a "common good" (Committee for Academic Nondiscrimination and Integrity, American Public Health Association); (3) they were government bodies or agencies directed by law to represent the "public interest" in litigation affecting their jurisdictions (President Carter's Administration, State of Washington).

Scope

Scope values assess the types of arguments and facts presented to the organization's policy makers. Were they obligated to examine the *political* dimensions of the issue: would the public or other political institutions accept the brief's answer to the question of governmental responsibility for rectifying past and continuing racial discrimination? Was the organization exposed to the *philosophical* ramifications of the case—the general issues of the appropriate blends of liberty and equality values to be endorsed as national principles? Did members of the association discuss the *social* implications of the case—the potential for exacerbating racial tensions, fears about "balkanizing" the nation, or suspicions about retrenchment in civil rights at the expense of the newly acquired status of minorities? Were they alerted to the comparatively narrow *legal* issue of what limitations are imposed by the Constitution on the attainment of racial justice? Those organizations in which the debate explicitly drew upon the political, philosophical, and social as well as the legal aspects of the case are placed in the "broad" category. Organizations that concentrated on only one aspect are characterized as "narrow" in their scope. Debates emphasizing two or three of these aspects are labeled "medium."

Leadership Style

Determining whether an organization was democratic or oligarchic in *Bakke* depended on five indicators: active membership involvement before the brief was filed; encouragement of dissenting opinions; alternative positions to the affirmative action issue offered; presence of an existing membership mandate on the issue; and the emphasis placed on "consensus" or amicable agreement within the organization. Descriptions of decision making within organizations were obtained through the interviews and other sources. No organization displayed fewer than four of the five indicators placing it in the "oligarchic" or "democratic" column.

Polarization

Polarization scores were determined by asking respondents to agree or disagree with the statement "Discussion about *Bakke* in my organization involved name calling, personal hostilities, and bitterness." Respondents "self-assigned" their organizations to the "high," "medium," or "low" categories depending on their degree of agreement or disagreement with the statement. Respondents from the same organization generally agreed in their assessments of the polarization level in the organization's discussion of *Bakke*. However, eleven of the three hundred sixty-one respondents replied "Don't know" (five being from oligarchic organizations, six from democratic organizations). In all but two cases, the "don't knows" were from organizations where at least three other respondents were willing to express their perceptions of organizational polarization. The exceptions were the Polish American Educators Association and the Student Bar Association of Rutgers School of Law. Follow-up interviews were conducted with members of each organization, and sufficient respondents were found to assign polarization scores to each ("low" for the Polish American Educators Association, "high" for the Student Bar Association).

Decision-making Behavior

The indicators used to determine *bargaining*, *compromise*, or *integrative* brief-making in *Bakke* relied on two sets of data. One indicator distinguished bargaining from other democratic behaviors. Respondents from democratic organizations were asked the questions: "Were there clear winners and losers in your organization after the *Bakke* discussion was concluded? Was there broad agreement among your organization's members about the brief's position?" If the struggle over the brief was seen as one with "clear winners and losers" with little common ground between them, then the organization's behavior was bargaining.

Compromise and integrative behaviors were distinguished by a second set of indicators. Respondents were queried about the nature of the agreement underlying the final policy statement issued by an organization in *Bakke*—either in its brief, or, if the organization joined a coalition brief, in other public statements. Did the agreement forged within the organization turn on an "interest" or "principle" orientation—the loss or gain to specific individuals or groups, or was it a broader agreement about the libertarian and egalitarian values at stake? A "principled" orientation was coded as broader than an "interest" orientation. The final decision, not the debate leading up to it, was the key datum. The indicator was thus concerned with the breadth of the *outcome* (the policy statement), not of the debate. Respondent's characterizations of the nature of the agreement were checked by an independent assessment of the public and private records of the organization's decision on *Bakke*.

Note that the "polarization" measure was similar to the "opposition" indicator; both tapped perceptions of the amount and nature of conflict within an organization. The difference between them, although subtle, was important. "Polarization" assessed the degree of *personalized* conflict—"name-calling, hostility, and bitterness"—within an organization. The "opposition" indicator, distinguishing bargaining from the other democratic behaviors, focused on the nature of the conflict—did participants see the *outcome* as one with a set of clear winners and losers. The criterion—"basis of agreement"—differentiating compromise from integrative behavior might appear to overlap with the "scope" indicator. But whereas "scope" assessed the breadth of the debate leading up to the decision, the "agreement" indicator emphasized the nature of the final decision. A debate narrow in scope might result in narrow agreement but need not. Several organizations, like the Equal Employment Advisory Council, had robust and wide-ranging debates, but in their final decision relied on a narrowed consensus based on the members' direct interest—usually occupational—in the litigation.

NOTES

Preface

1. Unless otherwise noted, all mimeographed materials, letters, and transcripts are also in my files. Coding scores for each organization are available in Appendix B to Timothy J. O'Neill, "The Politics of Equality," Ph.D. dissertation, University of California, Berkeley, 1981.

Introduction: Litigation As a Classroom

1. "The Democratic Character of Judicial Review," *Harvard Law Review* 66 (1963): 208.
2. "The Supreme Court as Republican Schoolmaster," *Supreme Court Review* (1967): 127–28.
3. Theodore J. Lowi, *American Government: Incomplete Conquest* (Hinsdale, Illinois: Dryden Press, 1976), p. 556.
4. These numbers include only those organizations which submitted amici briefs on the case's merits to the Supreme Court. They do not include briefs submitted by individuals, briefs filed in the lower courts, supplemental briefs, or briefs discussing the issue of granting *certiorari*.
5. Michael Walzer, "Political Decision-Making and Political Education," in Melvin Richter, ed., *Political Theory and Political Education* (Princeton: Princeton University Press, 1980), pp. 159, 162, and 171.
6. See "The Furor Over Reverse Discrimination," *Newsweek*, September 26, 1977, p. 52; "Bakke vs. UC Regents: A Landmark Case for High Court?" *Los Angeles Times*, January 23, 1977, p. E-3; "U.S. Stand on Bakke Case," *San Francisco Chronicle*, September 20, 1977, p. 1; and "Reverse Discrimination—Will *Bakke* Decide the Issue?" *National Journal*, September 17, 1977, p. 1436.
7. I use the term "affirmative action" to stand for the issue of whether preferential treatment should be accorded to members of groups traditionally the victims of unjust discrimination. Unfortunately, the phrase is overbroad. It is also used to designate all programs aimed at fostering minority participation in American society, be they preferential or exhortatory. Nevertheless, "affirmative action" is preferred here because other phrases offered to cover the issue posed by *Bakke*—e.g., "affirmative discrimination," "positive or benign discrimination," "reverse discrimination"—

tend to be code words representing specific points of view. "Affirmative action" is less likely to prejudge the issue.

8. *Caucasians Only: The Supreme Court, the NAACP, and the Restrictive Covenant Cases* (Berkeley: University of California Press, 1959). See also his earlier article, "Litigation as a Form of Pressure Group Activity," *Annals* 319 (1958): 20–31. Arthur Bentley and David Truman can lay claim to "discovering" the relevance of group activity to the legal process; Vose and later authors are responsible for turning those insights into the building blocks for a theory of interest-group activity in the judicial process. See Bentley's *The Process of Government* (Bloomington, Indiana: Principia Press, 1935), pp. 289–97, 382–99; and Truman's *The Governmental Process* (New York: Alfred A. Knopf, 1958), pp. 482–97. Compare with Vose's *Constitutional Change* (Lexington, Ma.: Lexington Books, 1972); Comment, "The Amicus Curiae," *Northwestern University Law Review* 55 (1960): 469–83; Samuel Krislov, "The Amicus Curiae Brief: From Friendship to Advocacy," *Yale Law Journal* 72 (1963): 694–721; and Nathan Hakman, "Lobbying the Supreme Court: An Appraisal of 'Political Science Folklore,'" *Fordham Law Review* 35 (1966): 15–50.

9. William K. Muir, Jr., *Law and Attitude Change* (Chicago: University of Chicago Press, 1973), p. ix.

10. Michael Oakeshott, "Political Education," in Peter Laslett, ed., *Philosophy, Politics and Society* (Oxford: Blackwell, 1956), p. 2.

11. See Dan Nimmo, *Popular Images of Politics* (Englewood Cliffs, New Jersey: Prentice-Hall, 1974), pp. 75–77; Fred I. Greenstein, *Children and Politics* (New Haven: Yale University Press, 1965); David Easton and Jack Dennis, *Children in the Political System* (New York: McGraw-Hill, 1969); and Kent Jennings and Richard Niemi, "Continuity and Change in Political Organizations," *American Political Science Review* 69 (December 1975): 1299–1315. It should be noted that Greenstein, Easton and Dennis, and Jennings and Niemi are not blind to the role of reflection in political socialization. But by emphasizing the development of political opinions in children, they concentrate on the external factors molding political perceptions rather than on the internal factors shaping personal values and behaviors.

12. See James MacGregor Burns, *Leadership* (New York: Harper and Row Colophon Books, 1978), p. 86.

13. See William K. Muir, Jr., "The State Legislature as a School of Political Capacity," in Walter Dean Burnham and Martha Wagner Weinberg, eds., *American Politics and Public Policy* (Cambridge: MIT Press, 1978), pp. 222–47.

14. *Democracy in America*, vol. I (New York: Alfred A. Knopf), pp. 191–198.

15. Philip E. Converse, "The Nature of the Belief Systems in Mass Publics," in David Apter, ed., *Ideology and Discontent* (New York: Free Press, 1964), pp. 206–61.

16. Sidney Verba and Norman H. Nie, *Political Participation in America* (New York: Harper and Row, 1972), p. 119.

17. Ibid., p. 118. Verba and Nie go on to conclude, however, that the key variable affecting participation is not race but socioeconomic status. Northern blacks and whites from similar social and economic backgrounds

exhibit minor differences in their willingness to participate (Ibid., pp. 125–40).

18. Herbert H. Hyman and Charles R. Wright, "Trends in Voluntary Association Memberships of American Adults," *American Sociological Review* 36 (April 1971): 191–206.

19. Lester W. Milbrath and M. L. Goel, *Political Participation* (Chicago: Rand McNally, 1977), p. 49.

20. Jean Piaget, *The Moral Judgement of the Child* (London: Routledge and Kegan Paul, 1932).

21. Joel Auerbach, "Alienation and Political Behavior," *American Political Science Review* 63 (March 1969): 86–91.

22. Burns, *Leadership*, p. 448.

23. See Richard C. Cyert and James G. March, *A Behavioral Theory of the Firm* (Englewood Cliffs, New Jersey: Prentice-Hall, 1963).

24. Gunnar Myrdal, *An American Dilemma* (New York: Harper, 1944). Frank Westie offers evidence that such inconsistencies do in fact result in modified behavior. Frank R. Westie, "The American Dilemma: An Empirical Test," *American Sociological Review* 30 (August 1965): 536–37.

25. Burns, *Leadership*, p. 450.

26. Denis G. Sullivan, Robert T. Nakamura, and Richard F. Winters, *How America Is Ruled* (New York: John Wiley and Sons, 1980), p. 37.

27. Malcolm E. Jewell and Samuel C. Patterson, *The Legislative Process in the United States* (New York: Random House, 1966), p. 415.

28. Aaron Wildavsky, *The Politics of the Budgetary Process*, 3rd ed. (Boston: Little, Brown, 1979), pp. 125–26.

29. Grant McConnell, *Private Power and American Democracy* (New York: Random House Vintage Books, 1966), pp. 113–15.

30. For example, David Lawrence found such a correlation between level of education and tolerance to unconventional forms of political activity. David G. Lawrence, "Procedural Norms and Tolerance," *American Political Science Review* 70 (March 1976): 88.

31. Burns, *Leadership*, pp. 448, 450.

32. See Sanford Levinson, "On Teaching 'Political Science,'" in Philip Green and Sanford Levinson, eds., *Power and Community* (New York: Random House Vintage Books, 1970), p. 61.

33. Philip Selznick, *Leadership in Administration* (Evanston, Illinois: Row, Peterson, 1957), pp. 37, 90, 153.

34. Lawrence Scaff, "Max Weber's Politics and Political Education," *American Political Science Review* 67 (March 1973): 128–41.

35. Burns, *Leadership*, pp. 425–32.

36. Joseph R. Gusfield, "The Problems of Generations in an Organizational Structure," *Social Forces* 35 (May 1957): 323–30.

37. Laurence H. Tribe, *American Constitutional Law* (Mineola, New York: Foundation Press, 1978), p. 13.

38. Yale Kamisar, Fred E. Inbau, and Thurman Arnold, *Criminal Justice in Our Time* (Charlottesville, Virginia: University Press of Virginia, 1965), p. 145.

39. Herbert Jacob, *Justice in America*, 3rd. ed. (Boston: Little, Brown, 1978), p. 38.

40. Telephone conversation with the Clerk of the United States Supreme Court, October 23, 1978 and April 28, 1980.
41. Vose, "Litigation as a Form of Pressure Group Activity," p. 21.
42. Krislov, "The Amicus Curiae Brief," p. 720. There are some who would argue that the amicus process is not as important as I have depicted it. Basing his analysis on cases pled before the Court from 1958 to 1965, Nathan Hakman concluded that amicus participation is exceptional rather than routine, and when it does occur the amicus is more likely to express "a specific and separate pecuniary interest" than espouse broad social policies. Admitting that civil rights and First Amendment freedom cases are most likely to attract organizational participation, Hakman nevertheless argues that "the notion that the judicial process is part of a continuing political process is one that needs serious qualification and refinement" (Hakman, "Lobbying the Supreme Court," pp. 15, 35, 39–43, 47, 49). To some extent, Hakman's criticisms are irrelevant to a study focusing exclusively on a case attracting 117 amici organizations. Landmark cases such as the *Restrictive Covenant Cases* (thirty-three organizations filed twenty-five briefs amici curiae), *Brown* v. *Board of Education* (thirty organizations, twenty-four briefs), and *Bakke*'s precursor, *DeFunis* v. *Odegaard* (sixty-two organizations, twenty-six briefs), attract the very kinds and numbers of participation that the standard judicial interest-group model presumes but that Hakman castigates as unsupported by the evidence.
43. *NAACP* v. *Button*, 371 U.S. 415 (1963).

Chapter I: Bakke, the University, and the Problems of Racial Equality

1. "Brief for Respondent," p. 3, *Regents of the University of California* v. *Bakke*, 438 U.S. 265 (1978). [This case hereafter cited as *Bakke* (U.S. Supr. Ct.)].
2. Robert Lindsey, "White/Caucasian—And Rejected," *New York Times Magazine*, April 3, 1977, p. 43.
3. Quoted in "Brief for Respondent," *Bakke* (U.S. Supr. Ct) pp. 3–4.
4. Report of Dr. Theodore West to the Davis medical school admissions committee, quoted in the *Record* of the lower court's findings (in *Bakke* v. *Regents of the University of California*, Superior Court of the State of California, County of Yolo, Super. Crt. No. 31287 (1974). [Hereafter cited as *Bakke* (Yolo Cty, Calif., Superior Ct)]) on file with the Office of the Clerk of the United States Supreme Court, pp. 224–25.
5. Lindsey, "White/Caucasian," p. 44. Unfortunately, there are no specific figures indicating how many applicants with scores lower than 470 were admitted in 1973. Neither the court record nor any of the briefs contain this information, and the Davis medical school admissions office refused to publish this data.
6. Letter to Dr. George Lowrey, Dean of Admissions, University of California, Davis Medical School, July 1, 1973, pp. 1–3.
7. Reynold Colvin, quoted in "Bakke Wins, Quotas Lose," *Time*, July 10, 1978, p. 15.
8. Quoted in Carol Benfell, "Should the Constitution Really be Colorblind?," *Barrister* 4 (Fall 1977), pp. 52–53.

9. Ralph Smith, "Examining the Merits of the Bakke Case," *The Daily Pennsylvanian* (the student newspaper of the University of Pennsylvania), March 4, 1977, p. 4. The letters exchanged between Bakke and Storandt are reprinted in Appendix A, "Brief of *Amici Curiae* for the National Urban League, et. al., on Petition for a Writ of *Certiorari* to the Supreme Court of the State of California," pp. 1a–8a.

10. Quoted in "The Furor Over Reverse Discrimination," *Newsweek*, September 26, 1977, p. 54.

11. Quoted in Benfell, "Should the Constitution Really be Colorblind?," p. 17.

12. Ibid., pp. 53–54.

13. See Ibid., p. 17, and letter from Peter Storandt to *Newsweek*, November 14, 1977, p. 6.

14. Letter from Allan Bakke to Peter C. Storandt, August 7, 1973, reproduced in "Brief of *Amici Curiae* for the National Urban League, et al." *Bakke* (U.S. Supr. Ct.), pp. 4a–6a.

15. *Record, Bakke* (Yolo County, Calif., Superior Ct.), pp. 228–29.

16. Ibid., pp. 225–26.

17. "To the extent Bakke's second rejection was predicated upon his political opposition to the University's special admissions project, the rejection raises serious First Amendment questions" ("Brief of the American Jewish Committee, et al., *Amici Curiae*", *Bakke* (U.S. Supr. Ct.), p. 8 n. 5).

18. "Brief for Respondent," *Bakke* (U.S. Supr. Ct.), pp. 9 and 13.

19. "Brief of Plaintiff, Respondent, and Cross-Appellant," *Bakke* v. *Regents of the University of California*, 553 P. 2d 1152 (1976), p. 41. [This case hereafter cited as *Bakke* (Calif. Supr. Ct.)].

20. "The Lawyer Fighting in Racial Case," *San Francisco Chronicle*, January 12, 1977, p. 3. Also telephone conversation with Colvin and Links, April 17, 1979.

21. "Brief for Repondent," *Bakke* (U.S. Supr. Ct.), p. 2.

22. *Record, Bakke* (Yolo County, Calif., Superior Ct.), pp. 15, 57–58, 159–60.

23. Ibid., pp. 64–66, 86, 168, 195–96, 201–33, 388.

24. Letter to the editor of the *Sacramento Bee* from Dr. Sarah D. Grey, past Task Force Chairperson, January 4, 1977, reproduced in Appendix B, "Brief of *Amici Curiae* for the National Urban League, et al.," p. 10a.

25. *Record, Bakke* (Yolo County, Calif., Superior Ct.), pp. 62–63, 150–59.

26. "Medical Dean Aids 'Special Interest' Applicants," *Los Angeles Times*, July 5, 1976, pp. 1, 3.

27. *Record, Bakke* (Yolo County, Calif., Superior Ct.), pp. 65–67, 161–68, 203–5, 210, 216–23, 388.

28. Memorandum to President Charles J. Hitch, May 14, 1974, p. 3.

29. Quoted in Benfell, "Should the Constitution Really be Colorblind?" p. 12.

30. *Shelley* v. *Kraemer*, 334 U.S. 1, 22 (1948).

31. *Strauder* v. *West Virginia*, 100 U.S. 303, 308 (1880).

32. Dissenting in *DeFunis* v. *Odegaard*, 416 U.S. 312, 337 (1974). [Hereafter cited as *DeFunis* (U.S.)]

33. *DeFunis* v. *Odegaard*, 82 Wash. 2d 11, 507 P. 2d 1169 (1973). [Hereafter cited as *DeFunis* (Wash.)]

34. Guido Calabresi, "Bakke as Pseudo-Tragedy," *Catholic University Law Review* 28 (1979): 433–34.
35. Justice Brennan, concurring in *United Jewish Organizations* v. *Carey*, 430 U.S. 144, 172 n. 2 (1977).
36. "Brief in Reply of Members of the Congressional Black Caucus, Members of the Congress of the United States to Brief of the United States, *Amici Curiae*," *Bakke* (U.S. Supr. Ct.), p. 7.
37. See *Keyes* v. *School District*, 413 U.S. 189 (1973); *Craig* v. *Boren*, 429 U.S. 190 (1976); and *United Jewish Organizations* v. *Carey*.
38. Kenneth L. Karst, "Foreword: Equal Citizenship Under the Fourteenth Amendment," *Harvard Law Review* 91 (November 1977): 3–4.
39. *Brown* v. *Board of Education*, 347 U.S. 483, 493–94 (1954).
40. *Slaughter-House Cases*, 83 U.S. (16 Wall.) 36, 81 (1873).
41. P. 308.
42. Senator Boutwell speaking against *Slaughter-House Cases*, 43rd Cong., 2nd Sess., 1875, *Congressional Globe*, pp. 1792–94, 1863.
43. *Korematsu* v. *United States*, 323 U.S. 214, 216 (1944); see also *Hirabayashi* v. *United States*, 320 U.S. 81 (1943).
44. Justice Rehnquist, dissenting in *Trimble* v. *Gordon*, 430 U.S. 762, 779 (1977).
45. The phrase is J. R. Pole's (*The Pursuit of Equality in American History* [Berkeley: University of California Press, 1978], p. 272). The same observation is made by Karst, "Foreword: Equal Citizenship Under the Fourteenth Amendment," pp. 4, 40; and by Terrance Sandalow, "Racial Preferences in Higher Education," *University of Chicago Law Review* 42 (1975): 672 n. 57.
46. Following Owen M. Fiss, "Groups and the Equal Protection Clause," *Philosophy and Public Affairs* 5 (Winter 1976): 108–9.
47. Ibid., p. 113.
48. Ibid., pp. 112, 119–22.
49. *Lochner* v. *New York*, 198 U.S. 45, 72 (1905) (Justice Harlan, dissenting, speaking of the Fourteenth Amendment's due process clause).
50. See *Hirabayashi* v. *United States* and *Korematsu* v. *United States*.
51. Gerald Gunther, "Foreword: In Search of Evolving Doctrine on a Changing Court," *Harvard Law Review* 86 (1972): 8.
52. *Dunn* v. *Blumstein*, 405 U.S. 331, 364 (1972) (Dissent).
53. For a discussion of the constitutional goal of effective but limited government, see Lief H. Carter, *Reason in Law* (Boston: Little, Brown, 1979), pp. 166–210.
54. Martin Shapiro, *Freedom of Speech* (Englewood Cliffs, New Jersey: Prentice-Hall Spectrum, 1966), pp. 29–30.
55. Alexander Bickel, *The Least Dangerous Branch* (Indianapolis: Bobbs-Merrill, 1962), p. 258.
56. Sandalow, "Racial Preferences in Higher Education," pp. 700–1.
57. The theoretical rationale for this argument is developed by Karst, "Foreword: Equal Citizenship Under the Fourteenth Amendment," pp. 6, 64; and Fiss, "Groups and the Equal Protection Clause," pp. 147–70. Authors emphasizing the "stigma" approach typically cite *Strauder* v. *West Virginia*, 100 U.S. 303, 308 (1880), to justify and clarify the concept:

"The very fact that colored people are singled out . . . by a statute is practically a brand upon them, affixed by law; an assertion of their inferiority, and a stimulant to . . . race prejudice."

58. See John Ely, "The Constitutionality of Reverse Racial Discrimination," *University of Chicago Law Review* 41 (1974): 730 n. 36.
59. "Brief for Respondent," *Bakke* (U.S. Supr. Ct.), p. 34.
60. Ibid., p. 47.
61. "Notice of Intended Decision," reprinted in Alfred A. Slocum, ed., *Allan Bakke versus Regents of the University of California*, vol. 1 (Dobbs Ferry, New York: Oceana Publications, 1978), pp. 165–91.
62. "Findings of Fact and Conclusions of Law," reprinted in ibid., p. 163.
63. "Notice of Intended Decision," reprinted in ibid., p. 192.
64. Interview with Professor David Feller, University of California (Boalt Hall) Law School, Berkeley, California, June 6, 1977.
65. Telephone conversation with Mr. Frank Pohlhaus, general counsel, NAACP's Washington, D.C. bureau, December 1, 1978. Mr. Pohlhaus's remarks were confirmed by a member of the Sacramento, California office of the NAACP.
66. "Reply Brief of Appellant and Cross-Respondent," *Bakke* (Calif. Supr. Ct.), pp. 7–8.
67. "Opening Brief of Appellant and Cross-Respondent," *Bakke* (Calif. Supr. Ct.), p. 22.
68. Ibid., pp. 37–38. However, the university retreated from this position in its "Petition for a Writ of *Certiorari*" to the United States Supreme Court, December 14, 1976. "[I]n a report to the Department of Health, Education and Welfare in response to a complaint filed by Bakke, the chairman of the admissions committee declared: 'Had additional places been available, individuals with Mr. Bakke's rating could likely have been admitted. . . .'" in 1973 (p. 11 n. 4). The assertion that no applicant with a score less than 470 was admitted in 1973 has been challenged by two investigative reporters. See Lindsey, "White/Caucasian," p. 44; and "Medical Deans Aid 'Special Interest' Applicants," pp. 1, 3.
69. *DeFunis* (U.S.), p. 350. The California majority opinion quoted the first line of Brennan's cautionary admonition. See *Bakke* (Calif. Supr. Ct.), p. 1160.
70. Interview of Justice Mosk by Leah Cartabruno, television station KVIE, Sacramento, California, June 10, 1977. Reports of the interview can be found in "UC's Handling of the Bakke Case Defended by Justice Mosk," *Berkeley Gazette*, June 10, 1977, p. 4; and Steven Pressman, "Coblentz Defends Minority Admissions," *Daily Californian*, June 13, 1977, pp. 1, 16.
71. *Bakke* (Calif. Supr. Ct.), p. 1155.
72. Ibid., p. 1172.
73. *Shelley* v. *Kraemer*, quoted in ibid., p. 1163 n. 17.
74. Ibid., pp. 1164 n. 18, 1161 and 1165. The quotation is from Justice Douglas's dissent in *DeFunis* (U.S.), p. 342.
75. Ibid., pp. 1161, 1165 and 1171.
76. Ibid., pp. 1162, 1170, and 1165–66.
77. "UC's Handling of the Bakke Case Defended by Justice Mosk," p. 4.

78. *Bakke* (Calif. Supr. Ct.), pp. 1182–83, 1188, 1180 and 1184.
79. Quoted in K. Connie Kang, "Senior Justice Counts His Blessings," *San Francisco Chronicle*, October 9, 1977, p. A-4.
80. *Bakke* (Calif. Supr. Ct.), p. 1191.
81. Christopher F. Mooney, *Bakke: Law, Equality and the American Conscience*, unpublished manuscript, University of Pennsylvania Law School, 1979, p. 18.
82. *Bakke* (Calif. Supr. Ct.), p. 1165.
83. The United States Supreme Court granted *certiorari* when DeFunis appealed the Washington court's decision, but vacated the case as moot because DeFunis was in the last year of law school by the time the Supreme Court heard oral arguments. *DeFunis* v. *Odegaard*, 414 U.S. 1038 (1973), vacated as moot, 416 U.S. 312 (1974).
84. 39 N.Y. 2d 326, 348 N.E. 2d 537, 384 N.Y.S. 2d 82 (1976).
85. *Anderson* v. *San Francisco Unified School District*, 357 F. Supp. 248 (N.D. Cal. 1972).
86. *Flanagan* v. *President and Directors of Georgetown College*, 417 F. Supp. 377 (D.D.C. 1976).
87. William Coblentz, chairperson of the University of California Board of Regents, provided this explanation during network television news coverage of the United States Supreme Court's decision on *Bakke*. "CBS Evening News," June 29, 1978.
88. Interview with Carol Mock, former student member of the Board of Regents, March 18, 1978. The University of California, Davis Law School faculty voted 16 to 1 against appeal. Letter from Pierre R. Loiseaux, Dean, University of California, Davis Law School, to David S. Saxon, President of the University of California, November 3, 1976.
89. Letter from Donald L. Reidhaar to Archibald Cox, August 4, 1977, p. 2.
90. Quoted in "The Wake of the Bakke Case is Felt on the East Coast, Too," *Pennsylvania Gazette*, June 8, 1977, p. 2.
91. Quoted in Beverly T. Watkins, "Efforts in *Bakke* Case Called 'Less than Competent'; Applicants from Minority Groups Fall Off Sharply," *Chronicle of Higher Education*, April 4, 1977, p. 1.
92. Ibid., p. 4.
93. Ibid.
94. Quoted in Benfell, "Should the Constitution Really be Colorblind?," p. 13.
95. David S. Saxon, "UC's Minorities Plan Serves Public Needs," *Los Angeles Times*, January 23, 1977, p. E-3.
96. "Brief *Amici Curiae* for the National Urban League, et al.," *Bakke* (U.S. Supr. Ct.).
97. "Angry Groups' Plan to Overcome *Bakke* Decision," *San Francisco Examiner*, January 16, 1977, p. 1; "3000 Demonstrate Against Bakke," *The Daily Californian*, October 10, 1977, p. 1.
98. "Anti-Bakke Crowd Burns Paper," *Berkeley Gazette*, October 13, 1977, p. 1.
99. See the transcript of the September 2, 1977 "MacNeil/Lehrer Report" entitled "*Bakke* Case" for one such confrontation. Participants were Kenneth S. Tollett, Director of the Institute for the Study of Educational

Policy at Howard University; Howard Squadron, Senior Vice-President, American Jewish Congress; and Dr. John Cooper, President, Association of American Medical Colleges.

100. Paul Melnicoff, "D.C. Labor Council Passes Anti-Bakke Resolution," *United Labor Action*, September 1977, p. 1.

101. McGeorge Bundy, "The Issue Before the Court: Who Gets Ahead in America?," *Atlantic Monthly* (November 1977): 43.

102. Sixty-four percent of nonwhites opposed, twenty-six percent supported preferential treatment. "Most Against Preference for Non-Whites, Women," *Current Opinion* V (June 1977): 67, quoting a March 25–28, 1977, Gallup Poll.

103. Quoted in Seymour M. Lipset and William Schneider, "The *Bakke* Case: How It Would Be Decided at the Bar of Public Opinion," *Public Opinion* I (March/April 1978): 42.

104. Constitutional recognition of the status of liberty can be found in the Preamble's promise of securing "the Blessings of Liberty"; Article I, section 3's apportionment of "Representatives and direct Taxes" according to each state's population of "free Persons"; Article I, section 9, paragraph 2's guarantee of the common law "privilege of Habeas Corpus," and paragraph 3's prohibition of bills of attainder and ex post facto laws; Article IV, section 3's protection against religious tests as qualification for public office; and the specific guarantees of personal liberty contained in the first ten amendments.

105. See Ronald P. Sokol, *The Puzzle of Equality* (Charlottesville, Virginia: Michie, 1967), pp. 48–68.

106. See Albert Weale, *Equality and Social Policy* (London: Routledge and Kegan Paul, 1968), pp. 120–21.

107. Samuel H. Beer, "Fabianism Revisited," *Review of Economics and Statistics* 25 (August 1953): 206.

108. Charles Frankel, "The New Egalitarianism and the Old," *Commentary* 56 (September 1973): 57. Emphasis in the original.

109. John Rawls, *A Theory of Justice* (Cambridge, Massachusetts: Belknap Press of Harvard University Press, 1971), pp. 73–80, 511–12.

110. See Jerome Karabel, "Open Admissions," *Change* 4 (May 1972), pp. 38–43.

111. Abraham Lincoln, "Message to Special Session of Congress, July 4, 1861," reprinted in Richard N. Current, ed., *The Political Thought of Abraham Lincoln* (Indianapolis: Bobbs-Merrill, 1967), p. 188.

112. David M. Potter, *People of Plenty* (Chicago: University of Chicago Press, 1954), pp. 91–92, 96.

113. Irving Kristol, "Equality as an Ideal," *International Encyclopedia of the Social Sciences*, vol. 5 (New York: Macmillan, 1969), pp. 108, 110.

114. Elliott Zashin, "The Promise of Black Americans in Civil Rights: The Past Two Decades Assessed," *Daedalus* 107 (Winter 1978): 241.

115. David Danzig, "The Meaning of the Negro Strategy," *Commentary* 41 (February 1964): 22.

116. Bayard Rustin, "From Protest to Politics: The Future of the Civil Rights Movement," *Commentary* 42 (February 1965): 27.

117. Executive Order 10925, 26 *Federal Register*, 1977 (March 6, 1961).

118. Executive Order 11246, 30 *Federal Register* 12319 (September 24, 1965).
119. Both quotations are reprinted in Lyndon B. Johnson, *The Vantage Point: Perspectives on the Presidency, 1963–1969* (New York: Holt, Rinehart and Winston, 1971), p. 166.
120. See *Contractors Association of Eastern Pennsylvania* v. *Secretary of Labor,* 422 F. 2d 159 (3rd Cir. 1971), cert. denied, 404 U.S. 584 (1971).
121. United States Bureau of the Census, *Characteristics of the Population, United States Summary,* vol. 5 (Washington, D.C.: U.S. Government Printing Office, 1971), pp. 1–100.
122. United States Bureau of the Census, *Current Population Reports, The Social and Economic Status of the Black Population in the United States, 1974* (Washington, D.C.: U.S. Government Printing Office, 1975), p. 65.
123. *San Francisco Chronicle,* October 11, 1977, p. 8.
124. See Hugo Adam Bedau, "Compensatory Justice and the Black Manifesto," *The Monist* 56 (1972): 20–42.
125. William Julius Wilson, "The Declining Significance of Race," *Society* 15 (January/February 1978): 56–62.
126. Kenneth Clark, "Is the Significance of Race Declining?" *Current,* no. 203 (May/June 1978): 3–26.
127. Erik Olin Wright, "Race, Class, and Income Inequality," *American Journal of Sociology* 83 (May 1978): 1368–97; and John L. McCoy and Davis L. Brown, "Health Status Among Lo-Income Elderly Persons: Rural-Urban Differences," *Social Security Bulletin* 41 (June 1978): 14–26.
128. "Bakke Wins, Quotas Lose," p. 9.
129. Ibid.
130. Tape recording of U.S. Supreme Court proceedings of June 28, 1978 (Washington, D.C.: Motion Picture and Sound Recording Branch, Audiovisual Archives Branch, National Archives, 1978).
131. *Bakke* (U.S. Supr. Ct.), pp. 412–414. Title VI reads: "No person in the United States shall, on the grounds of race, color, or national origin, be subjected to discrimination under any program or activity receiving Federal financial assistance," 42 *United States Code* (*U.S.C.*) section 2000d. The Davis Medical School, as does virtually every other medical school in America, receives substantial funding from the federal government.
132. *Bakke* (U.S. Supr. Ct.), p. 325. See also, pp. 328–40, and 352.
133. Ibid., pp. 324–25, 369.
134. Ibid., p. 357.
135. Ibid., pp. 360–62.
136. Ibid., pp. 284–87, 305.
137. Ibid., pp. 311–13, 321–24.
138. Ronald Dworkin, "The *Bakke* Decision: Did It Decide Anything?," *New York Review of Books,* August 17, 1978, pp. 20–25.
139. William J. Bennett and Terry Eastland, "Why *Bakke* Won't End Reverse Discrimination," *Commentary* 46 (September 1978): 34.
140. Quoted in ibid., p. 29.

141. Quoted in "The Landmark Bakke Ruling," *Newsweek*, July 10, 1978, p. 31. Yale law professor Bruce Ackerman was less charitable. "It was a landmark occasion, but the court failed to produce a landmark decision." Quoted in "Bakke Wins, Quotas Lose," p. 16.

Chapter II: The Imperatives of Organizational Survival

1. See table 11 below.
2. Definitions of the terms "interest group," "minority-defense organization," and "public-interest advocates" are elaborated later in the text of this chapter. See Appendix for a discussion of the indicators I used to assign organizations to specific categories.
3. See Appendix for categorization of *scope*.
4. Theta (Freedman's coefficient of differentiation) was only .08. (See table 12.)
5. The discussion of the amici organizations in this section relies on interviews with, among others, Douglas S. McDowell, Kenneth C. McGuiness, and Robert E. Williams (for the Equal Employment Advisory Council); Paul King, Stephen V. Bomse, and Daniel E. Titelbaum (for the National Association of Minority Contractors); Wade Henderson, Alfred A. Slocum, and Richard G. Huber (for the Council on Legal Education Opportunity); and J. Stanford Smith, Lee R. Marks, and Martha Jane Shay (for the National Fund for Minority Engineering Students).
6. Equal Employment Advisory Council, "Statement of Purposes, Background Activities, and Organization" (Mimeographed, Washington, D.C., August, 1977), p. 1.
7. Interview with informant preferring anonymity, New York City.
8. Kenneth C. McGuiness, ed., *Preferential Treatment in Employment— Affirmative Action or Reverse Discrimination?* (Washington, D.C.: Equal Employment Advisory Council, 1977). The book was originally intended to aid the board's decision whether to enter three preferential employment cases then pending before the federal courts. However, *Bakke* reached the Supreme Court before any of the employment cases, and the decision on whether and how to intervene in *Bakke* became the policy basis for deciding to enter the other cases when they reached the court of appeals.
9. Interview with informant preferring anonymity, Chicago.
10. Ibid.
11. Ibid.
12. Interview with Douglas McDowell, associate counsel, Equal Employment Advisory Council, Washington, D.C., September 20, 1977.
13. Interview with informant, New York City.
14. Ibid.
15. "Brief *Amicus Curiae* of the Equal Employment Advisory Council," *Regents of the University of California* v. *Bakke*, 438 U.S. 265 (1978) [Hereafter cited as *Bakke* (U.S. Supr. Ct.)], pp. 5–6 (emphasis in the original).
16. 30 Fed. Reg. 12319, as amended 32 Fed. Reg. 14303 and 34 Fed. Reg. 12985. Title I, section 103 of Public Law 95-28, May 13, 1977 (42 U.S.C. 6701).

TABLE 11 Organizational Use of Litigation, 1967–1977

Rate of Participation in Litigation	Percentage of Organizations	
Never	24%	(28)
Seldom (0–4 cases)	41%	(47)
Occasional (5–9 cases)	10%	(11)
Frequent (10 or more cases)	25%	(29)
Total	100%	(115)

NOTE: "Participation in litigation" is defined as having been an amicus, party, or unnamed sponsor in any court case excluding *Bakke*.

TABLE 12 Interest Orientation and Scope

	Interest Orientation of Organizations (N = 115)		
Scope	Interest-Group (30)	Minority Defense (61)	Public-Interest (24)
Narrow (65)	18	35	12
Medium (15)	3	11	1
Broad (35)	9	15	11

$$\theta = \frac{(\Sigma fb - \Sigma fa)}{T_2} = \frac{304}{4014} = .0757$$

17. Telephone conversation with Steven Bomse, counsel, Minority Contractors Association of Northern California, Inc., San Francisco, March 2, 1978. The Northern California chapter wrote the brief endorsed by the national association.
18. "Brief *Amici Curiae* of the National Association of Minority Contractors and Minority Contractors Association of Northern California, Inc., In Support of Petitioner," *Bakke* (U.S. Supr. Ct.), pp. 5, 27.
19. The La Raza National Lawyers Association became a sponsoring organization in 1972.
20. Kenneth J. Brown, Jr., "CLEO: Friend of Disadvantaged Minority Law Students," *American Bar Association Journal* 61 (December 1975): 1483.
21. "CLEO: A Narrative Report," memorandum from Alfred A. Slocum, executive director, and Richard G. Huber, chairman, Council on Legal Education Opportunity, to George G. Bailey, chairman, ABA Program Coordinating Committee, January 31, 1977, pp. 2, 5.
22. Ibid., p. 6.
23. "CLEO: Participation Data, 1976–1977" (Mimeographed, Washington, D.C., November 4, 1976), p. 3.
24. "All About CLEO" (Pamphlet, Washington, D.C., 1977), pp. 1–2.
25. Title IX, Part D, Sections 961–66 of the Education Amendments of

1972 (Public Law 92-318, 92nd Cong., June 23, 1972), amended by the Education Amendments of 1976 to the Higher Education Act of 1965 (July 22, 1974).

26. "CLEO: A Narrative Report," p. 4.

27. "Interest of the *Amicus Curiae*," in "Brief of the Council on Legal Education Opportunity as *Amicus Curiae*," *Bakke* (U.S. Supr. Ct.), pp. 2–3.

28. Interview with Wade Henderson, associate director (now executive director), Council on Legal Education Opportunity, Washington, D.C., September 20, 1977.

29. Quoted in "Bar Group Entering Bakke Case Appeal," *San Francisco Chronicle*, May 23, 1977, p. 5.

30. Telephone conversation with Frederick R. Franklin, staff director, Section on Legal Education and Admissions to the Bar; American Bar Association; Chicago, Illinois; January 24, 1978. See also letter from Justin A. Stanley, president, American Bar Association, to Leonard F. Walentynowicz, executive director and legal counsel, Polish-American Congress and National Advocates Society, Washington, D.C., June 6, 1977; and Justin A. Stanley, "President's Page," *American Bar Association Journal* 43 (May 1977): 587.

31. Reprinted in "Brief of the American Bar Association, *Amicus Curiae*," *Bakke* (U.S. Supr. Ct.), p. 2.

32. Interview with Henderson.

33. "A Proposed Justice Department Response to the Current Debate Over Affirmative Action in Higher Education" (Memorandum to Drew Days from Alfred A. Slocum, executive director, Council on Legal Education Opportunity, Washington, D.C., February 22, 1977), p. 8.

34. "Brief of the Council on Legal Education Opportunity," p. 6.

35. Ibid., p. 13.

36. Ibid., pp. 28, 31–33, 47.

37. Interview with Henderson.

38. Telephone conversation with Professor Henry Ramsey, Jr., University of California, Berkeley, March 10, 1978.

39. "Brief of the American Jewish Committee, American Jewish Congress, et al., *Amici Curiae*," *Bakke* (U.S. Supr. Ct.), p. 58.

40. "Petition for Leave to File Brief *Amicus Curiae*, and Brief of the American Federation of Teachers, *Amicus Curiae*," *Bakke* (U.S. Supr. Ct.), p. 14.

41. National Fund for Minority Engineering Students, Inc., Articles of Incorporation, Article III (Pamphlet, Washington, D.C., 1974).

42. Address by J. Stanford Smith to the Engineering Education Conference, Crotonville, New York, July 25, 1972. Quoted in "Brief of the National Fund for Minority Engineering Students, *Amicus Curiae*," *Bakke* (U.S. Supr. Ct.), pp. 3–4.

43. Planning Commission for Expanding Minority Opportunities in Engineering, *Minorities in Engineering: A Blueprint for Action* (New York: Alfred A. Sloan Foundation, 1974), p. 12.

44. National Fund for Minority Engineering Students, *Annual Report, 1978* (Pamphlet, Washington, D.C., 1978), pp. 1–5. See also the fund's "Statement of Purpose" (Pamphlet, 1976), pp. 1–3f.

45. *NFMES, Annual Report, 1978,*
46. Interview with informant requesting anonymity, New York City, September 13, 1977.
47. "Brief of the National Fund for Minority Engineering Students," *Bakke* (U.S. Supr. Ct.), p. 6 n. 4. The brief quoted *Bakke* v. *Regents of the University of California,* 553 P. 2d. 1152, 1160, 1161 (1976).
48. Ibid., pp. 6–7.
49. Ibid., pp. 4, 10.
50. Ibid., pp. 6, 12, 36.
51. Interview with Lee R. Marks and Martha Jane Shay; Ginsburg, Feldman and Bress; Washington, D.C.; September 21, 1977.
52. Interview with informant, New York City.
53. This discussion of minority-defense organizations in *Bakke* depends on interviews with, among others, Steven Berzon and Marian Edelman (Children's Defense Fund); Jack Greenberg, Eric Schnappen, Charles Stephen Ralston, and William Lee (NAACP Legal Defense and Educational Fund); Raul Yzaguirre, Elisa Sanchez, Vilma S. Martinez, and Peter R. Chacon (Mexican-American Legal Defense and Educational Fund); Robert Hermann, Jack John Olivero, and Oscar Garcia-Rivera (Puerto Rican Legal Defense and Education Fund); Anthony Krzywicki (Polish American Affairs Council); and Arthur Gajarsa and Ralph Perrotta (Italian-American Foundation).
54. Interview with Steven Berzon, former staff counsel, Children's Defense Fund; San Francisco, California; April 27, 1978. The coalition brief was titled "Brief *Amici Curiae,* National Council of Churches of Christ in the United States of America, et al."
55. Interview with Ira Gissen, director, National Discrimination Department, Anti-Defamation League, New York, September 15, 1977. The Anti-Defamation League organized a coalition brief representing five organizations.
56. James Q. Wilson, *Political Organizations* (New York: Basic Books, 1973), pp. 263–64.
57. Not all the legal defense funds were minority-defense organizations. Lacking the ties of shared cultural or occupational identities, the Pacific Legal Foundation and the Mid-American Legal Foundation were public-interest advocates.
58. Since 1983 the NAACP Legal Defense and Educational Fund Inc., has been named simply the Legal Defense and Educational Fund, Inc. See below in the text a description of how the "NAACP" was stripped from the organization by a federal court judge.
59. Nathan Hakman, "Lobbying the Supreme Court," *Fordham Law Review* 35 (1966): 46.
60. Clement Vose, *Constitutional Change* (Lexington, Ma.: Lexington Books, 1972), p. 317.
61. Jack Greenberg, director-counsel, NAACP Legal Defense Fund, quoted in Alan Weinstein, "Interview with Jack Greenberg," *Civil Liberties Review* 2 (June/July 1975): 109.
62. "Brief of the National Association for the Advancement of Colored People as *Amicus Curiae,*" *Bakke* (U.S. Supr. Ct.), p. 1 (emphasis added).

63. "Brief of the NAACP Legal Defense and Educational Fund, Inc., as *Amicus Curiae*," *Bakke* (U.S. Supr. Ct.), p. 1 (emphasis added).
64. Dr. H. Claude Hudson, quoted in Warren Brown, "NAACP Votes to Strip Name From Longtime Civil Rights Ally," *Washington Post*, June 26, 1979, p. 5.
65. Ibid.
66. See the remarks made by Benjamin Hooks, executive director of the NAACP, and Jack Greenberg in ibid.
67. The decision was handed down on March 28, 1983 by Judge Thomas P. Jackson. At the time these notes are being written, the legal defense fund is appealing the decision before the District Court of Appeals. See "NAACP Is Victim In Suit Over Name," *New York Times*, March 29, 1983, pp. A1, 19.
68. NAACP Legal Defense and Educational Fund, Inc., *Annual Report, 1978* (Pamphlet, New York, 1978), pp. 1–5, 8.
69. Jack Greenberg, quoted in Weinstein, "Interview with Jack Greenberg," p. 123.
70. See the exchange of letters between Derrick Bell, a Harvard Law School professor, and Julian LeVonne Chambers, the fund's president. The latter here is quoting Jack Greenberg's Cardozo lectures, *Civil Liberties Review* 3 (April–May 1976): 7, 85.
71. Interview with Charles Stephen Ralston and William Lee, NAACP Legal Defense Fund staff attorneys, New York, September 13, 1977.
72. Ibid.
73. Because of the breadth of the debate which created this policy, the fund was coded "broad" in scope.
74. The fund's *DeFunis* brief was one of the first to recognize that Marco DeFunis's challenge of the special admissions program at the University of Washington Law School had been "mooted" (deprived of practical significance) by DeFunis's impending graduation from the law school. "Brief of the NAACP Legal Defense and Educational Fund, Inc., as *Amicus Curiae*," *DeFunis* v. *Odegaard* 416 U.S. 312 (1974), p. 12.
75. "Brief of the NAACP Legal Defense . . . Fund," *Bakke* (U.S. Supr. Ct.), p. 2.
76. Interview with Charles Stephen Ralston and William Lee, NAACP Legal Defense Fund, New York, September 13, 1977.
77. Interview with Eric Schnappen, NAACP Legal Defense Fund staff attorney, New York, September 14, 1977. Mr. Schnappen was christened the "intellectual force" behind the brief by his colleagues.
78. "Brief of the NAACP Legal Defense . . . Fund," pp. 51, 10.
79. Ibid., pp. 2, 53–67, and Appendices A and B.
80. Alfred H. Kelly, "Clio and the Court: An Illicit Love Affair," *Supreme Court Review*, 1965, p. 144.
81. "Brief *Amici Curiae*, Anti-Defamation League, et al.," *Bakke* (U.S. Supr. Ct.), p. 25.
82. *Brown* v. *Board of Education*, 347 U.S. 483, 492–93 (1954). See also the Court's discussion of the "inconclusive" history of the Fourteenth Amendment's adoption and the confusing role played by the differing intentions of the supporters and opponents of the Amendment. The

Court also pointed out that "[w]hat others in Congress and the state legislatures had in mind cannot be determined with any degree of certainty" (p. 489).

83. The argument that the Fourteenth Amendment's requirement "[n]o State shall . . . deny to *any person* within its jurisdiction the equal protection of the laws" [emphasis added] should be taken seriously and means neither white nor black, Jew nor Catholic should be treated unequally by a state's laws or actions, was pursued in briefs submitted by the American Jewish Committee and the American Jewish Congress ("Brief of the American Jewish Committee, et al., *Amici Curiae*," p. 15); the Anti-Defamation League ("Brief *Amici Curiae* of Anti-Defamation League, et al., p. 23); the Fraternal Order of Police ("Brief *Amici Curiae* of the Fraternal Order of Police, et al.," p. 6); the Pacific Legal Foundation ("Brief *Amicus Curiae* for Pacific Legal Foundation in Support of Respondent," p. 7); the Sons of Italy ("Brief *Amicus Curiae* for the Order Sons of Italy in America in Support of Respondent," p. 10); and the Young Americans for Freedom ("Brief *Amicus Curiae* Young Americans for Freedom," p. 12).

84. "Brief of the NAACP Legal Defense . . . Fund," p. 9 n. 12. The Court in *Slaughter-House* qualified its doubts "whether any action of the State not directed by way of discrimination against the negroes as a class, or on account of their race, will ever be held to come within the purview of [the equal protection clause]" by asserting that "we do not say that no one else but the negro can share in this protection." *Slaughter-House Cases*, 83 U.S. 36, 72 (1873).

85. "Brief of the Mexican-American Legal Defense and Educational Fund as *Amicus Curiae*," *Bakke* (Calif. Supr. Ct.), p. 2.

86. "Brief *Amici Curiae* for the National Urban League, et al.," *Bakke* (asking the United States Supreme Court to deny *certiorari*), p. 4. "According to the United States census, there are at least 10.6 million 'persons of Spanish origin' in the United States." Ibid., p. 7.

87. "Brief of the Mexican-American Legal . . . Fund," *Bakke* (Calif. Supr. Ct.), pp. 9–10.

88. Ibid., pp. 13, 31.

89. See Chapter 1.

90. John Vasconcellos, Democrat and chairman of the California State Assembly Education Subcommittee on Post-Secondary Education.

91. "Brief of *Amici Curiae*, Mexican-American Legal Defense and Educational Fund, et al.," *Bakke* (U.S. Supr. Ct.), pp. 5ff.

92. Ibid., pp. 11, 29–30.

93. Jack Greenberg, quoted in Weinstein, "Interview with Greenberg," pp. 116–17.

94. Both quotes are in Fred Barbaro, "Ethnic Resentment," *Society* 11 (March–April 1974), p. 74.

95. Carl T. Rowan, "New Alliance," *Washington Star*, July 17, 1979, p. IV-5. Mr. Rowan did not endorse these suspicions, but only repeated the views of, in his words, a "substantial number of blacks."

96. Warren Brown, "Black, Hispanic Groups to Cooperate on Goals," *Washington Post*, November 14, 1978, p. 9.

97. See the remarks attributed to Representative John Conyers, D-Mich., in Rowan, "New Alliance."

98. "Brief of *Amicus Curiae*, Asian-American Bar Association of the Greater Bay Area in Support of Petitioners," *Bakke* (U.S. Supr. Ct.), pp. 12, 14.

99. "Brief of Native American Students of the University of California at Davis, et al., as *Amici Curiae* in Support of Petitioner," *Bakke* (U.S. Supr. Ct.), pp. 4, 5.

100. Interview with Robert Hermann, legal director, Puerto Rican Legal Defense Fund, New York, September 14, 1977.

101. Ibid.

102. "Puerto Ricans—Poorest of the U.S. Poor," *San Francisco Sunday Examiner and Chronicle*, February 19, 1978, p. 22.

103. "Brief of the Black Students Union of Yale University Law School, *Amicus Curiae*, in Support of Petitioner," *Bakke* (U.S. Supr. Ct.), p. 22.

104. Ibid.

105. "Brief *Amici Curiae* for National Council of Churches, et al.," *Bakke* (U.S. Supr. Ct.), p. 9.

106. "Brief of the Board of Governors of Rutgers, the State University of New Jersey, et al.," *Bakke* (U.S. Supr. Ct.), p. 30.

107. The phrase is Leonard Walentynowicz's, Executive Director, Polish-American Congress, Washington, D.C., January 10, 1977.

108. Well-articulated expressions of these fears may be found in Michael Novak, "Affirmative Action: Ethnic Perspective," pp. 1–21; Caroline Golab, "Comments: Ethnicity and Affirmative Action," pp. 37–42; and the Reverend John A. Limberakis, "Comments," pp. 48–50, all in *Affirmative Action: Ethnic Perspectives*, proceedings of a conference sponsored by the Nationalities Service Center and the Community College of Philadelphia; mimeographed, Philadelphia, Pennsylvania; October 29, 1976.

109. *United Jewish Organizations* v. *Carey*, 97 S.Ct. 966, 1014 (1977).

110. "Brief of the Polish-American Congress, et al., as *Amici Curiae*," *Bakke* (U.S. Supr. Ct.), pp. 7–8.

111. Code of Federal Regulations, Title XLI, Section 60-50.1 (b).

112. "Brief *Amicus Curiae* for the Order Sons of Italy in America in Support of Respondent," *Bakke* (U.S. Supr. Ct.), p. 4.

113. "Brief of the American Jewish Committee, et al.," *Bakke* (U.S. Supr. Ct.) p. 12.

114. Interviews with Anthony Krzywicki, legal counsel, Polish-American Affairs Council, Philadelphia, Pennsylvania, January 16, 1978; and with Arthur J. Gajarsa, general counsel, National Italian American Foundation, Washington, D.C., September 20, 1977.

115. Jeno F. Paulucci, "For Affirmative Action for Some Whites," *New York Times*, November 26, 1977, p. IV-3.

116. Nathan Glazer, *Affirmative Discrimination* (New York: Basic Books, 1975), p. 177 (emphasis in the original).

117. Interview with Krzywicki.

118. National Italian American Foundation, "Washington Newsletter," Washington, D.C., January/February 1977, p. 1. The "Italian-American Foundation" changed its name to "National Italian American Foundation" in December 1977.

TABLE 13 Differences in Scope Between Veteran and Neophyte Amici
Organizations

Amici Experience	Scope	
	Broad	Narrow
Veterans[a]		
Interest groups	7% (3)	13% (6)
Minority-defense	29 (13)	31 (14)
Public-interest advocates	11 (5)	9 (4)
Total	47% (21)	53% (24)
Neophytes[b]		
Interest groups	10% (7)	20% (14)
Minority-defense	7 (5)	41 (29)
Public-interest advocates	9 (6)	13 (9)
Total	26% (18)	74% (52)

NOTE: "Medium" scope organizations were disaggregated into those with two and those with three scope elements and collapsed into the "narrow" and "broad" categories respectively.
[a]"Veterans" denotes organizations that had participated in *DeFunis* as well as *Bakke*.
[b]"Neophytes" denotes organizations that participated only in *Bakke*.

119. Interview with Gajarsa.
120. John C. Calhoun, *A Disquisition on Government* (Charleston: Press of Walker and James, 1851), p. i.
121. Alexander Hamilton, James Madison, and John Jay, *The Federalist Papers* (New York: New American Library, 1961), No. 1, p. 33.
122. Some examples of such efforts are Carl J. Friedrich, ed., *The Public Interest* (New York: Lieber-Atherton, 1962); and Barry M. Mitneck, "A Typology of Conceptions of the Public Interest," *Administration and Society* VIII (May 1976), pp. 5–28.
123. Madison, *Federalist Papers*, No. 10, p. 78.
124. E. E. Schattschneider, The *Semi-Sovereign People* (New York: Holt, Rinehart and Winston, 1960), p. 23.
125. See table 13.
126. Interview with Samuel Rabinove, legal director, American Jewish Committee, New York, September 12, 1977.
127. Interview with David Reuben, general counsel's office, National Education Association, Washington, D.C., January 10, 1978.
128. This discussion of the American Civil Liberties Union relies upon interviews with, among others, Edward J. Ennis, Carl Cohen, John Shattuck, E. Richard Larson, and Frank Askin.
129. American Civil Liberties Union, *1976–1977 Annual Report* (Pamphlet, New York, 1977) pp. 1–10. These figures do not include the ACLU Foundation.
130. "Brief of the American Civil Liberties Union, the American Civil Liberties Union of Northern California, and the American Civil Liberties Union of Southern California, *Amici Curiae*," *Bakke* (U.S. Supr. Ct.), p. 1.
131. Stephen C. Halpern, "Assessing the Litigative Role of ACLU Chapters," *Policy Studies Journal* 4 (Winter 1975): 158.

132. Ibid. Jacob's distinction is made in his *Justice in America* (Boston: Little, Brown, 1978), p. 33.
133. Interview with E. Richard Larson, director of the American Civil Liberties Union *Bakke* task force, New York, September 12, 1977.
134. "Private Attorney Generals," *Yale Law Journal*, LVIII (1949): 581.
135. Interview with former chairman of the American Civil Liberties Union of Southern California, Los Angeles, May 17, 1978.
136. "Brief of the American Civil Liberties Union, . . . ," *Bakke* (U.S. Supr. Ct.), pp. 2–4.
137. The *Civil Liberties Review* ceased publication in 1979 because of financial problems.
138. Frank Askin, "Eliminating Racial Inequality in a Racist World," *Civil Liberties Review* 2 (Spring 1975): 96–105.
139. Carl Cohen, "Honorable Ends, Unsavory Means," in ibid., pp. 106–14.
140. American Civil Liberties Union Board of Directors, "Minutes," December 5–6, 1970; reprinted in the *1976 Policy Guide of the American Civil Liberties Union* (New York: American Civil Liberties Union, n.d.), p. 101.
141. Interview with Larson.
142. ACLU Board of Directors, "Minutes," p. 101.
143. "Brief of the Mexican-American Legal Defense Fund, et al.," *DeFunis* (U.S. Supr. Ct.), pp. 12, 31.
144. "News Release," November 27, 1972, reprinted in the *1976 Policy Guide*, p. 243. "Board Minutes," April 14–15, 1973, reprinted in ibid., pp. 247–48.
145. "News Release," September 29, 1969, reprinted in the *1976 Policy Guide*, p. 245. "Board Minutes," December 5–6, 1970, reprinted in ibid., p. 257.
146. "Board Minutes," September 24–25, 1977, reprinted in the *1977 Supplement to the American Civil Liberties Union Policy Guide* (Lexington, Massachusetts: Lexington Books, 1978), pp. 142–45.
147. Interview with former staff member, New York office of national ACLU in San Francisco, July 20, 1979.
148. E. Richard Larson, memorandum to "Interested ACLU Folks," May 11, 1977.
150. Ibid., pp. 12–13, quoting John Rawls, *A Theory of Justice*.
151. Ibid.
152. Ibid., pp. 9–10. The last sentence is a quotation taken from A. D. Lindsay, *The Modern Democratic State*.
153. Ibid., p. 10.
154. Larson, "Interested ACLU Folks," p. 1.
155. Quoted in Stephen Arons, "Friends of the Court . . . and the Man Who Started It All," *Saturday Review*, October 15, 1977, p. 13.
156. Interview with former staff member, July 20, 1979.
157. Interview with Larson. This statement was made in spite of the language in the *Policy Guide* quoted in footnotes 144 and 145 above.
158. Telephone interview with Frank Askin, general counsel, American Civil Liberties Union, New York, October 6, 1978.
159. Telephone conversation with a board member, Washington, D.C., November 8, 1979.

160. Ibid.
161. This conclusion draws upon discussions with Larson, Askin, a former staff member, the board member, and the former chairman of the Southern California affiliate of the ACLU.
162. Frank Askin, "Bakke Case: ACLU Files Amicus Brief Supporting Affirmative Action Program," *Civil Liberties*, July 1977, p. 5 (emphasis added).
163. "Nazi Defense by ACLU Has Cost 2,000 Members," *New York Times*, September 6, 1977, p. 16; Jim Mann, "Hard Times for the ACLU," *New Republic*, April 15, 1978, pp. 12–15. The *Times* cites as its source a member of the New York national office. Mann provides no sources for his numbers.
164. Interview with Larson.
165. Mann, "Hard Times for the ACLU," p. 13.
166. This was a judgment shared by the informants listed in footnote 161.
167. Wilson, *Political Organizations*, p. 239. Robert Salisbury, "An Exchange Theory of Interest Groups," *Midwest Journal of Political Science* 13 (February 1969): 1–30.
168. This personal observation is shared by observers such as Mann, "Hard Times for ACLU," p. 14. See more generally Wilson, *Political Organizations*, chaps. 2–4, 10–12, on the incentive structures of voluntary organizations.
169. Mayer Zald and Roberta Ash, "Social Movement Organizations: Growth, Decay, and Change," *Social Forces* 44 (March 1966): 330.
170. The ACLU's debate over affirmative action did not terminate with the *Bakke* case. The national board approved, and the 13th Biennial Convention of the ACLU ratified, a new affirmative action policy in 1979 which expanded the categories of individuals deserving affirmative assistance to include those with "physical or mental disability" and which explicitly endorsed the use of "numerical remedies," or quotas, for blacks, American Indians, Hispanics, Asian-Americans, and women. At least one member of the NAACP saw this as a dilution of the ACLU's affirmative action policy "by incorporating . . . a slew of other groups in a policy originally meant to deal with remedying racial/color discrimination. At the primarily white ACLU Biennial, the blacks lost." Letter from Michael Meyers to Jeannette Hopkins, September 1, 1982. See also "Biennial Conference in Washington, D.C., June 16–19," *Civil Liberties*, April 1979, p. 6; "ACLU Strengthens Its Affirmative Action Policy," *Civil Liberties*, June 1979, p. 2; Gara La Marche, "Biennial '79: New Faces, New Spirit," *Civil Liberties*, September 1979, p. 8; and Policy #306: "Affirmative Action in Employment and Education," *Policy Guide of the ACLU, 1981* (New York: ACLU, 1982), pp. 272–75.

Chapter III: The Oligarchic Impulse

1. The conventional citations are Plato's distinction between "timocracy," the regime animated by the love of honor, and "oligarchy," the political system "founded on property assessment . . . in which the rich rule and the poor man has no part in the ruling office" (*The Republic of Plato*,

translated with notes by Allan Bloom [New York: Basic Books, 1968], pp. 222–28); and Aristotle's defense of one of the three "true" or correct forms of political societies, aristocracy—"when the Few . . . rule with a view to the Common interest"—from its perverted or deviant form, oligarchy, the rule of the rich in the interests of the rich (*The Politics of Aristotle*, edited and translated by Ernest Barker [New York: Oxford University Press, 1946], pp. 114–17). Both perceptions emphasize the types of passion motivating political action: aristocracy presumes a life of virtue and a commitment to the politics of the common interest; oligarchy is motivated by the love of material interests and is dedicated to the preservation of special interests. A vivid depiction of the classical Greek understanding of the oligarchic mentality is captured in Thucydides' account of the Corcya civil war. Corcya, once a town blessed by the love of "simple honesty," becomes the battleground for the "love of power, operating through greed and through personal ambition" (*History of the Peloponnesian War*, translated by Rex Warner [Baltimore: Penguin Books, 1954], pp. 207–12).

2. Daniel Bell, "Meritocracy and Equality," *The Public Interest* 29 (Fall 1972): 66. See also Carl J. Friedrich, "Reason and Discretion," in Friedrich, ed., *Authority* (New York: Lieber-Atherton, 1958), p. 37.

3. *The Life and Work of John Adams*, edited by Charles Francis Adams, vol. 4 (Boston: Charles C. Little and James Brown, 1851), p. 427.

4. Robert Michels, *Political Parties* (New York: Collier Books, 1962). Michels's work shares this distinction with Gaetano Mosca's *The Ruling Class* and Vilfredo Pareto's *The Mind and Society*, but in terms of its impact it is, at least, first among equals.

5. Michels, *Political Parties*, p. 47.

6. Ibid., Parts I (chapters 1–3), II (chapters 1–2, 7), III (chapter 1), VI (chapter 2).

7. Carl J. Friedrich, *Constitutional Government and Democracy*, 4th ed. (Waltham, Mass.: Blaisdell Publishing Co., 1968), p. 439.

8. *From Max Weber: Essays in Sociology*, translated and edited by H. H. Gerth and C. Wright Mills (New York: Oxford University Press, 1946), p. 228.

9. Michels, *Political Parties*, p. 33.

10. Mayer Zald and Roberta Ash, "Social Movement Organizations: Growth, Decay, and Change," *Social Forces* 44 (March 1966): 338–39.

11. Elliott Rudwick and August Meier, "Organizational Structure and Goal Succession: A Comparative Analysis of the NAACP and CORE, 1964–1968," *Social Science Quarterly* 51 (June 1970): 9–24.

12. Henry J. Pratt, "Bureaucracy and Group Behavior: A Study of Three National Organizations," paper delivered to the American Political Science Association, 1972, cited in James Q. Wilson, *Political Organizations* (New York: Basic Books, 1973), pp. 226–27.

13. Seymour Martin Lipset, M. A. Trow, and James S. Coleman, *Union Democracy* (Garden City, New York: Anchor Books, 1956).

14. Samuel J. Eldersveld, "American Interest Groups: A Survey of Research and Some Implications for Theory and Method," in Henry W. Ehrmann, ed., *Interest Groups on Four Continents* (Pittsburgh: University of Pittsburgh Press, 1958), p. 185.

15. Lipset, Trow, and Coleman, *Union Democracy*, pp. 448–52.
16. Philip Selznick suggests that this phrase should properly read "the self-preserving consent of the governed."
17. Harold Lasswell and Daniel Lerner, *The Comparative Studies of Elites* (Stanford: Stanford University Press, 1952), p. 7.
18. Carol S. Greenwald, *Group Power: Lobbying and Public Policy* (New York: Praeger, 1977), pp. 303–4.
19. Daniel Reisman, *The Lonely Crowd* (New Haven: Yale University Press, 1961), p. 223.
20. Nelson W. Polsby, *Community Power and Political Theory* (New Haven: Yale University Press, 1963), p. 118.
21. Pluralism presumes that public issues "are separable, can be dealt with satisfactorily by piecemeal adjustment, and can be solved by limiting the scope of conflict, cooperating with others in searching for solutions, and accepting compromises." Both quotations are from Robert A. Dahl, *Democracy in the United States: Promise and Performance*, 4th ed. (Boston: Houghton Mifflin, 1981), p. 58.
22. Robert A. Dahl and Charles E. Lindblom, *Politics, Economics, and Welfare* (New York: Harper Torchbooks, 1963), p. 312.
23. The most readable counterargument to standard pluralist theory is C. Wright Mills's *The Power Elite* (New York: Oxford University Press, 1956). Other works criticizing the alleged conservative bias of pluralism are Henry S. Kariel, *The Decline of American Pluralism* (Stanford: Stanford University Press, 1961), chapter IX; and Grant McConnell, *Private Power and American Democracy* (New York: Random House, Vintage Books, 1966), chapter 4. Two critiques of the empirical adequacy of pluralist explanations are E. E. Schattschneider, *The Semi-Sovereign People* (New York: Holt, Rinehart and Winston, 1960), chapters 2 and 6; and Jack L. Walker, "A Critique of the Elitist Theory of Democracy," *American Political Science Review* 60 (June 1966): 285–95. One should also read Dahl's rejoinder (Robert A. Dahl, "Further Reflections on 'The Elitist Theory of Democracy'," ibid.: 296–305).
24. Giovanni Sartori, *Democratic Theory* (New York: Praeger, 1965), p. 81.
25. Robert A. Dahl, *Polyarchy* (New Haven: Yale University Press, 1971).
26. Jeffrey M. Berry, *Lobbying for the People* (Princeton: Princeton University Press, 1977), p. 210.
27. Lipset, Trow, and Coleman, *Union Democracy*, p. 1.
28. Grant McConnell, "Public and Private Government," in Sanford Lakoff and Daniel Rich, eds., *Private Government* (Glenview, Illinois: Scott, Foresman, 1973), p. 32.
29. V. L. Allen, *Power in Trade Unions* (London: Longmans, Green, 1954), pp. 10–11, 15.
30. Methods employed to classify organizations are described in the Appendix.
31. David Truman, *The Governmental Process* (New York: Alfred Knopf, 1965), p. 142.
32. Albert O. Hirschman, *Exit, Voice, and Loyalty* (Cambridge: Harvard University Press, 1970), pp. 21, 46, 82–86, 132–37.
33. See table 14.
34. See table 15.

TABLE 14 Bureaucratic Size and Membership Participation

Level of Membership Participation	Less than 1/100[a]	1–2/100	3 or more/100	Total
	Ratio of Staff to Organization Members			
Oligarchic organizations	42% (22)	40% (21)	19% (10)	101%[b] (53)
Democratic organizations	45 (21)	36 (17)	19 (9)	100 (47)
	(43)	(38)	(19)	(100)

θ = −.0241 = −.02

[a] Staff members per 100 organization members, rounded to nearest whole number.
[b] Does not equal 100% because of rounding.

TABLE 15 Leadership Style and Membership Participation

Leadership Style	Active[a] Participation	Passive or no Participation	Total
Oligarchic style[b]	24% (41)	76% (128)	100% (169)
Democratic style[c]	84 (127)	16 (24)	100 (151)
	(168)	(152)	(320)

NOTE: Managerial organizations are not included.
[a] Organizations were assigned "active" or "passive or no" participation scores according to responses from interviewees and assessment of public and private descriptions of organizational policy making in Bakke.
[b] Organizations whose respondents characterized the policy-making process in their organization as "elite domination" (decision made by executive officers and staff members).
[c] Organizations whose respondents characterized the policy-making process in their organization as "broad membership participation" or struggle among organizational elites.

35. Leadership style and degree of polarization were associated by a high lambda of .60. (See table 16.)
36. See table 17.
37. See table 18.
38. This section depends, in part, on interviews with Louis Pollak, Mason Harding, Iris Brest, Albert J. Rosenthal, Ralph Smith, and Oliver Williams.
39. Interview with Mason Harding, general counsel, Columbia University, New York City, September 9, 1977.
40. "Ivy Schools Plan to Give Opinions on Bakke Admission Quota Case," Daily Pennsylvanian (student newspaper of the University of Pennsylvania), March 9, 1977, pp. 1, 7.
41. Telephone conversation with Iris Brest, legal counsel, Stanford University, Stanford, California, August 10, 1977.
42. Letter from Allan Bakke to Peter C. Storandt, Assistant Dean of Admissions, University of California, Davis Medical School, August 7, 1973; reprinted in "Brief of Amici Curiae, the National Urban League, et al.,"

TABLE 16 Leadership Style and Polarization

Level of Polarization	Oligarchic Style	Democratic Style	Total
High polarization[a]	81% (127)	19% (30)	100% (157)
Medium polarization[b]	59 (31)	42 (22)	101[d] (53)
Low polarization[c]	6 (6)	94 (93)	100 (99)
	(164)	(145)	(309)[e]

$\lambda = .6005 = .60$

[a] Organizations whose respondents mildly or strongly agreed with statement "Discussion about *Bakke* in my organization involved name calling, personal hostilities, and bitterness."
[b] Organizations whose respondents neither strongly agreed nor disagreed with statement in footnote a.
[c] Organizations whose respondents mildly or strongly disagreed with statement in footnote a.
[d] Does not equal 100% because of rounding.
[e] Does not include respondents from managerial organizations or the "don't knows."

TABLE 17 Managerial Organizations and "Membership" Participation

"Did you consult with frequent contributors or clients of your organization about participating in *Bakke*?"

Respondents from managerial organizations saying:

Yes	63%	(26)
No	32	(13)
Don't Know	5	(2)
	100%	(41)

TABLE 18 Intraorganizational Conflict in Amici Organizations

Responses to the statement:

"How would you characterize the amount of differences of opinion (conflict) in your organization?"

High	35%	(127)
Medium	27	(96)
Low	18	(66)
None	17	(61) } 35% (127)
Don't Know	3	(11)
		(361)

(urging the United States Supreme Court to deny *certiorari* in *Bakke*), pp. 4a–6a.

43. Telephone interview with Brest.
44. Interviews with Harding; and with Albert Rosenthal, professor of law and one of the authors of the *Bakke* brief submitted by the University of Pennsylvania and Columbia, Harvard, and Stanford Universities, at Columbia University Law School; New York City; September 9, 1977.
45. Interview with Harding.
46. Robert Lucid, chairman of the University Council Steering Committee, quoted in "Ivy Schools Plan to Give Opinions on Bakke," p. 7. Some faculty leaders asked to review the brief before its submission, but most faculty members did not become upset until after they read in the press that a brief had been filed without their approval.
47. Interview with Oliver P. Williams and James Piereson, Department of Political Science, University of Pennsylvania; Philadelphia; February 27, 1979. Similar comments are reported in ibid.
48. Ibid.
49. Ibid.
50. "Brief of Columbia University, Harvard University, Stanford University, and the University of Pennsylvania as *Amici Curiae*," *Regents of the University of California* v. *Bakke* 438 U.S. 265 (1978) [Hereafter referred to as *Bakke* (U.S. Supr. Ct.)], p. 2 n. 1.
51. The perplexing character of the university as an association is exacerbated by what Cohen and March have called its "organized anarchy." The university "does not know what it is doing. Its goals are either vague or in dispute. Its major participants wander in and out." Michael Cohen and James G. March, eds., *Leadership and Ambiguity* (New York: McGraw-Hill, 1974), p. 3.
52. This discussion of the American Federation of Teachers' involvement in *Bakke* relies on discussions with, among others, Lawrence Poltrock, James Ballard, William Simons, Warren Kessler, and Raul Teilhet.
53. Bert Shanas, "Albert Shanker: The Politics of Clout," *New York Affairs* 6 (1978): 5, 8.
54. Albert Shanker, speaking on the NBC "Today" show, August 25, 1977.
55. "Brief for the American Federation of Labor and Congress of Industrial Organizations as *Amicus Curiae*," *DeFunis* v. *Odegaard*, 416 U.S. 312 (1974), pp. 4–5. Although Shanker pressed for an AFL-CIO brief in *Bakke*, the leadership resisted, officially because the organization's concern about the seniority issue and other Title VII questions had been settled by the courts since 1974, leaving the AFL-CIO with no specific interest in the outcome of the case. However, a more plausible explanation was the fear of inflaming the divisions within the union over the issue of affirmative action. Despite the firm policy against member unions offering briefs opposing one another in court cases, the AFT decided to file a brief on Bakke's side while the American Federation of State, County, and Municipal Employees; the International Union of Electrical, Radio, and Machine Workers; and the United Farm Workers of America—all AFL-CIO affiliates—joined the anti-Bakke coalition brief headed by the National Council of Churches. Interview with Law-

rence Poltrock, general counsel, American Federation of Teachers; Chicago, Illinois; January 28, 1978.

56. Interview with Poltrock.

57. This paragraph draws upon the interview with Poltrock and a conversation with a staff member in the Washington, D.C., office of the AFT, March 14, 1979.

58. Owen M. Fiss, "Groups and the Equal Protection Clause," *Philosophy and Public Affairs* 5 (Winter 1976): 107, 109.

59. While the AFT's argument was contradicted by the success of Asian-American applicants to Davis (between 1970 and 1975, Asian-Americans won eleven of the seventy special admission slots and forty-one of the 450 regular admission slots), it may not have been too far off-base as regards black applicants. Only one black during the five-year period won admission through the regular process; twenty-six were admitted during the same period through the special admissions program. In 1973 and 1974, Chicanos were successful in both programs (fifteen special admissions, six regular). See Table 1, Chapter 1. However, one might plausibly rebut the AFT position by pointing out that in the absence of a special program, educationally or economically disadvantaged blacks might have won no slots in the admissions contest.

60. "Brief of the American Federation of Teachers, *Amicus Curiae,*" *Bakke v. Regents of the University of California,* 553 P.2d 1152 (1976), pp. 16−17.

61. "Brief of the American Federation of Teachers, *Amicus Curiae,*" *Bakke* (U.S. Supr. Ct.), pp. 12−15.

62. Interview with Poltrock.

63. "Teacher Union Refuses to Back Minority Quotas," *New York Times,* August 19, 1977, p. 13. Mr. Teilhet's remarks were made during a public debate on *Bakke* held on the campus of the University of California, Berkeley, October 12, 1977.

64. See "Bakke: UPC Disagreement with AFT," *Advocate* (November−December 1977), p. 8.

65. "Brief of the American Federation of Teachers," *Bakke* (U.S. Supr. Ct.), pp. 1−2.

66. The first statement is attributed to Ned Hopkins, the second to John O'Neill. Quoted in Shanas, "Albert Shanker," p. 14.

67. Greenwald, *Group Power,* p. 42.

68. Adolph A. Berle, Jr., and Gardiner C. Means, *The Modern Corporation and Private Property* (New York: Harcourt Brace Jovanovich, 1968).

69. Mancur Olson, Jr., *The Logic of Collective Action* (Cambridge: Harvard University Press, 1971), pp. 55−56.

70. Seymour Martin Lipset, *The First New Nation* (Garden City, New York: Doubleday Anchor, 1963), p. 232.

71. Wilson, *Political Organizations,* p. 239.

72. Stephen K. Bailey, *Education Interest Groups in the Nation's Capital* (Washington, D.C.: American Council on Education, 1975), p. 28.

73. Carter's margin of victory in New York State was 288,000 or two percent of the votes counted, but he won New York City by over 650,000 votes, enough to offset Gerald Ford's majorities in the suburbs and up-

state New York. Bert Shanas estimated that the AFT "can deliver a half million votes in New York City alone, and maybe ten times that many nationally." A Harris Poll discovered that eighty-five percent of the AFT membership voted in accord with the union's recommendations in the 1976 presidential election. Shanas, "Albert Shanker," pp. 5–6, 9.

74. Ibid.

75. Ibid., p. 8.

76. This discussion relies on conversations with Raul Teilhet and others.

77. This discussion of the Legal Services Corporation relies on interviews with, among others, Alice Daniels, Revius O. Ortique, Jr., Stephen S. Walters, and Jeffrey Segel.

78. 42 *U.S.C.* sections 2996–2996K. Congress extended the Corporation's charter in 1977 (Public Law 95-222).

79. The original legal service program was initiated by officials of the Office of Economic Opportunity under the authority of Title II of the Economic Opportunity Act of 1964, Public Law 88-452 (August 20, 1964), codified at 42 *U.S.C.* sections 2701-2994d (1970). The program was specifically authorized by Congress with the passage of the Economic Opportunity Amendments of 1966, Public Law 89-794, section 222 (a) (November 8, 1966), codified at 42 *U.S.C.* section 8809 (1970).

80. Note, "The Legal Services Corporation: Curtailing Political Interference," *Yale Law Journal* 81 (1971): 247–59.

81. Arlie Schardt, "Legal Services, Round II," *Civil Liberties Review* 2 (Winter 1975): 41–42.

82. H.R. 6360, 92d Congress, 1st Session (March 18, 1971).

83. H.R. 8163, 92d Congress, 1st Session (May 5, 1971).

84. U.S. Congress, House, Committee on Appropriations, "Statement of Thomas Ehrlich, President, Legal Services Corporation," *Departments of State, Justice, and Commerce, the Judiciary, and Related Agencies Appropriations for 1979, Hearings Before a Subcommittee of the Committee on Appropriations*, 95th Congress, 2d Session, 1978, Part 3, p. 767.

85. Interview with Stephen S. Walters, legal counsel, Legal Services Corporation, Washington, D.C., September 19, 1977.

86. "Interest of *Amicus Curiae*," in "Brief of the Legal Service Corporation, *Amicus Curiae* on Behalf of Petitioner," Bakke (U.S. Supr. Ct.), pp. 2–4.

87. Telephone interview with Alice Daniels, general counsel, Legal Services Corporation; Washington, D.C.; September 19, 1977.

88. U.S. Congress, House, Statement of Representative John Ashbrook of Ohio on the LSC Reauthorization Bill, H.R. 6666, 95th Congress, 2d Session, June 27, 1977, *Congressional Record (Daily Digest)*, 123: 111, pp. H6535, H6539-H6545. Ashbrook's proposed amendment would have prohibited explicitly the presentation of any legal assistance by the LSC in cases "involving any program of affirmative action or any other system of quotas or goals . . ." (H6539). The Congressman also offered an amendment which would require the liquidation of the Corporation by September 30, 1979. That amendment was defeated by a floor vote.

89. Ibid., pp. H6540, H6542.

90. U.S. Congress, Senate, Debate on Hayakawa Amendment to Senate Bill 1303, 95th Congress, 2d Session, October 10, 1977, *Congressional Record (Daily Digest)*, 123: 162, pp. S16805-S16808.

91. Interview with Daniels.

92. Telephone interview with Jeffrey Segel, staff counsel, Project Advisory Group, Washington, D.C., January 30, 1979. The PAG is a voluntary association of local legal services programs that attempts to give organizational voice to local interests in LSC operations.

93. See Philip Selznick's discussion of the leader as "law-giver" and the requisites of "institutionalization" in his *Leadership in Administration* (Evanston, Illinois: Row, Peterson, 1957), pp. 5–28.

94. Interview with Daniels.

95. "Statement of Thomas Ehrlich," p. 763.

96. U.S. Congress, House, Statement of Representative Thomas Railsback of Illinois, 95th Congress, 2d Session, June 27, 1977, *Congressional Record (Daily Digest)*, 123:111, p. H6541. (The pertinent subcommittee is the Subcommittee on Courts, Civil Liberties, and the Administration of Justice of the House Committee on the Judiciary.)

97. "The President's Message to Congress Proposing Establishment of the Independent Corporation," *Weekly Compilation of Presidential Documents* 7 (May 5, 1971): 727.

98. Schardt, "Legal Services, Round II," p. 42.

99. U.S. Congress, Senate, *State, Justice, Commerce, the Judiciary, and Related Agencies Appropriations, 1978, Hearing Before the Committee on Appropriations*, 95th Congress, 1st Session, 1977, Part 3, p. 585.

100. Judith Shklar, *Legalism* (Cambridge: Harvard University Press, 1964), p. 1.

101. "Brief *Amici Curiae* for the National Council of Churches, et al.," *Bakke* (U.S. Supr. Ct.), Appendix A, p. 5A.

102. National Legal Aid and Defender Association, *Annual Report, 1976/1977* (Washington, D.C.: National Legal Aid and Defender Association, n.d., n.p.). This discussion of the NLADA relies on interviews conducted with, among others, Jeffrey Isralsky.

103. "Brief of the Legal Aid Society of Alameda County and the National Association for the Advancement of Colored People, et al., as *Amici Curiae*," *DeFunis* (U.S. Supr. Ct.), pp. 5–6.

104. This paragraph relies on a telephone interview with Jeffrey Isralsky, deputy director, Defender Division, National Legal Aid and Defender Association; Washington, D.C.; January 12, 1978.

105. Ibid., and interview with Segel.

106. Lewis Anthony Dexter, *How Organizations Are Represented in Washington* (Indianapolis: Bobbs-Merrill, 1969), chapter 1.

107. Greenwald, *Group Power*, p. 54.

108. Interview with Isralsky.

109. Telephone interview with an NLADA member, New York City, August 17, 1978.

110. Selznick, *Leadership in Administration*, p. 58.

111. Theodore Lowi, *The End of Liberalism* (New York: W. W. Norton, 1969), p. 93.

112. Interview with Williams.

113. Truman, *The Governmental Process*, p. 199.

114. Ibid. is an example of such a discussion, see pp. 199–201.

115. The first quotation comes from a letter from the president of a union, and the second quotation comes from an interview with the executive director of a Washington-based organization. Both preferred anonymity. Interview conducted on January 11, 1978.
116. Norman Luttberg and L. Harmon Zeigler, "Attitude Consensus and Conflict in an Interest Group: An Assessment of Cohesion," *American Political Science Review* 60 (September 1966): 655–66.
117. *Regents of the University of California v. Bakke*, 438 U.S. 265, 311–13, 316–17, 321–24 (1978).
118. "The Landmark Bakke Ruling," *Newsweek*, July 10, 1978, p. 25. See McGeorge Bundy, "The Issue Before the Court: Who Gets Ahead in America?", *Atlantic Monthly* 240 (November 1977):41–42, 53.
119. Telephone conversation with a member of the Development Office, University of Pennsylvania, Philadelphia, September 9, 1977.

Chapter IV: The Anagrams of Democracy

1. James MacGregor Burns, *Leadership* (New York: Harper and Row Colophon Books, 1978), p. 425.
2. Taken from interviews with informants who were members in, respectively, the Jewish Labor Council, the Equal Employment Advisory Council, the Order Sons of Italy in America, the Committee for Academic Nondiscrimination and Integrity, the American Indian Bar Association.
3. The vocabulary of "bargaining," "compromise," and "integration" is from Mary Parker Follett, *Dynamic Administration* (New York: Harper, 1941), pp. 213–21. I have taken considerable liberties in redefining these concepts for my own use. (See Appendix.)
4. Philip Selznick, *Leadership in Administration* (Evanston, Illinois: Row, Peterson, 1957), p. 58.
5. See table 19.
6. See table 14, Chapter 3, note 33.
7. See table 20.
8. See table 21.
9. The discussion that follows is based on several different sources: interviews with members of the Justice Department, the Department of Health, Education, and Welfare, and the White House staff, most of whom requested anonymity; interviews with representatives of advocacy organizations that pressed the Administration to file a *Bakke* brief; the almost daily accounts of the struggle over the brief in the pages of the *New York Times* and the *Washington Post*; John Osborne's article "Carter's Brief" (*The New Republic*, October 15, 1977); and James W. Singer's account of the controversy in the September 17 and October 1, 1977 issues of the *National Journal*.
10. Samuel Krislov, "The Role of the Attorney General as Amicus Curiae," in *Roles of the Attorney General of the United States* (Washington, D.C.: American Enterprise Institute, 1968).
11. Philip Perlman, quoted in Clement Vose, *Caucasians Only: The Supreme Court, the NAACP, and the Restrictive Covenant Cases* (Berkeley: University of California Press, 1959), p. 170.

TABLE 19 Interest Orientation and Style of Democratic Decision Making

Interest Orientation (Structure of Interest)	Decision-Making Style			Total
	Bargaining	Compromise	Integration	
Interest-group	14% (1)	71% (5)	14% (1)	99%ᵃ (7)
Minority-defense	20 (7)	60 (21)	20 (7)	100 (35)
Public-interest advocate	20 (1)	20 (1)	60 (3)	100 (5)
	(9)	(27)	(11)	(47)

λ = .0625 = .06

ᵃDoes not equal 100% because of rounding.

TABLE 20 Polarization in Democratic Organizations

Democratic Decision-Making Style	Degree of polarization			Total
	High	Medium	Low	
Bargaining	78% (7)	11% (1)	11% (1)	100% (9)
Compromise	11 (3)	26 (7)	63 (17)	100 (27)
Integrative	0 (0)	9 (1)	91 (10)	100 (11)
	(10)	(9)	(28)	(47)

λ = .2564 = .26

NOTE: Each type of democratic organization was assigned a polarization score based on responses to the statement "Discussion about *Bakke* in my organization involved name calling, personal hostilities, and bitterness." Organizations whose respondents strongly or mildly agreed with the statement were categorized as "High polarization." Those whose respondents neither strongly agreed or disagreed were identified as "Medium polarization." Those who strongly or mildly disagreed were labeled "Low polarization."

12. Daniel Berman, *It Is So Ordered* (New York: W. W. Norton, 1966), p. 57.
13. The incoming Eisenhower Administration also endorsed the brief. This paragraph's account of the intragovernmental struggle over the suggested *DeFunis* brief is based largely on interviews with three members of the Justice Department and a former staff aide to the President. See also Robert M. O'Neil, *Discriminating Against Discrimination: Preferential Admissions and the DeFunis Case* (Bloomington: Indiana University Press, 1975), pp. 29–30.
14. Letter from Donald Reidhaar, general counsel for the University of California, to Albert Meyerhoff, May 5, 1977.
15. Nancy Hicks, "Califano Says Quotas Are Necessary to Reduce Bias in Jobs and Schools," *New York Times*, March 18, 1977, pp. 1, 18.
16. David Bird, "Califano Concedes Error in Advocating Job Quotas," *New York Times*, April 1, 1977, pp. 1, 27. A letter addressed to the secretary by the Committee on Academic Non-Discrimination and Integrity demanding he repudiate his March 17 statement may have been the cata-

Table 21   297

TABLE 21 Leadership Behavior and Style of Democratic Decision Making

Democratic decision-making style	(1 Strongly Agree)	(2)	(3)	(4)	(5 Strongly Disagree)	(Don't Know)	Total
			Percentage of respondents				
Bargaining	20% (6)	30% (9)	30% (9)	17% (5)	3% (1)	0% (0)	100% (30)
Compromise	28 (24)	42 (36)	15 (13)	8 (7)	2 (2)	5 (4)	100 (86)
Integrative	54 (19)	31 (11)	6 (2)	9 (3)	0 (0)	0 (0)	100 (35)
	(49)	(56)	(24)	(15)	(3)	(4)	(151)

NOTE: Data on decision-making procedures were elicited by use of the following question: Do you agree with the statement "My organization's leaders acted to insure the fullest discussion of *Bakke*, communicated the alternatives we could pursue, and responded positively to membership preferences."

lyst for a telephone conversation with Bird in which Califano retracted his original statements.

17. Memorandum to Secretary Califano from St. John Barrett, acting general counsel; Albert Hamlin, acting director, Office for Civil Rights; Mary Berry, Assistant Secretary for Education; and Ernest Boyer, Commissioner of Education, March 25, 1977.
18. Letter from St. John Barrett to Drew Days, March 29, 1977.
19. "Briefs on *Bakke*," Newsletter for the Institute for the Study of Educational Policy, Howard University, Washington, D.C., June, 1977, mimeographed, p. 3.
20. The American Jewish Committee, American Jewish Congress, Anti-Defamation League, Jewish Labor Committee, Jewish War Veterans, Agudath Israel of America, National Council of Jewish Women, and the National Jewish Community Relations Advisory Council.
21. Memorandum to the National Committee on Nondiscrimination of the Anti-Defamation League from Ira Gissen, Civil Rights Committee, New York, July 13, 1977.
22. Rowland Evans and Robert Novak, "The Quarrel Over Quotas," *Washington Post*, August 29, 1977, p. C-5.
23. "Transcript of President's News Conference on Foreign and Domestic Matters," *New York Times*, July 29, 1977, p. 8.
24. Quoted in "Justice Department Aids UC on Bakke," *Daily Californian* (student newspaper of the University of California, Berkeley), August 25, 1977, p. 1. See also Jean Heller, "Attorney General Bell—Either Loved or Hated?", *San Francisco Chronicle*, October 3, 1977, p. 22.
25. David E. Rosenbaum, "Carter Said to Back Bar to Race Quotas," *New York Times*, September 12, 1977, pp. 1, 24.
26. "Blacks Urge Carter to Back Affirmative Action," *New York Times*, September 10, 1977, p. C-49.
27. Interview with Leonard Walentynowicz, executive director, Polish-American Congress, Washington, D.C., January 10, 1978.
28. "Blacks Warn Carter on Bakke Case," *San Francisco Chronicle*, September 13, 1977, pp. 1, 20.
29. David E. Rosenbaum, "Carter Called Firm Against Race Quotas," *New York Times*, September 14, 1977, p. 15.
30. "Blacks Pressure Carter on Bakke," *Berkeley Gazette*, September 13, 1977, pp. 1, 4.
31. Margaret Gentry, "Carter Plays Safe on Race Issue," *Berkeley Gazette*, September 15, 1977, p. 11.
32. "Brief of the United States as Amicus Curiae," *Regents of the University of California* v. *Bakke*, 438 U.S. 265 (1978) [Hereafter cited as *Bakke* (U.S. Supr. Ct.)], pp. 29 and 62. The brief is quoting a March 23, 1973 policy statement of the Justice Department, Labor Department, the Civil Service Commission, and the Equal Employment Opportunity Commission.
33. "Brief of the United States," p. 65 and pp. 71–73.
34. Quoted in Rosenbaum, "Carter Said to Back Bar to Race Quotas," pp. 1, 24.
35. *Record, Bakke* v. *Regents of the University of California*, Office of the Clerk of the United States Supreme Court, pp. 203–205, 210.

36. Berman, *It Is So Ordered*, pp. 83–86.
37. Attorney General Bell, quoted in Robert Reinhold, "U.S. Backs Minority Admissions But Avoids Issue of Racial Quotas," *New York Times*, September 20, 1977, pp. 1, 34.
38. A "Justice Department source," quoted in "Carter's Dog-Day Afternoon," *Time*, September 5, 1977, pp. 12–13.
39. An unnamed Justice Department attorney, quoted in Osborne, "Carter's Brief," p. 13.
40. "Justice Backs Veterans' Job Law; White House Aides Upset," *Washington Post*, December 5, 1978, p. 2.
41. Allan P. Sindler, *Bakke, DeFunis, and Minority Admissions* (New York: Longman, 1978), p. 253.
42. "Brief *Amicus Curiae* of the American Jewish Congress, et al.," *Shelley v. Kraemer* 334 U.S. 1 (1948). Vose, *Caucasians Only*, pp. 142, 155, 163–73, 194, 241.
43. "Brief *Amicus Curiae*," *Brown v. Board of Education*, 347 U.S. 483 (1954). Berman, *It Is So Ordered*, p. 57.
44. "Private Attorney-Generals: Group Action in the Fight for Civil Liberties," *Yale Law Journal* 58 (1949): 589–92. The Commission is now entitled the Commission on Law, Social Action and Urban Affairs.
45. This discussion of the American Jewish Congress relies on interviews with, among others, Joseph Robison, Richard Cohen, and Norman Dershowitz.
46. "Where We Stand: Quotas and Goals," resolution adopted by the National Biennial Convention of the American Jewish Congress, May 12, 1972 (Pamphlet, New York, n.d.).
47. Interview with Richard Cohen, associate executive director, American Jewish Congress, New York, September 9, 1977.
48. Telephone conversation with AJC member and former vice-president, Brooklyn chapter, New York, December 27, 1979.
49. Interview with Cohen.
50. Ibid.
51. The Union of American Hebrew Congregations, "Programs and Services" (undated pamphlet, New York), pp. 14–15.
52. "Draft Resolution from the Task Force on the Bakke Case," Minutes of the Commission on Social Action, New York, April 24–25, 1977. See also, "*Bakke*: No Easy Answers," *Reform Judaism*, October 1977, p. 1.
53. General Assembly of the Union of American Hebrew Congregations, "Statement on Affirmative Action," mimeographed, adopted November 18–22, 1977, San Francisco, California.
54. Interview with two members of the Council's executive board, New York City, January 12, 1978.
55. "Brief of the American Jewish Congress, in Support of Petitioner," *DeFunis v. Odegaard*, 416 U.S. 312 (1974), pp. 3–4, 12–13.
56. "Resolution on Quotas and Affirmative Action," adopted by the Governing Council of the American Jewish Congress, Philadelphia, Pennsylvania, October 20, 1974.
57. Interview with Joseph Robison, director emeritus, Commission on Law and Social Action, American Jewish Congress, New York, September 9, 1977. Hyman Bookbinder, the American Jewish Committee's Washing-

ton representative, echoed Robison's sentiments, stating that *Bakke* was his "most painful" experience in forty years of political life (Quoted in Steven V. Roberts, "Bakke Case Divides Rights Group," *San Diego Union*, September 25, 1977, p. 5).

58. "Resolution on Quotas and Affirmative Action," pp. 1–2.

59. The non-Jewish endorsers were the Hellenic Bar Association of Illinois, the Italian-American Foundation, the Polish American Affairs Council, the Polish American Educators Association, the Ukrainian Congress Committee of America (Chicago Division), and UNICO. The AJC's strategy was explained by Joseph Robison.

60. Quoted in "The Bakke Briefs: Old Allies Split," *New York Times*, October 20, 1977, p. B-5. The same bewilderment was voiced to me by writers of briefs representing black, Latino and feminist groups.

61. "The 'Affirmative Action' Debate; Can Justice Be Color-Blind?," *City* 6 (Summer 1972): 29–30. Another critic of the Jewish "retreat" from an aggressive civil rights posture is more charitable, ascribing it to a strong affirmation of the twin doctrines of individualism and meritocracy and to an ignorance of the "unique historical experiences of blacks" that make the experiences of other minority groups irrelevant. Martin Kilson, "The Elusive Contours of Postwar Race Relations," *Civil Liberties Review* 5 (March/June 1978): 40.

62. Leonard Fein, "The War Inside the Jews," *The New Republic*, October 16, 1977, p. 16.

63. A. L. Stevenson's study of discriminatory "help wanted" ads during the first quarter of the twentieth century shows a rise in advertisements specifically excluding Jews from less than one percent in 1911 to over 13% in 1926 (Discussed in L. Harmon Zeigler and Wayne Peak, *Interest Groups in American Society* (Englewood Cliffs: Prentice-Hall, 1972), p. 27).

64. Herbert A. Simon, *Administrative Behavior* (New York: Free Press, 1957), p. 14.

65. 319 U.S. 624 (1943). See David R. Manwaring's description of the AJC's role in *Render Unto Caesar: The Flag-Salute Controversy* (Chicago: University of Chicago Press, 1962).

66. "Resolution on Quotas and Affirmative Action," p. 1 (emphasis added).

67. "Brief of the American Jewish Committee, et al.," *Bakke* (U.S. Supr. Ct.), p. 8.

68. Fein, "The War Inside the Jews," p. 18.

69. Joseph B. Robison, "Giving Reality to the Promise of Job Equality," *Law in Transition Quarterly* 1 (1964): 115–17.

70. This discussion of the NAACP depends on interviews with, among others, Roy Wilkins, Nathaniel Jones, Nathaniel Colley, Clarence Mitchell, Frank Pohlhaus, and William Wells.

71. "Brief of the National Association for the Advancement of Colored People as *Amicus Curiae*," *Bakke* (U.S. Supr. Ct.), p. 4.

72. "Brief of the Appellant," *Brown* v. *Board of Education*, p. 187.

73. "Brief of the Appellant," *Bolling* v. *Sharpe*, 347 U.S. 497 (1954), p. 10.

74. Quoted in Diane Ravitch, "Color-Blind or Color-Conscious?," *The New Republic*, May 5, 1979, p. 17.

75. Interview with Roy Wilkins, former executive director, NAACP, Washington, D.C., November 2, 1978.

76. Memoranda addressed to "staff" dated March (no day), 1968, and October 8, 1969.

77. Telephone interview with Frank Pohlhaus, legal counsel, Washington, D.C. bureau of the NAACP, December 1, 1978.

78. Thomas Sowell, *Black Education: Myths and Tragedies* (New York: McKay, 1972), p. 292 (emphasis in the original).

79. J. A. McPherson, "The Black Law Student: A Problem of Fidelities," *Atlantic Monthly* 225 (April 1970):99.

80. Gallup Poll, March 25–28, 1977, quoted in "Most Against Preference for Non-Whites, Women," *Current Opinion* 5 (June 1977): 67. The Gallup Poll asked, "Some people say that to make up for past discrimination, women and minority groups should be given preferential treatment in getting jobs and places in colleges. Others say that ability, as determined by test scores, should be the main consideration. Which point of view comes closest to how you feel on this matter?"

81. *New York Times*/CBS News Poll, October 1977, quoted in Seymour M. Lipset and William Schneider, "The *Bakke* Case: How Would It Be Decided At the Bar of Public Opinion," *Public Opinion* 1 (March/April 1978): 42.

82. ABC News/*Washington Post* Poll, February 26–March 6, 1981, quoted in "Where the Races Differ," *Public Opinion* 4 (April/May 1981):38.

83. Interview with former board member, NAACP, Philadelphia Pennsylvania, September 19, 1977.

84. Quoted in Gloster B. Current, "The 'Hot' Sixtieth—A Memorable Convention," *The Crisis*, August–September 1969, p. 276.

85. Interview with Wilkins.

86. Nathaniel R. Jones, "The Future of Black-Jewish Relations," *The Crisis*, January 1975, p. 26. Mr. Jones expressed the same sentiments in a telephone conversation on September 7, 1977 in New York.

87. Interview with Wilkins.

88. This change is most clearly seen in editorials published in *The Crisis*, the official journal of the NAACP. See, for example, "Quotas, Goals and Parity," *The Crisis*, October 1972, p. 257.

89. "Resolutions Adopted By the 65th Annual Convention of NAACP at New Orleans, LA, July 1–5, 1974," reprinted in *The Crisis*, April 1975 Supplement, p. 127. Also telephone conversation with Clarence Mitchell, November 17, 1978, Washington, D.C.

90. Quoted in Gloster B. Current, "NAACP at 65—Still On The Drive," *The Crisis*, October 1974, p. 261.

91. Quoted in Gloster B. Current, "NAACP 66th Annual Convention—'You Gotta Belong!'" *The Crisis*, October 1975, p. 278.

92. In a resolution entitled "Bakke" ("Resolution Adopted At The 68th Annual Convention of NAACP at St. Louis, Missouri, June 27–July 1, 1977," *The Crisis*, December 1977 Supplement, p. 3).

93. Interview with Nathanial Colley, general counsel, NAACP Sacramento, California office, April 17, 1977.

94. Interview with William Wells, assistant general counsel, NAACP, New York, September 14, 1977.

95. Bayard Rustin, "From Protest to Politics: The Future of the Civil Rights Movement," *Commentary* 42 (February 1965): 26.
96. Quoted in Jones, "The Future of Black-Jewish Relations," p. 26.
97. Paul Delaney, "The Struggle to Rally Black America," *New York Times Magazine*, July 15, 1979, pp. 20–22, 87, 90–93.
98. Interviews with Pohlhaus, Mitchell, and the former board member.
99. Alexander Hamilton, James Madison and John Jay, *The Federalist Papers* (New York: New American Library, 1961), no. 10, p. 78; no. 51, p. 325.
100. Gallard Hunt, ed., *The Writings of James Madison*, vol. 6 (New York: Putnam, 1900–1910), pp. 67–69.
101. *Federalist Papers*, no. 61, p. 284; no. 57, p. 352; no. 51, p. 322.
102. "There is no maxim, in my opinion which is more liable to be misapplied than . . . that the interest of the majority is the political standard of right and wrong" (Letter to James Monroe, 1786). The principle "that the voice of the majority binds the minority . . . does not result . . . from a law of nature, but from compact found on utility" (Letter to Thomas Jefferson, February 4, 1790). Hunt, *Writings of James Madison*, vol. 3, p. 273; and vol. 5, p. 440.
103. John P. Roche, "Equality in America," in John P. Roche, ed., *American Political Thought: From Jefferson to Progressivism* (New York: Harper Torchbooks, 1967), p. 140.
104. See *Federalist Papers*, nos. 10, 14, 43, and 51.
105. See table 19 in note 5 above.

Chapter V: The Lawyer As an Organizational Leader

1. Interview with Leonard F. Walentynowicz, executive director, Polish-American Congress, and former counsel to the National Medical and Dental Association.
2. Examples of these predictions are Robert Borosage, et al., "The New Public Interest Lawyers," *Yale Law Journal* 79 (1970): 1069–1151; Jonathan D. Casper, *Lawyers Before the Warren Court* (Urbana: University of Illinois Press, 1972); and Stuart Scheingold, *The Politics of Rights* (New Haven: Yale University Press, 1974).
3. Richard C. Cortner, *The Apportionment Cases* (Knoxville: University of Tennessee Press, 1970), p. 37.
4. Charles H. Sheldon, *The American Judicial Process* (New York: Dodd, Mead, 1974), p. 108.
5. Richard Kluger, *Simple Justice* (New York: Vintage Books, 1975), pp. 291–94.
6. Robert M. O'Neil, *Discriminating Against Discrimination: Preferential Admissions and the DeFunis Case* (Bloomington: Indiana University Press, 1975), pp. 28–29.
7. Samuel Krislov, "The Amicus Curiae Brief: From Friendship to Advocacy," *Yale Law Journal* 72 (1963): 694–721; David R. Manwaring, *Render Unto Caesar: The Flag-Salute Controversy* (Chicago: University of Chicago Press, 1962).
8. Kluger, *Simple Justice*; Ruth B. Cowen, "Women's Rights Through Litigation," *Columbia Human Rights Law Review* 7 (1976): 373–412.

9. The studies suffer also from the liability of being overly theoretical (Scheingold), or more impressionistic than systematic in their discussions of the lawyer's roles (Borosage). Two exceptions are Vose and Casper, but both seem more concerned with the lawyer's effect on the legal process than in the internal workings of the litigant organization. See Clement Vose, *Constitutional Change* (Lexington, Massachusetts: Lexington Books, 1972).

10. Scheingold, *The Politics of Rights*, pp. 9, 131–33.

11. Borosage, "The New Public Interest Lawyers," p. 1079 n. 19.

12. Scheingold, *The Politics of Rights*, pp. 6, 141–42.

13. Philip Selznick, *Leadership in Administration* (Evanston, Illinois: Row, Peterson, 1957), pp. 37, 90, 153.

14. See table 22.

15. See table 23.

16. See table 24.

17. Relevant portions of the code are cited in Borosage, "The New Public Interest Lawyers," p. 1131.

18. Philippe Nonet, *Administrative Justice* (New York: Russell Sage, 1969), pp. 110–11.

19. Ibid., p. 114.

20. Talcott Parsons, "A Sociologist Looks at the Legal Profession," in Talcott Parsons, *Essays in Sociological Theory*, revised edition (Glencoe, Illinois: Free Press, 1954), p. 384.

21. Interview with Robert Hermann, legal director, Puerto Rican Legal Defense and Education Fund; New York; September 14, 1977.

22. Philip Selznick, *TVA and the Grass Roots* (New York: Harper Torchbooks, 1966), p. 254. See also Michel Crozier, *The Bureaucratic Phenomenon* (Chicago: University of Chicago Press, 1964), pp. 175–208.

23. We have already seen a particularly dramatic form of organizational blindness in the Legal Services Corporation (Chapter 3).

24. Judith Shklar, *Legalism* (Cambridge: Harvard University Press, 1964), p. 10.

25. Donald L. Horowitz, *The Courts and Social Policy* (Washington, D.C.: Brookings Institution, 1977), p. 25.

26. Wesley Newcomb Hohfeld, *Fundamental Legal Concepts* (New Haven: Yale University Press, 1946), pp. 27–31.

27. Jerold S. Auerbach, *Unequal Justice* (New York: Oxford University Press, 1976), p. 85.

28. Jonathan Black, *Radical Lawyers* (New York: Avon, 1971), p. 14. See also Paul E. Corcoran, *Political Language and Rhetoric* (Austin: University of Texas Press, 1979), p. 4.

29. Lawrence M. Friedman, *The Legal System* (New York: Russell Sage, 1975), pp. 262–63.

30. Corcoran, *Political Language and Rhetoric*, p. 2.

31. Interview with David M. Rabban, associate secretary and associate counsel, American Association of University Professors; Washington, D.C.; September 16, 1977.

32. Memorandum to Professors Finkin, Sandalow, Sofaer, Tollett, and Van Alstyne, from David M. Rabban, "AAUP 'Policy' in Issues Raised by the *Bakke* Case," April 5, 1977.

TABLE 22 Types of Agenda Setters in Amici Organizations

Agenda Setter	Percentage of Respondents	
Civilian participant[a]	20% (77)	
Civilian ally[b]	1 (4)	
Lawyer participant[c]	72 (276)	} 78% (301)
Lawyer ally[d]	6 (25)	
Don't know	1 (3)	
Total	100% (385)[e]	

NOTE: Data elicited by use of following question: "Who (name, title, address) first suggested participating in *Bakke*?" (Probe: "Was he/she a lawyer or law trained?")
  [a] Non–legally trained leader or member of the organization.
  [b] Individual important to the organization but not officially affiliated with it.
  [c] Leader, member, or staff member with law training.
  [d] Lawyers providing *pro bono* services to the organization; other legally trained individuals not officially affiliated with the organization.
  [e] Total is 385 because of multiple responses.

TABLE 23 Agenda Setters in Legal and Nonlegal Amici Organizations

Agenda Setter	Legal Organizations[a]	Nonlegal Organizations[b]	
Civilian participant	13% (23)	27% (54)	
Civilian ally	1 (2)	1 (2)	
Lawyer participant	82 (149)	63 (127)	} 72% (145)
Lawyer ally	4 (7)	9 (18)	
Total	100% (181)	100% (201)	

NOTE: Table 23 is based on data presented in table 22.
  [a] Organizations composed primarily of lawyers or pursuing litigational objectives.
  [b] Organizations composed predominately of non–legally trained persons or pursuing nonlitigational activities.
  [c] Total is less than 385 because "Don't knows" have been dropped.

TABLE 24 Lawyers as "Entrepreneurs" in Legal and Nonlegal Amici Organizations

"Entrepreneur"	Legal Organizations	Nonlegal Organizations	Total
Civilian leader	14% (24)	47% (92)	32% (116)
Lawyer leader	86 (142)	53 (103)	68 (245)
Total	100% (166)	100% (195)	100% (361)

NOTE: An "entrepreneur" is defined as a person actively seeking support for specific policy on *Bakke* within the organization.

33. Telephone conversation with Kenneth Tollett, Howard University, Washington, D.C., October 2, 1978.
34. Interview with Rabban.
35. Interview with a former member of the San Francisco office of the AAUP, Berkeley, California, November 28, 1977.
36. See table 25.
37. See table 26.
38. "Brief for Petitioner," *Regents of the University of California* v. *Bakke*, 438 U.S. 265 (1978) [Hereafter *Bakke* (U.S. Supr. Ct.)], p. 47.
39. "Oral Arguments in the Supreme Court of the United States," *Bakke* (U.S. Supr. Ct.) (Mimeographed, 1977), p. 17. On file in the Office of the Clerk of the United States Supreme Court.
40. "Brief of the Black Law Students Union of Yale University Law School, *Amicus Curiae*, in Support of Petitioner," *Bakke* (U.S. Supr. Ct.), pp. 21, 23.
41. Interview with William Wells, assistant general counsel, NAACP, New York, September 14, 1977.
42. *Anderson* v. *San Francisco Unified School District*, 357 F. Supp. 248 (N.D. Cal. 1972), quoted in "Notice of Intended Decision, F. Leslie Manker, Judge of the Superior Court of Yolo County, California, November 22, 1974." This document appears in Alfred A. Slocum, ed., *Allan Bakke versus Regents of the University of California*, vol. 1 (Dobbs Ferry, New York: Oceana Publications, 1978), p. 189.
43. *Bakke* v. *Regents of the University of California*, 553 P. 2d. 1152; 1163 n. 17; and 1161.
44. Justice Tobriner, dissenting, ibid., pp. 1185, 1188. First emphasis in the original; the second is added.
45. *Bakke* (U.S. Supr. Ct.), p. 374 n. 58. See also p. 375.
46. Ibid., p. 401.
47. Ibid., p. 403.
48. Ibid., p. 319 n. 53, pp. 289–90.
49. See, Samuel Beer, "In Search of a New Public Philosophy," in Anthony King, ed., *The New American Political System* (Washington, D.C.: American Enterprise Institute, 1978), pp. 11–13.
50. Laurence A. Tribe, *American Constitutional Law* (Mineola, New York: Foundation Press, 1978), p. 993, n. 18.
51. Owen Fiss, "Groups and the Equal Protection Clause," *Philosophy and Public Affairs* 5 (Winter 1976): 123, 147–58.
52. On a corporation's due process rights, see *Santa Clara County* v. *Southern Pacific Railroad Co.*, 118 U.S. 394 (1886); and *Minneapolis and St. Louis Railroad* v. *Beckwith*, 129 U.S. 26 (1888). On its First Amendment rights, see *Grosjean* v. *American Press Co.*, 297 U.S. 233 (1936); *Joseph Burstyn, Inc.* v. *Wilson*, 343 U.S. 495 (1952); and *First National Bank* v. *Bellotti*, 435 U.S. 765 (1978).
53. Ronald Dworkin, "The Bakke Case: An Exchange," *New York Review of Books*, January 26, 1978, p. 44.
54. Timothy J. O'Neill, "The Language of Equality in a Constitutional Order," *American Political Science Review* 75 (September 1981): 626–35.
55. Woodrow Wilson, *Constitutional Government in the United States* (New York: Columbia University Press, 1908), p. 69.

TABLE 25 Perception of *Bakke* by Organizational Leadership Style

| | Do you agree with the statement "*Bakke* is primarily a question of law, not of politics or philosophy"? | | | | | | |
	(1 Strongly Agree)	(2)	(3)	(4)	(5 Strongly Disagree)	(Don't Know)	Total
Oligarchic organization respondents	11% (18)	43% (72)	39% (66)	3% (5)	4% (7)	1% (1)	101% [a] (169)
Democratic organization respondents	2 (3)	20 (30)	25 (38)	40 (60)	13 (19)	1 (1)	101 [a] (151)
Managerial organization respondents	10 (4)	22 (9)	32 (13)	34 (14)	2 (1)	0 (0)	100 (41)
Total	(25)	(111)	(117)	(79)	(27)	(2)	(361)

[a] Does not equal 100% because of rounding.

TABLE 26 Perception of Lawyers by Organizational Leadership Style

Role of lawyers	Oligarchic Organization Respondents		Democratic Organization Respondents		Managerial Organization Respondents		Total	
Guardians of the Constitution	63%	(65)	28%	(11)	40%	(6)	52%	(82)
Expert interpreters of the law	37	(38)	65	(26)	60	(9)	46	(73)
Mechanics	1	(1)	8	(3)	0	(0)	3	(4)
Total	101%[a]	(104)	101%[a]	(40)	100%	(15)	101%[a]	(159)[b]

NOTE: Data elicited by use of the following question: "What special values or interests, if any, did the lawyers in your organization bring to the discussion of *Bakke* and the issue of affirmative action?" (Asked of those responding "Strongly agree" or "Agree" to question in Table 9.)

[a] Does not equal 100% because of rounding.

[b] Total is 159 because of multiple responses.

56. See John T. Noonan, *Persons and Masks of the Law* (New York: Farrar, Straus, and Giroux, 1976), p. 4.
57. Alexis de Tocqueville, *Democracy in America*, vol. 1 (New York: Knopf, 1945), pp. 283–90.
58. Auerbach, *Unequal Justice*.
59. Richard L. Engstrom and Patrick F. O'Connor, "Lawyer-Legislators and Support for State Legislative Reform," *Journal of Politics* 62 (1980): 266–76.
60. Albert P. Melone, "Rejection of the Lawyer Dominance Proposition: The Need for Additional Research," *Western Political Quarterly* 33 (1980): 225–32.
61. The harshest language was used by Justice Stevens, usually one of the more congenial members of the Court. In the opening footnote to his rejection of the Davis program, he pointed out: "Four Members of the Court have undertaken to announce the legal and constitutional effect of this Court's judgment. . . . It is hardly necessary to state that only a majority can speak for the Court or determine what is the 'central meaning' of any judgment of the Court." *Bakke* (U.S. Supr. Ct.), p. 408 n. 1.

Chapter VI: Beyond *Bakke*

1. *United Steelworkers* v. *Weber*, 443 U.S. 193, 197 (1979). The case was actually three cases in one. The United Steelworkers of America, the Kaiser Aluminum and Chemical Corporation, and the United States all appealed the Fifth Circuit's holding in support of Brian Weber. The three cases were consolidated for joint disposition.
2. Section 703 (d) of the Civil Rights Act of 1964, 64 *U.S.C.* S2000e-2(d).
3. *Weber*, pp. 200, 204, and 208.
4. Ibid., p. 230 (emphasis in original).
5. Ibid., p. 209.
6. *Fullilove* v. *Klutznick*, 448 U.S. 448, 449 (1980).
7. See also Justice Powell's concurrence, *Fullilove* v. *Klutznick*, p. 514. Powell also noted the temporary nature of the set-aside, p. 513.

8. Ibid., pp. 473–76, 478, 480, 482 and 484.
9. Ibid., p. 521.
10. "[T]he Court . . . [has] held that the Due Process Clause of the Fifth Amendment imposes the same equal protection standard upon the Federal Government that the Fourteenth Amendment imposes on the States." Ibid., p. 525 n. 3.
11. Ibid., pp. 527, 531.
12. Ibid., pp. 533–34, 537–39.
13. See "Affirmative Action Coordinating Center, et al., Amici Curiae," *United Steelworkers* v. *Weber.*
14. Henry Siegman, executive director, AJC, "Why AJ Congress Did Not Enter the Weber Case" (News release, American Jewish Congress, New York, n.d.), p. 2. See also "American Jewish Congress Won't Enter Weber Case; Cites Possible History of Employer Discrimination" (News release, American Jewish Congress, New York, n.d.), pp. 1–3.
15. The Leadership Conference billed itself as "a coalition of national organizations—civil rights, religious, labor, civic, fraternal, women and the handicapped—established in 1949 to work for the enactment and enforcement of effective civil rights and social welfare legislation." (News release, dated Monday, November 7, 1978, from the Washington office of the Leadership Conference for Civil Rights).
16. News release, dated Monday, November 20, 1978, from the office of David S. Saxon, President of the University of California.
17. Warren G. Hill, executive director, Education Commission of the States, "*Bakke* and Beyond: A Report of the Education Commission of the States and the Justice Program of the Aspen Institution," Report no. 112; Denver, Colorado; July, 1978; p. viii.
18. Jonathan D. Casper, *Lawyers Before the Warren Court* (Urbana: University of Illinois Press, 1972), p. 197.
19. Richard Kluger, *Simple Justice* (New York: Vintage Books, 1975), p. 742.
20. Louis Hartz, *The Liberal Tradition in America* (New York: Harcourt Brace and World, 1955); Robert A. Dahl, *A Preface to Democratic Theory* (Chicago: University of Chicago Press, 1956).
21. For example, Frank M. Coleman, "The Hobbesian Basis of American Constitutionalism," *Polity* 7 (Fall 1974): 57–89; Francis E. Devine, "Absolute Democracy or Indefeasible Right: Hobbes versus Locke," *Journal of Politics* 37 (August 1975): 736–68.
22. Alexander Hamilton, James Madison, and John Jay, *The Federalist Papers* (New York: New American Library, 1961), no. 6, p. 54.
23. Ibid., no. 55.
24. John Rees, *Equality* (London: Macmillan, 1971), p. 37.
25. "Brief of the American Civil Liberties Union, et al., Amici Curiae," *Regents of the University of California* v. *Bakke*, 438 U.S. 265 (1978) [Hereafter *Bakke* (U.S. Supr. Ct.)], p. 10. Compare, "Brief of American Jewish Committee, American Jewish Congress, et al., Amici Curiae," *Bakke* (U.S. Supr. Ct.), pp. 15–16, 19–51.
26. The report is cited as "Minority Report Upon Proposed Civil Rights Act of 1963, Committee on Judiciary Substitute for H.R. 7552, 1964 U.S. code, "Cong. and Admin. News," p. 2437. "Brief of the National Associa-

tion for the Advancement of Colored People as *Amicus Curiae*," *Bakke* (U.S. Supr. Ct.), p. 27 n. 21.

27. *Bakke* (U.S. Supr. Ct.), p. 320.

28. Nathan Glazer, "Why Bakke Won't End Reverse Discrimination," *Commentary* 66 (September 1978): 38, 41.

29. Hanna Fenichel Pitkin, *The Concept of Representation* (Berkeley: University of California Press, 1972), p. 240.

INDEX

and Municipal Employees, AFL-
CIO, xii, 191
American Federation of Teachers, AFL-
CIO, (AFT), xii, 102, 141–149,
160, 182
absence of mass defections from, 145–
148, 169
associational and promotional values
of, 147–148
brief to California Supreme Court, 40,
142–143, 144
brief to U.S. Supreme Court, 142–144,
166
as civil rights advocate, 141–142
constituency of, 141
dissension over *Bakke* in, 144–145,
148–149, 167
leadership style of, 135, 141, 144–
145, 164, 167, 216, 218
political effectiveness of, 147
remedial education supported by, 75
utilitarian incentives and, 146–148,
162–163
American Indian Bar Association, xi, 84
American Indian Law Center, xiv
American Indian Law Students Association, xi
American Indian Legal Defense and Education Fund, 221
American Jewish Committee, xi, 25, 192,
208, 252
coalition brief of, in *Bakke*, 84, 100
scope of debate in, 105
American Jewish Congress (AJC), xi, 5,
115, 160, 191–201
absent from *Weber*, 252
affirmative action and quotas discussed
in, 5, 108, 192–196, 197–199,
200–201
anti-Semitism combated by, 192
Bakke brief of, 84, 89, 200–201, 259,
260
Commission on Social Action of, 192,
197, 234
DeFunis and, 89, 192, 194–196,
197–198, 234
integrative decision making in, 191,
192–196, 211
interest advocacy of, 102
learning promoted in, 194–195
legal staff of, 233, 234
NAACP and, 191–192, 216
proportional representation notion rejected by, 100
remedial programs advocated by, 75
selfish motives ascribed to, 199–201

American Medical Student Association,
xii, 40
American Nazi Party, 116, 117, 168
American Public Health Association, xii,
61
Americans for Democratic Action (ADA),
xii, 83, 157, 158
American Subcontractors Association,
xii, 63, 218
amici briefs, 7, 18–19
in *Bakke*, 7, 65–67, 68, 72, 73–76,
78–80, 86, 89–92, 94–95, 97–
102, 107, 112–114, 142–144,
165–167, 172, 186–187, 200–201,
230
effectiveness of, 165–167
litigants' briefs vs., 144
traditional justification for, 172
see also coalition briefs
amicus process, political education and,
17–19
Amsterdam News, 60
Anti-Defamation League, xi, 40, 192
in alliance for educational opportunity,
252–253
Bakke brief of, 91
antidiscrimination principle, 35–37, 226
Antioch School of Law, xii, 219
aristocracy, 120–121
Aristotle, 10, 125
Arnold, Thurman, 17–18
Ashbrook, John, 152
Ash Commission on Executive Reorgani-
zation report, 151
Asian American Bar Association of the
Greater Bay Area, xi, xvii, 96, 191
Askin, Frank, 108–110, 111, 114, 115
Aspen Institute, Justice Program of, 253
Aspira of America, xiii, 84, 221–223
Association of American Law Schools, xi,
40, 69, 253
Association of American Medical Col-
leges, xi, 40
Association of Mexican American Edu-
cators, xii, 84
Athens, city-state (*polis*) of, 125
Atlantic Monthly, 166
Auerbach, Joel, 10

Bakke, Allan Paul:
appeal filed by, *see* Supreme Court of
California, Bakke's suit appealed to
lawsuit filed by, 23–24, 25–26; *see
also* Yolo County Superior Court,
Bakke's lawsuit in
medical school applications of, 20–23,
24–25

ABOUT THE AUTHOR

Winner of the 1982 Edward S. Corwin Award in Public Law of the American Political Science Association, Timothy J. O'Neill is assistant professor of political science at Wellesley College. He has been assistant professor at Tulane University and research fellow at the Brookings Institution and has also taught at the University of California at Santa Cruz. From 1973 to 1976 he was a National Science Foundation Graduate Fellow in Political Science at the University of California, Berkeley. He is a graduate of Claremont Men's College (B.A. 1971) and of the University of California at Berkeley (M.A. 1974, Ph.D. 1981). His home is in Wellesley, Mass.

ABOUT THE BOOK

Bakke has been composed in Linotron 202 Sabon by G & S Typesetters of Austin, Texas, and was printed on 60 pound Glatfelter and bound by Braun-Brumfield of Ann Arbor, Michigan.